D0074826

EVICTED!

EVICTED!

Property Rights and Eminent Domain in America

David Schultz

Praeger
An Imprint of ABC-CLIO, LLC

A B C  C L I O

Santa Barbara, California • Denver, Colorado • Oxford, England

Library of Congress Cataloging-in-Publication Data

Schultz, David A. (David Andrew), 1958–
    Evicted: property rights and eminent domain in America / David Schultz.
        p. cm.
    Includes bibliographical references and index.
    ISBN 978-0-313-35344-4 (hard copy : alk. paper) — ISBN 978-0-313-35345-1 (ebook)
1. Eminent domain—United States. 2. Right of property—United States.
3. Eviction—United States. I. Title.
    KF5599.S38   2010
    343.73'0252—dc22   2009030411

ISBN: 978-0-313-35344-4
EISBN: 978-0-313-35345-1

14   13   12   11   10   1   2   3   4   5

This book is also available on the World Wide Web as an eBook.
Visit www.abc-clio.com for details.

Praeger
An Imprint of ABC-CLIO, LLC

ABC-CLIO, LLC
130 Cremona Drive, P.O. Box 1911
Santa Barbara, California 93116–1911

This book is printed on acid-free paper ∞

Manufactured in the United States of America

The author thanks *Touro Law Review* for kindly allowing him to reprint portions of his article "The Property Rights Revolution That Failed: Eminent Domain in the 2004 Supreme Court Term," *Touro Law Review* 929–988 (2006) in chapter 7. It is reprinted with permission of *Touro Law Review*.

Contents

CHAPTER ONE

Why Should Anyone Care about Eminent Domain?

> *Rick:* How can you close me up? On what grounds?
> *Renault:* I'm shocked, *shocked* to find that there is gambling going on here!
> *Croupier:* Your winnings, sir.
> *Renault:* Oh, thank you very much.
>
> —*Casablanca* (1942)

The topic of eminent domain rarely is the subject of dinner time or cocktail party conversation. Eminent domain—the power of the government to take private property for some public use—does not generate much interest or excitement for most people. Instead, talk of this topic is generally confined to a select group of individuals in rarified settings. It might be government lawyers seeking to acquire some property to build a school, widen a highway, or perhaps even to remove some eyesore or unsafe building. Or it might be the topic of conversation among real estate appraisers who are seeking to determine the fair-market value of a piece of property that the government may wish to acquire. Or perhaps it might even be brought up in a first-year law school property or constitutional law class where students are quizzed about ownership rights, the Bill of Rights, or some other arcane topic. Whatever the context, discussion of eminent domain is rarely a front page news story or the subject of much political debate and controversy.

Yet the 2005 U.S. Supreme Court's decision in *Kelo v. City of New London*, 545 U.S. 469 (2005), upholding the use of eminent domain to take private property from one owner and give it to another in order to promote economic development, exploded the topic into the mainstream and pop culture. Much in the same way the character Renault (played by Claude Rains) in the movie *Casablanca* was shocked that there was gambling afoot in his city, others were similarly shocked that the government had the power to take the property of some and give it to others in order to facilitate economic development. The Court's decision shocked and angered many, producing an enormous outcry in the media. Even though the decision did not make any new law in the sense that the government had long had the authority to take private property for economic development and other purposes, the reaction to the *Kelo* decision was a surprise. The backlash drew new attention both to property rights that individuals hold in their houses, and to the power of the government to take one's house to serve community interests. It also invented a new rallying cry for property rights advocates—"eminent domain abuse."

Prior to and as a result of the *Kelo* decision, "eminent domain abuse" conjured up ages of governments bulldozing homes and forcing people out on the streets. Big bad government was teaming up with big bad big business and rich fat cats bent on screwing over the little guy. It was about David versus Goliath, the sanctity of a home, the challenge to the American dream, and a threat to the adage that one's home is one's castle.

Suzette Kelo, the homeowner in the *Kelo* case, became the poster child for eminent domain abuse. Books such as *Eminent Domain: Use and Abuse*, published by the American Bar Association, in part told Ms. Kelo's story.[1] Other titles such as *Bulldozed: "Kelo," Eminent Domain, and the American Lust for Land*, and *Little Pink House: A True Story of Defiance and Courage*, also recounted the saga of Ms. Kelo, painting her the victim and little guy (or woman) defending her home against big bad government and the evil Pfizer Pharmaceutical Company.[2] After *Kelo*, numerous states passed laws seeking to make it harder for the government to take private property, at least perhaps single-family homes, for economic development purposes. State and local governments banned the taking of owner-occupied homes, barred the use of eminent domain for economic development, or sought to limit the concept of a "public use" to "traditional government functions" or purposes such as to build schools or highways. Other laws increased the compensation owners were entitled to receive for their property or stipulated additional hearings or hoops that the government had to jump through before it could take property. Even some in Congress sought to adopt laws that would make future *Kelos* impossible. Overall, the backlash against *Kelo* was intense and angry.

The criticism of *Kelo* stated that what we were facing in America was "eminent domain abuse." By that was meant somehow government had run amuck and its use of eminent domain was simply the most visible sign that Big Brother had won. Now for the first time the government could oust us from our homes. If it could do that, what's next? Take away our guns or other personal freedoms? *Kelo* was the embodiment of a big, bloated, oppressive government that picked on individual freedoms. In addition, many advocates representing the poor and people of color also saw the decision as a form of the chickens coming home to roost. They argued that the government had always been using eminent domain as a form of "urban removal" directed at racial minorities and the less affluent. It was used to break up their neighborhoods to build roads or highways or to otherwise take their property and give it to affluent whites. In short, eminent domain was a major tool encouraging gentrification of many communities across the country.

But *Kelo* was also a story about special interest politics and the evils of what happens when government and big business team up together. In the case of the Kelos, the City of New London, Connecticut, wanted their property in order to provide parking and other amenities for Pfizer Pharmaceuticals in an industrial park. New London was economically depressed and desperate, with an eroding tax base, a loss of jobs and population, and the flight of businesses from their community. There was also a fear that Pfizer would soon flee and the creation of the industrial park would be a way not only to retain existing industries but also to expand employment opportunities. The taking of the Kelos' property simply looked like a form of corporate thuggery, with the government doing Pfizer's bidding.

Similarly, back in the early 1980s when the City of Detroit was economically reeling from the job losses and the hemorrhaging of the automobile industry, it capitulated to the demands of General Motors to use its eminent domain authority to provide land for a new assembly plant or face the prospect of the auto giant going elsewhere to expand. As a result, in *Poletown Neighborhood Council v. City of Detroit*, 410 Mich. 616, 304 N.W. 2d 455 (Mich. 1981) the Michigan Supreme Court upheld the City of Detroit's use of its eminent domain authority to level a city neighborhood, relocate 1,362 households, and acquire more than 150 private businesses in order to accommodate the desire of General Motors Corporation to build a new assembly plant on 465 acres of land.[3] On top of this land acquisition, the City of Detroit also provided more than $200 million in tax breaks and other subsidies to GM to support this project, only to find the promised creation of 6,000 new jobs to be illusionary.[4]

Kelo and *Poletown* highlight the unsolved problem of eminent domain—how to prevent corporate thuggery.[5] By that, what are the checks to prevent powerful corporate interests from blackmailing politicians into using the government's takings power to further private interests? Political economist Charles Lindblom once described the marketplace as prison.[6] Governmental entities and the political decision-making process are an island embedded within a larger economic sea that leaves in the hands of private economic players the power to make business investment decisions. Developers can use this tool—invest or withhold investment and flee from a jurisdiction—if they do not secure the benefits they desire from a community. Such a threat has been successful in corporations extracting tax credits and breaks for business relocation decisions even though the empirical evidence suggests such incentives are minor factors affecting the location of facilities. Similarly, sports teams use the threat of relocation along with fan base loyalty to wrestle new publicly financed stadiums from cities and other local governments.

The point here is that there is a well-trod path of eminent domain being used on behalf of powerful interests to secure their needs, with the occasion of *Midkiff* takings (the breaking up land monopolies to benefit tenants, as will be discussed later in the book) the exception to the rule. What perhaps infuriated the Kelos and other families in Connecticut so much was not simply that their property was being taken, but that they felt they were being ganged up on by developers, a corporate giant, and the city. For the Kelos, as well as many others across the country who see developers and city officials working together to push them out of their homes, the problem is that democracy has broken down and they see no way that the political process is going to listen to them or respect their voice. The Kelos, no doubt, thought they were the victims of thuggery.

Yet underlying the numerous reasons various parties were upset with the *Kelo* decision, it also struck a nerve in American pop culture. At its core, the view captured was "our home is our castle" and that we should be able to do what we want with it. No one should be able to tell us what we can do with our property, especially our home, and no one should be able to force us out of what, for most of us, is our most prized and important possession. In fact, home ownership typifies a common (but, as we will see, an incorrect) perception about property rights. That perception is that if I own something it is *mine* and I have a right to do anything I want with it. When the Kelos lost their home they lost their castle, so to speak, and millions of people across America identified with them and fretted that they too could be the victims of eminent domain abuse. Thus, the *Kelo* decision prompted a flurry of books advocating for the enhanced or renewed protection of property rights.

Yet when one cuts through all the hype, hysteria, and hullaba-loos surrounding *Kelo*, there is one basic question: Are property rights and eminent domain irreconcilably in conflict? In order to answer that question, several other issues need to be addressed. First, what is "property" and what rights do we have to things that we own? Second, are ownership or property rights as fragile as many commentators claim? Third, what is "eminent domain" and what type of power does the government have to take property? With that question, there are issues surrounding why the government takes property. What does the law or the Constitution say about this power? Are there any limits to eminent domain? Is there a process that must be followed when the government takes private property for its use? Additionally, given the reaction to *Kelo*, one can also ask if the decision forged any new ground. Did it, for example, make new law and declare a new principle that *now*, for the first time, government could take property for economic development reasons, or was the government always able to do that, or when did the government acquire the power or authority to do that? Finally, perhaps a last question to ask: was there overreaction to *Kelo*? Was the case misunderstood? Did the courts not get it when it came to property rights or did legislators, owners, and the media simply engage in a knee-jerk response to the decision? Finally, perhaps the most important questions are "what is eminent domain abuse?" and "does it exist?" These and perhaps others are all good questions.

This book seeks to cut through all the misinformation about eminent domain and answer the above questions. It aims to offer a comprehensive discussion of eminent domain. It will also discuss how eminent domain has changed from the earliest days of the United States and show how it has been an important tool for a variety of governmental purposes, including economic development. In providing this discussion, the book will show if and how *Kelo* was a major change in the law and whether—as Renault pretended to be in *Casablanca*—we should have been shocked by that decision. The discussion is also meant to provide important detail and explanation of the deeper issue underlying this topic, specifically what "property" is and what rights owners have in it. There is no way one can discuss or explain eminent domain without defining "property" and what ownership means.

In order to accomplish the above tasks, the book breaks down the topic of eminent domain. Chapter 1 provides an overview of property law, explaining what it means to have property and what we can own. This discussion addresses topics that are often covered in law school such as when or how something becomes one's property. But, more important, the discussion weaves between what people think property is and what the law says it is. The goal here is comprehensive: provide explanation of why we have property and what it means to us both personally and legally.

Chapter 2 discusses the limits on property ownership, not only what rights are associated with ownership but also what limitations. The primary focus here is historical; how has property been viewed over the course of American history? Despite the rhetoric describing property as an absolute "right," this right has always been subject to limitations. Much of the discussion here will focus on the often huge gap between American political rhetoric that describes property as absolute and the reality of law and practice that have found significant limits on ownership rights. In effect, just because it is your property does not mean you can do whatever you want with it.

Chapter 3 is a general history of eminent domain as it evolved from medieval England and came to the United States, which will explain conceptually and in practice what eminent domain is and why governments have the power to take private property. The discussion here in many ways is philosophical in the sense that it addresses questions about the nature of government and why it even exists. Eminent domain is discussed in terms of the broader purposes of government alongside of what powers it needs in order to protect individuals and secure the public good. The reason for this chapter is simple—to clarify why governments do what they do and where the regulation of property may fit in.

Chapter 4 provides a constitutional history of eminent domain in America. It focuses on the takings clause of the Fifth Amendment of the Bill of Rights, seeking to explain what the constitutional mandates or says about eminent domain. Clearly, one chapter cannot provide an exhaustive historical analysis of this topic, but this one does offer a discussion of the major cases and historical trends affecting power of the government to take private property. The chapter serves as perhaps the "greatest hits" of eminent domain law, seeking to show its evolution over time and leading up to *Kelo*. Among the major points to be discussed is how eminent domain has long been an important and often aggressively used tool to promote a variety of public goods, including the building of railroads, public highways, and schools, and even to promote economic development. In fact, the chapter will underscore that many of the major accomplishments and milestones of this country required the use of eminent domain.

Chapter 5 turns specifically to a discussion of the public use justification for the taking of private property. One of the criticisms of *Kelo* both before and after it was decided was that the courts and the law failed to provide adequate protection for property rights. The chapter will concentrate on looking at a series of decisions prior to *Kelo* that gave many property rights advocates hope that the U.S. Supreme Court would become a more vigilant advocate for property rights, and why then the Court failed to do that in *Kelo*.

Chapter 6 is a description of the eminent domain process. It starts with the assumption that the government wants to take your home. What would it have to do (at least prior to *Kelo*) to do that? The chapter examines the steps in the eminent domain process. It looks at the three conditions that government must meet to take property, ascertaining (1) what constitutes a taking, (2) what is considered a valid public use, and (3) what constitutes just compensation for the taking. Among the topics emphasized will be what techniques are employed to determine the value of your home. The discussion reviews the legal requirements for the use of eminent domain but, more important, it examines how economic development, land use regulation, and eminent domain must all be understood as part of a broader planning process within the political process. The chapter essentially provides a primer or summary about what shall be called the ABCs of the eminent domain process.

Chapter 7 sets the legal context for the *Kelo* case and discusses it in the context of two other property rights cases also decided by the Supreme Court that year. But it looks at *Kelo* as part of a broader political agenda to defend property rights and limit the scope and role of the government in the economy. The overall purpose of this chapter is to cut through the rhetoric and really determine what the Court said in *Kelo*, what the case meant, and to what extent it changed the law to make it easier to condemn your property. Did *Kelo* really make new law and set a new precedent? Addressing this issue is the purpose of the chapter.

Chapter 8 examines the aftermath of *Kelo*. It looks at the reaction to the case politically and legally, especially in terms of the new laws that were adopted to make future *Kelo*s impossible. The chapter will in part examine several court cases (at the state level) before *Kelo* seeking to understand how well judges and courts were able to reach out and protect property owners facing eminent domain. One perhaps surprising answer is that, contrary to claims of rampant eminent domain abuse and feverish land grabs by local developers, courts are actually quite good at smoking out abuses and protecting property rights. The chapter will also then make a different argument that the eminent domain abuses that came out in *Kelo*, and which new laws sought to address missed the real problem. Specifically, the real abuse in *Kelo* and in many eminent domain cases or scenarios is what shall be called "corporate thuggery," the teaming up of local corporate interests with the government to press the agenda of the former at the expense of the public or other landowners.

Finally, the conclusion provides some recommendations regarding what is right and what is wrong with the current use of eminent domain laws. A major question to ask is whether eminent domain law needs to be fixed and do we need to place new limits on the ability of the government to take property in order to protect our rights? This chapter assesses the current debates in eminent domain law and offers some ideas on what is good or bad in current law and what needs to be done to remedy it. In effect, the chapter asks whether eminent domain abuse exists, what it is, and what can be done to address it. More specifically, can eminent domain and property rights be reconciled? The simple answer here is that critics of eminent domain have articulated the wrong problem. The issue is not whether eminent domain and property rights can be reconciled. It is whether eminent domain and individual rights can be reconciled. The answer here is yes.

Overall, the book perhaps reaches both a middle ground and takes a different path when it comes to thinking about eminent domain. On the one hand, it rejects more hysterical assertions or fears of eminent domain abuse and instead argues that eminent domain is an important and powerful tool to further the public good if it is properly employed. A wrecking-ball approach to vastly limiting eminent domain power (as current efforts seem to call for) is antidemocratic and will certainly cost taxpayers a lot of money in the long run. However, eminent domain is subject to abuse and the corporate thuggery problem, and some limits need to be imposed on the way eminent domain is used so that local governments are not merely pawns of broader interests when seeking to use this power.

My interest in this topic dates back to the early 1980s when I served as a city director of code enforcement in New York enforcing state and local housing and zoning laws. In doing that job, I became interested both personally and professionally in why we have housing laws and how governments legitimately limit property rights. This interest was further reinforced through employment with an organization that worked with low-income individuals and people of color to help organize them to defend their communities. Later, when writing a dissertation in the late 1980s, I explored the topic of eminent domain. Thus as a professor, housing and economic planner, and scholar, I have studied land use issues. Overall, this book and its observations are the product of 25 years of thinking about eminent domain and how to balance the rights of owners and the community with the needs to occasionally take property to promote important social objectives. My hope is that this book, unlike many of the others that reach a fever pitch when it comes to discussing eminent domain and property rights, will bring these many years of reflection to an examination of this topic.

CHAPTER TWO

It's My Property and I Will Do What I Want with It

(with apologies to Lesley Gore)
It's my party, and I'll cry if I want to.
—"It's My Party" as sung by Lesley Gore

What is property and what rights are attached to something I own? Perhaps this is the most fundamental question that needs to be asked when trying to understand the power of eminent domain. The reason for this is that if the power of eminent domain, as stated in the Fifth Amendment to the U.S. Constitution, is the authority to take private property for a public use, then one needs to understand what property is. Think about it. If something cannot be owned, then it cannot be considered property.

If one were to consider the world around us, there are many things that might possibly be objects of property. For example, our house or home is our property, as are our cars, trucks, television sets, computers, and clothes that we wear. However, what about things such as the air around us, a contract to buy a house, a lease, a possible inheritance in a will, or an IOU that a friend gives you after borrowing money? Are they property? Unlike the first set of items mentioned, which were tangible or real, this second list is less "real" and more intangible. One can touch a house, car, a television, or a computer, but can one really touch a contract, lease, or IOU beyond the paper it is written on? But what if the IOU is verbal and not even written on a piece of paper? Does that render it even less of a form of property than if it was written down on a piece of paper? For many, the IOU might be a valuable form of property, much in the same way that a contract for something in the future, such as medical care or Social Security, might constitute some type of property. But unlike a physical object that one can hold and possess, these other items cannot really be held in a physical way. Are they property?

Now think about some other things about us. Do we own our bodies? Can we buy and sell body organs or parts? How about blood? Human eggs or sperm? If we consider them property, then perhaps we should be allowed to sell them. In some ways, slavery was once based upon the notion that humans could be property, bought and sold no differently than buying or selling any other object. Additionally, think about your household pet. Do you own your cat and dog? Are pets simply property in the same way that cows or pigs raised for food are considered property? The simple answer from the perspective of the law is yes, all these entities are property, or at least have historically been considered to be forms or types of property.

But even if there is an agreement that something is property, what can one do with it? If we think about property in an ordinary sense that many people adopt, owning something means I can do whatever I want with it. Lesley Gore sang in the 1960s, "It's my party and I'll cry if I want to." For some, owning something implies "it's my property and I'll do what I want with it." This means I can hoard it, use it up, sell it, trade it, exclude others from using it, and perhaps even blow it up. To own something means I can do whatever I want with it. Yet that is not necessarily the case. I own my pets, for example. Can I torture or kill them as I want? What about my body? If I own it, cannot I sell it or any parts of it? Should I not be able to sell my body as prostitutes do, or sell blood or plasma as many individuals? What about selling a body organ such as a kidney? If our bodies are our property, then why not permit all these actions?

But beyond looking at property in one's body or pets, think about other forms of property and what you might be able to do with something you own. I can buy and sell my house. However, can I use my house in a way that disturbs others? What if I own a gun? Guns are property, but can I use them in ways to hurt others? The answer, of course, is no. There are limits to ownership depending on what type of property one is discussing.

Answering the questions regarding what property is and what rights I have over things that I own is the touchstone for understanding eminent domain. But understanding what property is is not easy. Literally there are tens of thousands of books, articles, and laws that try to clarify what it is. If one had time to review all this material it would be clear that there is no one fixed definition of property. *Property* as a concept has multiple meanings. Property can also be divided up into different forms of property, and property or ownership has associated with it many different forms of rights. Property may also be historically and culturally specific. At different times in history and across different cultures, what is considered property has had distinct meanings.

In law school, property law is generally a required class when one is a "1L," or a first-year student. Law school classes seek to examine and clarify what property is, at least in the United States, by discussing what property means from a legal point of view. Yet property also has other meanings beyond the law, extending to cultural and political perspectives. But from a legal point of view, property can be understood as containing many different forms and rights.

WHAT IS PROPERTY AND WHERE DOES IT COME FROM?

As a starting point one might ask: Where do property rights come from? Although this is a good historical and anthropological question, ultimately it may not be possible to answer it. The reason for that is that the concept of property that we are familiar with in the United States traces its legal origins back to English common law. There, the law about ownership and who could own what evolved over time, giving it the particular characteristics that many individuals in the United States have come to understand. The rules of English common law are different from those of other European countries, and they also stand in stark contrast to theories of property found elsewhere in the world.

For example, the rights to property in ancient Rome were very different than in modern America.[1] To own something, such as a burial plot or a religiously sacred spot, did not grant one the ability to exclude others from using the property in some cases. But more important, when settlers first arrived in North America during the fifteenth and sixteenth centuries, they encountered what they perceived to be land either not owned by anyone or owned by the various Native Americans who occupied the continent (the same was true also for Central and South America). These two perceptions about the status of the land led to two different actions, even if the results were the same. In one instance, where it was perceived that no one owned the land, the British (and the French and Spanish) claimed the land to be theirs.[2] Since the land was considered wild, unoccupied, or unclaimed, they followed traditional practice under British law and they declared it theirs and subject to the English Crown. Native Americans who may have occupied the land were then forcibly removed or slaughtered as the Europeans viewed them as trespassers or invaders upon their now-claimed property.

The other approach that settlers took was to purchase the land from the Native Americans. History books in the United States long chronicled the story of Peter Minuit purchasing the island of Manhattan from Native Americans for beads and trinkets worth just a pittance. In exchanging the beads and trinkets, the Dutch believed they were purchasing the rights to the land, including sole use or occupation, and the right to dispose of the property any way they wanted, including excluding the Native Americans from it. However, it is not clear that this is what the Native Americans thought. For them, the earth was not something that could be owned or possessed in the same way that someone owned or possessed a piece of personal clothing. The lands of the earth were something that one used, and the exchange of beads and trinkets was not a selling of Manhattan to the Europeans, but perhaps instead merely recognition that they could also peacefully use the lands alongside the Native Americans. Simply put, the Native Americans did not have the same conceptions of property as did the Europeans—they did not legally own the earth and therefore could not legally sell it. Or, to put it in modern legal analysis, they did not have legal title to the property and therefore could not convey it. (One could also say that in contract law terms there was no legal contract to sell the island because the Dutch and the Native Americans did not have a "meeting of the minds" regarding the terms of the contract and therefore there was no valid agreement, even if the Native Americans could sell the land.)

The point of this discussion is twofold. First, the rules of property appear to be different across cultures and time. Or at least anthropological studies and history seem to suggest that.[3] Second, the discussion of the Native Americans and property leads to the question about how property rights are initially acquired. Both of these questions point to an important distinction between possession and property.

As children, we chanted "possession is nine-tenths of the law" when something was found or, more important, when we wanted to hoard a toy and not share it with someone else! Claiming that possession was nine-tenths of the law meant that since we held it in our arms, we owned it and therefore it was ours. While our chants meant little (except to the extent that we dared someone else to take the toy away from us), the phrase had a ring of truth to it, in that it spoke to an important distinction between possession and property rights.

Possession of something seems to imply physical control over something. I possess a piece of property because I can defend it and prevent others from using it. This simple type of possession might be limited to the physical might and strength that I have, and it might also be limited to the amount of geography that I can easily defend. However, this type of possession is very unstable. There is no certainty that what I possess today will be held tomorrow. Possession is subject to my ability to hold something against all outsiders.

Possession contrasts with property. With property, at least the way it has evolved in the West and in the United States, my ownership conveys certain rights. What these rights are shall be discussed below, but my property means that the law legally recognizes my possession and it or, rather, the state or the government will protect my ownership. This means that an individual's rights to some property are not limited to the physical ability to defend and control the land. Instead, I can leave the property or acquire more acres than I can physically defend, and the property will still be mine. If someone seeks to take it away from me I can call the police to have that person removed, or I can go to court to have him evicted or charged with trespassing. Property rights, while perhaps initially and subsequently connected or related to possession, are more secure and certain than is mere possession of something.

How, then, did property as a legal convention come about? There are many theories about this and it could take an entire book alone to discuss the various ideas about its origins. However, a handful of theories can best capture the different approaches taken.

The first theory is that property is simply a social convention or tradition grounded in habit. David Hume, a famous eighteenth-century British philosopher, described property as the product of habit and convention in his *A Treatise of Human Nature.*[4] Hume, like many of his contemporaries, sought to explain the origin of society. This included discussing why laws exist, why they should be obeyed, and who should be entitled to rule a country. His writings occurred at a time when the power of kings was being questioned and parliaments and popular governments were beginning to develop. One popular tool for describing the origins of society and its rules was an appeal to a "social contract." Some writers argued that there had been a time when there were no laws or government.[5] At some point and for some reason, individuals gathered to create society by way of a social contract, or an agreement among individuals to create a society, government, and rules to order both. The parallel might be to think of social contracts as a form of constitutional convention. For many social contract theorists, property rights were a product of these conventions.

David Hume criticized the social contract thinking along several scores. First, he argued that such a contract was a historical and anthropological fiction. He doubted that there was some such point that could be described as presocial and that then there was some express agreement to form a society and a set of rules. Instead, rules of justice, societies, and governments were the product of habit and convention.[6] This means that people simply came to accept over time some relationships, including what was considered to be just and fair. Moreover, Hume criticized the idea of a social contract as simply a "convention." The entire idea of forming an agreement and keeping one's word to obey it is also a social convention.[7] Thus, social contract theorists who argued that the social contract created society would also have to explain how these contracts came to be created and accepted as binding. There is almost a reduction to the absurd here. To agree to a social contract, one must first need to create the concept of a contract, and that would imply creating the concept of agreements, which would imply creating the concept of keeping agreements, and so on.

Hume's alternative proposal was that society was the product of habit and convention. This is also true with property. Property arises first out of a security of possessions that is gradually respected by others.

> After this convention, concerning abstinence from the possessions of others, is enter'd into, and every one has acquir'd a stability in his possessions, there immediately arise the ideas of justice and injustice; as also those of property, right, and obligation. The latter are altogether unintelligible without first understanding the former. Our property is nothing but those goods, whose constant possession is establish'd by the laws of society; that is, by the laws of justice. Those, therefore, who make use of the words property, or right, or obligation, before they have explain'd the origin of justice, or even make use of them in that explication, are guilty of a very gross fallacy, and can never reason upon any solid foundation. A man's property is some object related to him. This relation is not natural, but moral, and founded on justice. Tis very preposterous, therefore, to imagine, that we can have any idea of property, without fully comprehending the nature of justice, and shewing its origin in the artifice and contrivance of man. The origin of justice explains that of property. The same artifice gives rise to both. As our first and most natural sentiment of morals is founded on the nature of our passions, and gives the preference to ourselves and friends, above strangers; 'tis impossible there can be naturally any such thing as a fix'd right or property, while the opposite passions of men impel them in contrary directions, and are not restrain'd by any convention or agreement.[8]

Property rights, for Hume, arise out of natural possession of objects. At some point the rules of justice come to respect our possession of property. This means we no longer have to keep it within physical possession at all times and be on constant patrol to protect it from all intruders. Property rights are conventional, but they are also respected and protected by society and government.

A second theory of property is critical of it as an institution. Specifically, property along this perspective is viewed as some sort of evil institution. Pierre-Joseph Proudhon, a famous nineteenth-century anarchist, once wrote a book with an answer that captured this sentiment—*Property Is Theft!*[9] Modern Western conceptions or beliefs that property is illegitimate can be traced to eighteenth-century French philosopher Jean-Jacques Rousseau, a social contract theorist who tried to explain the origin of society by appealing to an ancient compact reached among individuals. This compact, too, created the institution of property, thereby making it, as Hume said, a human or social convention. But property for Rousseau was not depicted in a positive light. Instead, property, along with all of society and government, were described in his *Discourse on the Origins and Foundations of Inequality* (often referred to as the *Second Discourse*) as a trick by the rich and powerful over the poor.

> The first man who, having enclosed off a piece of land, got the idea of saying *"This is mine"* and found people simple enough to believe him was the true founder of civil society. What crimes, what wars, what murders, what miseries and horrors would someone have spared the human race who, pulling out the stakes or filling in the ditch, had cried out to his fellows, "Stop listening to this imposter. You are lost if you forget that the fruits belong to everyone and the earth belongs to no one." It seems very likely that by that time things had already come to the point where they could no longer continue as they had been. For this idea of property, which depends on many previous ideas which could only have arisen in succession, was not formed in the human mind all of a sudden. A good deal of progress had to take place—acquiring significant industry and enlightenment, transmitting and increasing them from one age to the next—before arriving at this last stage in the state of nature. So let us resume these matters further back in time and try to gather under a single point of view this slow succession of events and knowledge, in their most natural order.[10]

For Rousseau, the original social contract and the property that it created was the first step in the gradual and eventual enslavement of individuals. Elsewhere in the *Second Discourse*, Rousseau sees the first step in creation of property as leading to even further social conflicts and distinctions. The institution of property leads to the family, with current family relations also based on artificial distinctions and inequalities.

> This was the age of a first revolution which led to the establishment and differentiation of families, which introduced a form of property, and from which perhaps arose many quarrels and fights.

However, as the strongest were probably the first to make themselves lodgings they felt capable of defending, it is plausible that the weak ones found it quicker and safer to imitate them rather than to try to dislodge them. And as for those who already had huts, each one must have rarely sought to take over his neighbour's, less because it did not belong to him than because it was useless to him and he could not have seized it without exposing himself to a lively fight with the family who occupied it.[11]

Private property enslaves. As Rousseau would state later in his most famous book, *The Social Contract*: "Man is born free, but he is everywhere in chains."[12] While in nature humans are free and equal, social institutions such as private property take away this natural freedom.

One can see in Rousseau's writings the sentiments of critiques of property found later in the writings of Karl Marx and the Marxists. In the 1848 *Communist Manifesto*, Marx called for the abolition of private property because he saw in it the roots of the oppression of the working class. Lenin, too, criticized private property as a form of theft and slavery, and when the Russian revolution took place in 1917, it moved to abolish property ownership and collectivize or nationalize it.[13]

A third depiction of property departs significantly from both Hume and Rousseau and deems property ownership both as natural (as opposed to Hume's conventional approach) and as a positive good or right that should be protected (as opposed to Rousseau's denunciation of property as a trick). This perspective is best described by John Locke, an eighteenth-century British philosopher, in his 1690 *Two Treatises on Government*. The *Two Treatises* is an attempt to refute claims for absolute monarchial power and to justify both parliamentary authority and a revolution to limit the authority of the Crown. To undertake this task, Locke also invokes social contract reasoning or metaphors to make an argument about government and society.

Locke's starting point is to assume a presocial state of nature.[14] This state of nature is a condition of natural liberty where all are free and equal. No human laws or rules exist in this state of nature. However, this does not mean that there are no rules of justice. Instead, Locke writes about the existence of natural laws or rule of justice. More important, he indicates that individuals in the state of nature possess certain natural rights, including the right to self-defense, to defend other rights, and to act in ways to preserve oneself and defend items that we have come to take into possession. While Locke seems initially to agree with Hume and Rousseau that property did not exist in a state of nature, his notion of possession, property, and how people acquire ownership of items emerges in the *Two Treatises*:

> Though the earth, and all inferior creatures, be common to all men, yet every man has a property in his own person: this no body has any right to but himself. The labour of his body, and the work of his hands, we may say, are properly his. Whatsoever then he removes out of the state that nature hath provided, and left it in, he hath mixed his labour with, and joined to it something that is his own, and thereby makes it his property. It being by him removed from the common state nature hath placed it in, it hath by this labour something annexed to it, that excludes the common right of other men: for this labour being the unquestionable property of the labourer, no man but he can have a right to what that is once joined to, at least where there is enough, and as good, left in common for others.[15]

In this passage Locke describes individuals as having a natural property right in their bodies. To some extent, our bodies are our property and we can own them (although Locke would later say that, because God created humans, there is a limit to what we can do with our bodies, such as commit suicide). Property seems to be a natural right. We come to acquire things first by labor. As Locke states:

> Thus the grass my horse has bit; the turfs my servant has cut; and the ore I have digged in any place, where I have a right to them in common with others, become my *property*, without the assignation or consent of any body. The *labour* that was mine, removing them out of that common state they were in, hath *fixed my property* in them.[16]

By that, if we gather, harvest, or make something, it is ours. As little kids we used to say "finders keepers, losers, weepers." If I find something, it is mine. For Locke, the sentiment is similar but instead it is "if I make something it is mine." This theory about human labor is important for a couple of reasons. First, it seems to establish some theory of entitlement or rights that connects work or labor to ownership. Mixing my body or labor with something entitles me to possess the object. This idea is at the root of many theories of property.[17] If I capture wild animals, gather gold nuggets while prospecting, or simply build or make anything, then I own it. This theory is also important to economists because it establishes what they call the labor theory of value. This theory states that the value of items is based upon the labor that produces it. Moreover, Locke's theory and the labor theory of value also explain how and why individuals should be paid for working. If I work in a factory or in an office I sell my labor or my labor power in exchange for a wage or salary. Therefore, by working I exchange something of value (my labor) for money from the employer.[18]

But in the above passage Locke also states that the rights to take possession of things or to make them property are limited by the need to leave enough for others. Thus, at least here there is no unlimited right to acquire property to the disadvantage of others. Yet elsewhere in this book Locke states that the natural limits to acquiring property are defined or circumscribed by spoilage. That is, gathering too much fruit, acorns, or other goods might lead to situations where I gather more than I can use and therefore they might spoil. But the introduction of money changes that. Money makes possible the unlimited acquisition of property without running the risk of spoilage.[19] Money also makes possible situations where all individuals can acquire as much property as they want. I no longer have to leave some fruits or acorns (Locke uses acorns as a frequent example) for others. If others do not have acorns and they want them, they can buy them from me if they have money. The introduction of money thus describes a second way people can acquire goods—buy them. More specifically, they can acquire them through voluntary exchange. If I have something you want, you can make me an offer to buy it. If the two of us agree on a price, we have a deal. Locke's theory of ownership thus is at the basis of modern theories of contract law and some political theorists such as C. B. Macpherson also see in Locke the basic process or rules of a free market capitalist economy. Specifically, Robert Nozick, a twentieth-century philosopher, argued that the rules of the property and the market can be easily summarized. His rules are paraphrased here.[20]

1. Whatever I make with my own labor is mine.
2. Whatever is the produce of voluntary exchange (no force or fraud) is mine.
3. Whatever I come to acquire from repeated applications of rule one and two are mine.

Locke's theory about labor and ownership are important, but even more significant is his linkage elsewhere in the *Two Treatises* between property, liberty, and government. While Locke describes a state of nature as one of perfect freedom and a place where individuals have natural rights, these rights are unclear.[21] Moreover, while in the state of nature I may come to acquire possession of items; again, the exact rights to these objects are occasionally insecure. Others may try to take things from me, steal them if they are left unguarded, or seek to subdue me to take my possessions. Left unchecked, the state of nature can turn into anarchy or a state of war. Here is where the social contract and government come in. Individuals enter into a social contract to protect their natural rights. The social contract, civil society, or government gives clarity to natural rights. This includes the right of property. The preservation of property is the chief goal of civil society.

> Man being born, as has been proved, with a title to perfect freedom, and an uncontrouled enjoyment of all the rights and privileges of the law of nature, equally with any other man, or number of men in the world, hath by nature a power, not only to preserve his property, that is, his life, liberty and estate, against the injuries and attempts of other men. . . . But because no political society can be, nor subsist, without having in itself the power to preserve the property . . . every one of the members hath quitted this natural power, resigned it up into the hands of the community in all cases that exclude him not from appealing for protection to the law established by it.[22]

Property is an all-inclusive concept that extends to one's personal liberty, possessions, and even life. The goal of the social contract in creating civil society is protecting property in this broadly defined sense. The law, in effect, gives legal meaning, status, and protection to property. Later on in the *Two Treatises*, Locke also declares that individuals possess a right to revolution and to change their government if it fails to protect their rights, including those to property.

Locke's political philosophy and theory of property have been tremendously influential in America and England.[23] His views about natural rights and a right to revolution to protect life, liberty, and estate influenced the American founding fathers, such as Thomas Jefferson, in the writing of the Declaration of Independence.[24] But his views also define a theory of property rights that sees them as natural. Individuals have specific ownership rights attached to property, and governments are limited in what they can do. In fact, the Fifth Amendment eminent domain clause, as will be discussed later, is partially based on Locke in that it defines limits on what the government can do when taking property and what it has to do to preserve individual rights to ownership. Locke's theory of property has also influenced other thinkers, including economist Milton Friedman, who connected the protection of private property to democracy and freedom.[25] Overall, the significance of John Locke's writings on government and society has been to endorse perhaps one of the most influential views about ownership that exists in the United States.

Beyond the arguments of Hume, Rousseau, and Locke, there are other theories or claims about the origin or justification of property rights. A theory of moral philosophy called utilitarianism arose in Britain in the nineteenth century and included thinkers such as James Mill, Jeremy Bentham, and John Stuart Mill. The core of utilitarianism is that the ideas of justice or what is right and wrong are based upon maximizing utility, that is, producing the greatest good for the greater number of individuals. Property rights are supported as an institution that promotes security, liberty, and other goals. Protecting property rights best produces the greatest good for the greatest number of individuals.[26] However, this utilitarian theory also means that if in some situations limiting property rights would also yield a greater social good, then they could be limited. It is a utilitarian theory of property rights that may also underscore the justification of eminent domain and the taking of private property away from one person and giving it to another for economic development reasons. This was the rationale for the taking in the *Kelo* case.

Another theory of property is found in the writings of nineteenth-century German philosopher G. W. F. Hegel. Hegel, similar to Locke, sees property as important to personal freedom. But he takes the argument even further. In his *Philosophy of Right*,

Hegel sees how one's senses of humanity, personality, or even identity are realized in private property. For Hegel: "Since my will, as the will of a person, and so as a single will, becomes objective tome in property, property acquires the character of private property." It may be an exaggeration to state that he argued that we are what we own, but there is a sense in which that is the direction he is headed. Individuals acquire a concrete sense of who they are through their property. Ownership secures a sense of freedom, security, and an embodiment of who an individual is. As Hegel states: "[P]roperty is the first embodiment of freedom and so is itself a substantive end."[27] Among contemporary writers Margaret Radin, in her *Reinterpreting Property*, has drawn upon Hegel to make similar arguments.[28] She contends that property helps define who individuals are. What is more important, this linkage of property and personhood also seems to establish ideas about privacy and claims that perhaps even if the government does pay for property taken, the mere taking of it is damaging to identity. Thus, perhaps to take one's home is only to take a possession. But for many, taking a private home is also a taking of something very near and dear and which for many is closely connected to a sense of identity. In effect, property is more than a "thing" in some cases. Contrary to Locke, not all forms of property are fungible into money or have a cash value. As a famous credit card commercial states, some things are just "priceless." One cannot always be adequately compensated for the loss of a home or a community.

The point in developing a discussion about the origins and justification of property rights is not simply to engage in abstract academic discussion. Instead, different theories about the origins of property help also to clarify why property rights exist and what the limits to those rights are. Depending on the theory selected, property rights are more or less secure, and the government would have different powers to use to deprive individuals of things that they own.

Property in America

Various philosophical and political traditions have influenced visions of property rights in the United States. Briefly, it is worth noting these traditions.[29]

As stated earlier, John Locke's writings were perhaps the most influential upon early America and this influence has been noted by many scholars. Locke argues that the protection of property is the goal of civil society. Property is a natural and prepolitical institution given to humanity by God, and a property interest gives the owner a singular and absolute control over something which no one, including the state, could violate. Property ownership of a thing was based upon ownership of one's body and labor such that anything that our labor mixed with became personal property. But property included more than the possessions of individuals. Property referred to one's "Life, Liberty, and Estate." "Property" was a general political term referring to all the personal and political rights of individuals with ownership of one's body and talents premised upon the natural freedom of individuals. These comments, along with the placing of property in a state of nature, indicate that property was meant to affirm the natural political rights and liberties of individuals against the state, and not necessarily be the only tool of economic development. These natural rights are not lost to the state, but instead:

> The Supream Power cannot take from any Man any Part of his Property without his own consent. For the preservation of Property being the end of Government, and that for which Men enter into Society, it necessarily supposes and requires, that the People should have Property.[30]

Thus, when Locke argues that the protection of property is the end or goal of government, or that each individual should have property, he is arguing that government should protect the political liberties of individuals. Property is protected because it is associated with the political liberties of individuals, and important to individual self-expression, identity, or personality. Many colonial American readings of Locke's theory of property noted this connection between personal political liberty and property ownership, and agreed with Locke that property rights deserved a somewhat absolute protection against government regulation.

In addition to Locke, J. G. A. Pocock argued in *The Machiavellian Moment: Florentine Political Thought and the Atlantic Republic Tradition* that a second description of property that influenced the American colonists is found in the neoclassical Republican tradition.[31] This Republican tradition can be traced back to the classical writings of Aristotle, the Romans, and Machiavelli and other sixteenth-century humanists in Florence, Italy.

The primary Republican influence upon colonial America, however, is James Harrington. His utopian 1656 treatise *Oceana* is indebted to and part of the Florentine tradition that links the maintenance of Republican government, liberty, and popular government to the distribution of property within a community. Harrington describes the political institutions necessary to maintain a Republican form of government. He argues in *Oceana* for the need to achieve a balance of power in a commonwealth among the king, the nobility, and the people if tyranny is to be avoided and a limited Republican form of government is to be sustained.[32] Crucial to that balance of power, or the "doctrine of balance" in Harrington's words, is the equal distribution of property among the three groups. To grant any one group, such as the king, a disproportionate amount or control over property would be to give him excessive power in the republic.

Harrington saw the doctrine of balance as necessary to limit the Crown's power. The doctrine of balance is rooted in the traditional neoclassical fear of excessive or maldistributions of wealth as a sign of an unhealthy commonwealth.[33] A free republic could only be maintained if excessive concentrations of wealth in the possession of few could be avoided. Dispersed and relatively equal ownership of property was crucial to limiting political power and promoting freedom.

Harrington adopted this Republican view on property and drew linkages between one's personal property and political power. While Harrington and Locke agreed that property is important to one's independence and status in society, Harrington did not agree that the end of society was the protection of property, or that the state could not regulate it. Harrington also did not believe that property distributions were natural. Property rules were conventional and distributions could be altered or regulated to promote Republican forms of government. Harrington protected individual liberty not by protecting the natural property rights in individuals, but by redistributing property to ensure a Republican and limited form of government.

According to Pocock, Harrington's doctrine of balance was subsequently interpreted by his followers to be an argument against executive patronage and power. This concept of balance translated into an important ideological tool of opposition for the

American colonials against the king.[34] Harrington's Republicanism, then, was a clear influence upon the early formulation of American politics such that the American Founding can be linked to the Atlantic Republican Tradition.

While Locke's and Harrington's influence upon America are often noted, ignored is a third thinker or tradition that influenced early American politics, law, and thoughts on property. Sir William Blackstone's views on property in his *Commentaries on the Laws of England* are often overlooked yet another important influence on early American views of property. Blackstone's views were more legalistic and conventional than either Locke's or Harrington's, yet at times it appears that the jurist's views were similar to those of Locke. For example, in volume 2 of the *Commentaries* Blackstone states:

> There is nothing which so generally strikes the imagination and engages the affections of mankind, as the right of property; or the sole and despotic dominion which one man claims and exercises over the external things of the world, in total exclusion of the right of any other individual in the universe.[35]

In this passage and others Blackstone describes property as an absolute right. Protection of this right, as well as all other absolute rights, is the "principal aim of society." More generally, in language reminiscent of Locke's, Blackstone states that the three absolute rights civil society should protect are security, liberty, and property. In volume 1 of his *Commentaries*, Blackstone agreed with Locke that the protection of property is important and necessary for freedom and property is also described as an absolute right of Englishmen. Again reminiscent of Locke, in *Commentaries*, volume 2, Blackstone described property ownership as an absolute dominion. Overall, Blackstone's influence is well noted in American history, and some colonists invoked what they read as his apparent defense of the absolutist view of property to support many of their political claims.[36]

Property was clearly an important concept in America and was well discussed by many individuals. James Madison described property broadly to include even one's opinions and beliefs. He argued that property as well as personal rights are an "essential object of the laws" necessary to the promotion of free government. Alexander Hamilton stated that the preservation of private property was essential to liberty and Republican government. Thomas Jefferson depicted property as a "natural right" of humankind and linked ownership to public virtue and republic government. John Adams described a proper balance of property in society as important to maintaining Republican government and connected property ownership to moral worth. Thomas Paine felt that the state was instituted to protect the natural right of property, and Daniel Webster would later link property to virtue, freedom, and power.[37] Numerous Anti-Federalists described a society as free when it protected property rights or equalized property distributions. For example, Samuel Bryan, in his *"Letters of Centinel,"* argued that a "republican, or free government, can only exist where the body of the people are virtuous, and where property is pretty equally divided."[38] Hence, many colonial American readings of Locke's theory of property also noted the connection between personal political liberty and property ownership, and agreed with Locke that property rights deserved a somewhat absolute protection against government regulation. Additionally, others followed Harrington and articulated the importance of property divisions in preserving state Republican governments. Still others cited Blackstone to defend more absolutist conceptions of property. Clearly there were many early Americans who described property as the end of society, as absolute, as linked to other important political rights, or as natural. Conversely, threats to property were considered destructive to freedom and Republican government.

While property was described in near absolute terms in the rhetoric of many of the founding fathers, the reality was that property was far less secure in practice. Historian Frank Bourgin stated it clearly when he indicated that "the prevalent interest in the Lockean doctrines emphasizing the restraints on government and the sanctity of private property has probably obscured the full significance of the influence of mercantilism in shaping the contours of our federal constitution."[39] Arthur Schlesinger Jr. has similarly concluded that "the American colonies had long been accustomed to government intervention in economic affairs" and that

> the colonies had become accustomed to governmental intervention by the British, who followed the policies of mercantilism. When independence was achieved, given their lack of capital and a later

start in manufacturing, it was hardly a surprise that their leaders would use the resources of government to promote economic development.[40]

Both of these historians note how the "coincidence of *The Wealth of Nations* and the Declaration of Independence both occurring in 1776 encouraged the notion that the stars of laissez-faire and of the American republic rose in unison."[41] In fact, Smith was hardly known in America until the 1790s. Instead of early America embracing Adam Smith, they pursued many policies that Smith wrote against. It was not until the Jacksonian era that laissez-faire ideas of Smith took hold; until then, mercantile policies were preferred.

Bourgin, Schlesinger, and other historians have noted the extensive regulation of the economy and market that occurred not just in early nineteenth-century America but even during the colonial and revolutionary era. State regulation of the economy included the promotion of manufacturing, and the confiscation of property for numerous public projects was common. Price fixing, as well as other forms of property regulation, was important. Regulation of monopolies, dormant land, urban land, and other economic policies were also employed. Hamilton's creation of a national bank, as well as advocacy to support and regulate commerce, are other examples of federal efforts to subordinate individual property interests to secure the public good.

There are significant other examples to support the claim (or the belief among many conservatives) that in early American law property rights did not occupy the absolutist position that the political rhetoric of the day suggested. Instead, consistent with Blackstone, use of one's property was subject to uses or regulation consistent with the public good and many state laws and constitutional provisions stipulated this "public good" limitation. The extensive use of eminent domain by state governments prior to and after the Revolution, often without compensation for property taken, challenged traditional property rights claims. The Mills Acts, laws that allowed the flooding of private land without compensation in order to build mills, starting in Massachusetts in 1795 and eventually encompassing many other states, similarly eroded some property claims in favor of others.[42] Even the judiciary, viewed perhaps as the one institution meant to safeguard property claims, permitted extensive limits on traditional property rights.

In many of the debates in the revision of the first state constitutions, there are indications that some states sought greater protection of property, while others saw property as privileged, and efforts to weaken its protections were undertaken. Finally, even legislation authored by Thomas Jefferson that abolished entail, primogeniture, or changed property rights qualifications necessary for franchise indicated that property rights were not static and they were not immune from government redistribution or control.

WHAT ARE PROPERTY RIGHTS?

Return to Lesley Gore: "It's my party and I'll cry if I want to." Is the same true with property and ownership? "It's my property and I will do what I want with it." The Lesley Gore reference implicates two questions when it comes to property. First, what rights are associated with property ownership? Second, can individuals do anything they want with their property? Answering both of these questions is important because it helps clarify what property is. What is more important, though, is to understand what rights are associated with ownership. Answering this question provides important clarification about how the government can regulate or interfere with property. Depending on what rights individuals have in ownership will determine, among other things, when the government can place limits on what people do with their property.

If individuals have extensive property rights, then the government may not be able to place many, if any, limits on what people do with their land. For example, a broad reading of property rights would suggest that perhaps an individual could tear down his home in a residential suburb and erect a factory on the land. Or perhaps an extensive reading of property rights would mean that individuals could blast loud music or pollute their property. Conversely, a narrow reading of property rights would suggest that the government could limit the ability of individuals to do any of the above in the interest, perhaps, of protecting others. The other reason for wanting to understand what property rights are is that, depending what "ownership" entails, some government actions may be a violation of these rights. Some regulations may be too extensive or an interference with property rights and therefore constitute a form of eminent domain known as a regulatory taking (this topic will be discussed later in the book). Additionally, if the issue is not a government regulatory taking, but eminent domain, the question is what rights do owners have when the government does in fact want to take someone's house or home and give the property to another private person? Simply put, "property rights" tell us what owners can do with the things they own, and describe the scope of governmental power over these rights.

When lawyers discuss or think about property rights, they do not describe ownership as a unitary right. Instead, property is often described as composed of a bundle of rights. The idea that property is a bundle of rights is attributed to an influential 1913 *Yale Law Journal* article written by Wesley Hohfeld.[43] To think of property as a bundle of rights, instead think of ownership as a bundle of sticks tied together. Each stick has a different length and width or diameter. Think of each stick as a property right. For someone to have complete rights, or all the rights associated with ownership, one has all the sticks in the bundle. The more sticks, the more rights. The length and width of the sticks refer to how extensive each one of those rights is. Ownership rights vary by the number of sticks and their lengths and diameters.

For example, a person who owns an apartment building has more rights in that building than does a tenant who is renting an apartment. The tenant has a limited use of her apartment for a duration of time, as determined by the lease or rental agreement. An individual who obtains a license to use something also has limited rights. If I am given a license or permission to enter someone's property to pick fruit in the fall, that right is limited to that. I do not have a right to build a house or exclude others from the property. Instead, this is a right reserved to the owner. Rights to music are a big issue in the age of the Internet, iPods, and MP3 players. Individuals may have a right to listen to music, but do they have a right to download, swap, or sell music? If I buy the new Bruce Springsteen DVD can I make a copy of it and sell or give it to my friends? The basic answer is no. Yes, I own the DVD but the ownership rights acquired with the purchase do not extend to me having the right to sell the music and personally profit. In buying the CD, I have a limited number of sticks and each stick may be a lesser length and thickness than Springsteen or the music company has.

What are the different sticks in the bundle of property rights? There are a few possible answers. Jeremy Bentham, an important nineteenth-century British philosopher, contended in his *The Principles of Morals and Legislation* that the right of property includes four rights: the right of occupation; the right of excluding others; the right of disposition, or the right of transfer in the integral right to other persons; and the right to transfer property after our deaths.[44] Put simply, to own something means an individual can occupy it, exclude others, give or sell it to others, or will it to others. Bentham's idea about what property is and the rights associated with it is good, but it has its limitations. First, his notion of property implies that it is a thing that is physical that can be occupied. Homes, real estate, cars, boats, are all real and can be occupied. Some of these entities may be what Bentham had in mind when he was thinking about property. But today property also includes nonphysical entities such as patents, copyrights, and licenses. The world of intellectual property is something not at all captured by Bentham's four rights. In addition, property may have more than these four basic sticks.

A. M. Honoré, a twentieth-century legal philosopher, argued that there are eleven sticks in the property rights bundle.[45] These sticks are both rights and responsibilities, and include the:

right to use;

right to manage;

right to possess;

right to an income;

right to security;

right to its capital;

right to transmissibility;

right to an absence of term;

responsibility to a prohibition of harmful use;

responsibility to a liability to execution; and

responsibility to residuary character.

These 11 rights cover a range of options regarding what owners can do with their property. It includes exclusion, use, and the right to sell or transfer property, but it also allows one to profit from it, be safe in its use, and otherwise divide up the bundle of rights in a variety of ways. This elevenfold classification of property offers a richer understanding of property for today. One person can own property and turn it over to another to manage; that person in turn can rent it to another or let even another use the property on a temporary basis. Music that I buy is still owned by the artist, sold and managed by a music company, and I acquire limited rights to play and listen to the music. I can give my CD to another but cannot make copies and sell to others. Owners thus hold many sticks in property and can transfer some of them to others, subject to limitations.

Referring to ownership as having these 11 characteristics is important in that it gives a more complete range of what one can do with property. On the one hand, the right to exclude is at the basis of many trespass laws and rules regarding copyright and patent, and intellectual property infringement cases. To own something means I can exclude others from using it. In effect, I can post a "Do not trespass" sign on my yard or over anything that I own. But three responsibilities are important also to note. They state that individuals cannot use their property to hurt others, that one's property can be taken by others to pay off debts, and that in general owners are responsible for how their property affects others. These different responsibilities are important to note, especially the one that says that owners cannot use their property to hurt others. In the British common law as it has come to be inherited and adopted in the United States, no one has a right to use his or her property in a way that it becomes a nuisance. Blaring loud music in the middle of the night or emitting pollution from my property hurts others. My right to use and enjoy my property may interfere with your right to use and enjoy yours. Limits on property rights have to be struck in a world where we live together, often in very close quarters or proximity. The sticks in the bundle of rights thus are limited in length and width in order to respect the rights of others.

The concept of property as a bundle of rights is critical to understanding contemporary ownership rights. While John Locke might have spoken of property as a natural right, he never gave a good description of what these rights included. His discussion of government being created to protect property rights seemed to imply the latter were nearly absolute. As pointed out earlier, that has never really been the case. The rights of others and the needs of the government (the public good) may limit what individuals can do with their property. In addition, even if one does have a full bundle of rights, does that mean that the government may never interfere with them? No. Eminent domain is based on the idea that if the government wants your property they may be able to secure it under some circumstances, so long as they pay you for it. However, there may be some limits on the reasons the government can offer to take property and there may be some requirements regarding the compensation offered to you. These topics are discussed later in the book.

TYPES OF PROPERTY

In the end we are still brought back to the question, what is *property*? Lawyers and the law have come up with numerous ways to classify property and to decide what it really is. Many first-year law school classes on property, as well as literally thousands of books and articles, all have fashioned ways to organize what property is.[46] It is impossible to repeat that discussion here, but some of these different classifications can be examined.[47]

One type of classification is to consider property as a "thing" or object, as opposed to a relationship. By that, most people think of property as some type of tangible or real object. A house is property because it is an object we can hold, touch, see, or occupy. The same is true for our vehicles, clothing, and other personal items. All of these items are real and we can touch them. They are, because of this physical quality, something that can become our property. However, property is not always a thing, or a "*res*" in Latin. Property is also a relationship. By describing property as a relationship it refers to certain rights individuals may have, focusing less on the thing than on the connections we have to something. By that, a home is property, but there are specific rights (the bundle of rights) attached to owning a home. There are also specific rights attached to having a mortgage, lease, a pension, or a bank account. All of these entities are property, but sometimes lawyers and the law prefer to focus on the relationship aspect of property, rather than the thing, in order to better capture the rights one may have.

Perhaps the main reason why thinking about property as a relationship and not a thing is important relates to a second distinction one can make regarding ownership. This is a distinction between thinking of property in terms of rights to a tangible versus an intangible entity. Again, homes, cars, and personal items such as clothing are all tangible or physical forms of property. Yet if the notion of property were simply to stop here, there are many types of things that we own that would not be captured by this conception of ownership. Individuals can have property rights in pensions, investments, contracts, licenses (such as to practice law or medicine), copyrights, patents, retirement accounts, and perhaps even in some type of bequests. In some situations, individuals have no property interests in air or light, but in some urban settings such a right has been recognized to exist if an adjoining building obstructs either of them. In addition, while there is generally no property right to air, ownership rights often include the airspace rights above the ground. Many of these intangible entities can be worth a significant amount of money even if they are not exactly something physical in the same way that a home is. The law considers all of these items to be property, too.

A third way to think about property is temporally. By that, individuals (when I speak of individuals I am not ignoring that corporations and other associations can also own property) can have a present as well as a future interest in property. In law school, first-year students are often perplexed by the different types of property interests. At the apex of property interests is what is called "fee simple absolute." From the days of British common law, a fee simple absolute was considered to be the firmest and most absolute right to property that could exist. In common law, a fee simple absolute was described as a freehold estate wherein one had "seisin," or an immediate right to possess the property and exclude all others. Fee simple absolute is the type of property interest most people think of today when they contemplate their own home, for example. It is a type of ownership that includes all the sticks in the bundle. It is a present possessory interest.

But fee simple absolute is not the only present possessory interest. There are lesser possessory rights. One can also have a nonfreehold estate in property. This type of interest grants someone the right to use property for a fixed number of years, such as with a lease. Another present possessory interest is life estate in property. By that, individuals can be given a right to use property for the duration of their life. When they die, the property interest goes to someone else. To whom that property goes addresses a different form of property—future interests. If the owner grants to me a life estate to use some property, who gets the property when I die? If the property returns back to the owner, the law calls this a reverter. By that, the property interest and possession reverts back to the owner. If instead the property, upon my death, transfers to a third party, then that person is said to have reversionary interest in the remainder of the property. That is, the third person may eventually receive the property, so long as the owner does not change her mind or alter the contract willing the property.

The point here is that it is possible to have an interest in some property that one does not presently possess. The critical issue is over the nature of the rights one has. As a rule, the law does not recognize a property interest unless it is vested. By vested, it means that the interest is secure and not subject to repeal or revision. A life estate is secure and vested, as is a fee simple absolute. However, remainders and reverters could change and not be vested. Future owners could die, deeds or contracts could change, or other circumstances might be altered. One good example of this deals with wills and bequests. If my uncle writes a will leaving me $1 million, I had better not run out and spend any money simply based upon the language of the will. There is no property interest of mine in that will (no matter how assuring my uncle is that he intends to leave me the money) because there is always a chance that the will could change. Moreover, if my uncle dies owning debtors more than $1 million, I also will not collect because debts have to be paid off before assets can be distributed. So long as my uncle is alive, my property interest in that inheritance has not vested. Once he has died and the will and assets are verified (this is the purpose of probate), then my interest has vested. At that point, if the money is available, then my interest in the $1 million has vested and I have a right to it. At that point the future possessory interest is now a present interest.

A full and rich discussion of property could effect many other distinctions and describe many different types of property interests. Fee simples (a lesser form of property rights than fee simple absolutes), life estates, reverters, and remainders all are subject to some qualifications or limits upon the rights they contain. Property might also include liens, licenses, contracts, court judgments, development rights, riparian or water rights, subsurface or airspace rights, copyrights, patents, and easements (or some limited rights to cross or use another's property). Ownership might be vested in one person, persons, associations, corporations, the government, or other entities or organizations. The range of *rei* (plural of *res*) that can be owned is infinite, and the types of relationships or bundle or rights attached to them are equally immense. As technology changes, new forms of property emerge and older forms of ownership may disappear or change. At one time, animals were thought of simply as property. If that is the case, then almost anything can be done to them. However, as social attitudes change and science provides new information about the sentient and cognitive capacities of animals, the law is shifting. Anticruelty laws now limit what one can do with or to animals. Moreover, if animals are property they cannot inherit our estate (our computer cannot inherit anything from us). But increasingly, property owners, such as Leona Helmsley, may wish to will a portion of their estate to their animals if the latter survives them, providing for them until they die.

New forms of patented life are considered to be a form of property. Both genetically modified foods and animals are considered presently to be forms of property. Whether cloned dogs or cats in the future will be treated that way is unclear. Presently the law still considers the human body a form of property in many situations. A corpse is the property of the estate or family of the deceased and my blood and plasma are my property, which can be sold. However, even if my kidney is my property, I cannot sell it, but if someone was to steal it from me it would be considered a form of theft. Moreover, as medical science gathers tissue or other specimens from human patients and doctors or drug pharmaceutical companies develop drugs from them, do individuals have a property interest in the profits derived from these new patents? Also, who owns frozen embryos, sperm, or ova? Divorce and probate proceedings in the United States struggle over these questions as they search for property law answers to addressing these questions.

The critical issues with all of these forms of property are threefold. First, does the law recognize the interest to be a property interest? If so, then what rights are associated with the property interest? Finally, the last question is about vesting. Specifically, has a right to the particular property interest vested or become so secure that a court could say, for example, that you clearly own it subject to some specified conditions? If all three of these

CHAPTER THREE

Property Rights in America

Anything that is not nailed down is mine.
Anything that can be pried loose is not nailed down.

Though we own property, even if it is fee simple absolute, that does not mean the king cannot take it. At least, that was true in medieval England. Private property has never been absolutely secure against the government, no matter what the rhetoric. The rights of ownership have always been conditioned or limited by the rights of others or by the government. There are many powers that the government has to limit the use of property, including the power to tax, the police power, and the power of eminent domain. The power to tax is well understood by most individuals and will not be discussed here. However, the police and eminent domain powers are less understood and they will be the focus of the discussion in this chapter.

The goal here will be to clarify how property rights were understood as they were transplanted into the United States from England. Additionally, the chapter examines the historical origins of eminent domain from England through colonial and early America.[1] The focus of this chapter will be the history of eminent domain though the middle of the twentieth century to offer readers an understanding of how eminent domain evolved and why it is often necessary for the government to take private property.

THREE BASIC POWERS OF THE GOVERNMENT

What do governments do? Numerous theories address this question, with no firm resolution. Oftentimes answers to this question are mostly matters of ideology or political philosophy, with different views on the task of government being a product of varying views on human nature or psychology.

For example, many ancient Greek philosophers, such as Socrates, Plato, and Aristotle, described humans as basically social creatures with a desire for knowledge and self-perfection.[2] Given this human psychology, Plato believed that the task of government was to achieve justice and to find the best role for everyone's talents or skills.[3] Plato believed that the human soul or psyche was composed of three elements: an emotive or spirited aspect, as well as an aspect that included human appetites or desires, and a rational or intellectual component. A perfectly balanced soul was one where the emotions and appetites were controlled by reason. However, not every person achieved this balance. Plato saw a world where some people were controlled by either their appetites or emotions. The leaders of his ideal republic, whom he called "philosopher kings," were the ones ruled by reason. The ideal republic—one where one's harmony or balance in the soul matched one's soul position or duties—was one where reason as embodied in the philosopher kings ruled the republic.

Other philosophers reached different conclusions about the proper role of government, also based upon the differing views they had about human nature. St. Augustine and many of the early Christian thinkers saw humans as basically base and sinful creatures.[4] Accordingly, their view of government was less noble and optimistic than the Greeks'. Government was often viewed as a "punishment and remedy" for human sin. This meant that the primary job of government was to keep peace, maintain order, and, as necessary, enforce moral and religious laws to prevent individuals from sinning if possible. Later, other Christian thinkers such as John Calvin adopted similar views. In the sixteenth century, famous British philosopher Thomas Hobbes adopted many of these Christian ideas when he wrote his book *The Leviathan*. Employing a social contract theory to explain the origins of government, like Locke and Rousseau, he envisioned that there was once a state of nature before there was government and civil society. However, this state of nature was a state of war where life, as Hobbes described it, was "solitary, poor, nasty, brutish, and short." It was a war of all against all. Individuals thus formed a social contract in order to protect themselves. What resulted, though, was a social contract to create a near-absolute monarchy.[5] For Hobbes, only a strong king with unlimited powers could keep order, given how contentious human nature was.

Rousseau and Locke, both of whom were discussed in chapter 2, also had their views on human nature. Rousseau seemed to assume that the state of nature was Eden-like, and that humans in this state of nature were naturally good, innocent, and uncorrupted. It was the invention of property and of social conventions that corrupted human nature. The behavior of humans as observed in society was not what they were really like, it was merely a corrupt view of men and women who were naturally more innocent and cooperative.[6] The government that formed as a result of tricking people into government was a tyranny whose goal was probably no more than the enslavement of the majority to serve the needs of the few.[7] For Locke, while humans and the state of nature may not have been as Eden-like as Rousseau believed, it was certainly not the state of nature of Hobbes. Humans were basically good but subject to misjudgments in how they enforce and protect their natural rights to property. Government was instituted to help clarify and protect these and other natural rights of individuals. In contrast to Hobbes, though, the social contract that individuals in the state of nature execute does not produce a monarchy. Instead, it is more of a limited government subject to what now might be called "constitutional limits."[8]

When the American founders were debating the creation of the republic and the Constitution of 1787, they were well versed in the political writings of the ancient Greeks, Christians, Rousseau, Hobbes, Locke, and other philosophers. Richard Hofstadter, a noted post–World War II American historian, penned at the beginning of his influential book *The American Political Tradition* that the U.S. Constitution "is based on the philosophy of Hobbes and the religion of Calvin."[9] By that, the framers of the Constitution seemed to believe Hobbes's contention that human nature was quarrelsome and that the chief task of government was to bring and maintain order. While Hofstadter's claim may overstate the case, there is no question that Hobbesian, Calvinistic, and also Lockean views influenced the American founders and their writing of the Constitution.

Perhaps one of the best statements regarding the political views and assumptions about human nature and politics that went into the Constitution can be found in the *Federalist Papers*. Written by James Madison, Alexander Hamilton, and John Jay for a newspaper to urge the New York legislature to adopt the new constitution in 1787, the 85 *Federalist Papers* are often viewed with reference when searching for clues about the Constitution. *Federalist* numbers 10 and 51, penned by Madison, describe a pessimistic view of human nature. They describe society as ever facing the threat of being drawn apart by factions. Factions are like special interest groups seeking their own private good at the expense of the majority of common good. But Madison describe the sources of faction as "sown in the nature of man." Humans fight about everything; "the most common and durable source of factions has been the various and unequal distribution of property."[10] Government is thus instituted to protect property and bring order. Government is necessary, as Madison stated in *Federalist* 51. In one of the most famous passages from this paper, Madison tells the reader:

> But what is government itself but the greatest of all reflections on human nature? If men were angels, no government would be necessary. If angels were to govern men, neither external nor internal controls on government would be necessary. In framing a government which is to be administered by men over men, the great difficulty lies in this: you must first enable the government to control the governed; and in the next place oblige it to control itself. A dependence on the people is, no doubt, the primary control on the government; but experience has taught mankind the necessity of auxiliary precautions.[11]

Government is necessary to protect property and check against actions and quarrels that are rooted in human nature. The only way to do that is to construct an elaborate constitutional system of checks and balances, separation of powers, federalism, and other mechanisms meant to break up and limit political power.

The importance of the *Federalist Papers* resides in the insights it provides to the minds of some of the framers and the Constitution. It underscores the importance attached to property and also the framers' vision for government, which stressed a limited government that had as its primary goals the maintenance of order, in order to promote liberty, property, and limit factions, For some, this vision of government is very democratic; for others, it is elitist. By that, some argue that the protection of property was meant to serve the interests of the wealthy. Charles Beard, writing in the early twentieth century, made this claim.[12] It is not important to resolve this debate here. It is sufficient to say that protection of property and maintaining public safety and order to further liberty for some or all is what the Constitution was about, and the way to do that was to place limits on what the government could do. This is the very essence of what a constitutional government is.

But is that all government is supposed to do? At a broad philosophical level that may be true, but one can get beyond broad generalities and ask what specific powers the Constitution gave the national government. A close reading of the document, especially Article I, reveals a host of specific powers regarding the regulation of commerce, national defense, and taxation, among other powers. Beyond the Constitution, states also were given or had their own powers to act. In fact, unlike the national government, states were viewed as having inherent powers. By that, state governments are viewed as having certain inherent powers to act to protect their citizens, whereas the national government does not have any inherent powers. Instead, the Constitution confers or creates federal power while state constitutions limit state power. In theory, this means that if the federal Constitution does not explicitly or implicitly grant the national government the authority to do something, then it cannot act. In theory, this also suggests a narrow construction of the powers of the national government. Conversely, this difference between state and federal power to act means that the former's power should be broadly construed. This difference may be critical also in explaining how the eminent domain authority of states versus the national government may be viewed, with the former being given more leeway to take property than the latter.

When thinking about the different powers that states and federal governments have, three critical powers come to mind: taxation, the police power, and eminent domain. Let us start with taxation. No one likes taxes but they are necessary for the government to operate. President Theodore Roosevelt is reputed to have described taxes as the price of civilization. One may not need to go that far in terms of praising them, but there is no question that armies, security, and law enforcement cannot pay for themselves.

In addition, a host of other functions, whatever they are and regardless of how expansive, need revenue. Taxes are one way to pay for government and these functions. The Constitution provides Congress and the national government with the authority to generate taxes to pay for its functions. One place it does that is in Article I, Section 8, wherein it states: "The Congress shall have power to lay and collect taxes, duties, imposts and excises, to pay the debts and provide for the common defense and general welfare of the United States."

Elsewhere, the Sixteenth Amendment expressly provides for Congress to impose and collect income taxes. This amendment became necessary after an odd Supreme Court decision in the nineteenth century appeared to question the constitutional authority of the federal government to impose a tax on income. While there are a few tax scammers and antigovernment types who question the validity of this amendment, no one seriously believes the federal government lacks the authority to tax income. The same is true for states. While both may face some limits in terms of how taxes are levied, requiring them to be uniform for the same class of individuals or taxpayers, governments have the power to tax.

The local governments' tax authority permits them to devise a variety of mechanisms to generate income. When it comes to the power of taxation and how it affects one's property, it is clear that taxes take away something that individuals own—some of their income or wealth. Taxes are a permitted limitation or taking of property in order to further the common good or goals of government. It may be ironic, but individuals may be required to give up some of their property in order to protect the rest of their property.

A second power of governments is referred to as the police power. The police power may be described as the inherent power of states to regulate for the health, safety, welfare, and morals of its citizens. Only states have police power; the federal government does not. The Supreme Court in *New York v. Miln*, 36 U.S. 102 (1837), developed the legal concept of police power as an importance attribute of state sovereignty. The police power gives states the authority to legislate for a whole host of issues, allowing states to pass laws to protect the environment, arrest speeders, regulate marriage and abortion, and to build roads, highways, and bridges. It is also the police power that permits states to enact zoning laws. The police power is important because, as the name implies, it allows the state to police its borders to protect its citizens. It is allowed to enact laws that prevent one person from harming another.

Many laws enacted under the police power authority might affect how property is used. For example, laws that prosecute trespass (making it illegal to enter someone else's property without the owner's permission) is one way that the police power regulates or protects owners. Conversely, laws that limit how individuals use their property to ensure that they do not create a nuisance fit into this category, such as preventing loud noises from blaring from a stereo in the middle of a night, requiring vacant property to be boarded up, or other rules that prevent one from polluting. Zoning laws might limit what types of buildings or structures are built in some neighborhoods, preventing toxic waste dumps or garbage burning plants from being built in the middle of residential neighborhoods. Zoning laws might also limit where adult entertainment is located.

Zoning laws and other police-power regulations may impose significant limitations upon how property is used. But not all forms of regulation are permitted. If, on the one hand, one is truly using her property as a nuisance, the government has nearly unlimited authority to abate the nuisance. But in some situations the nuisance requires only some modest legislation. Are there situations in which regulation can be too extensive? Yes. Zoning and other forms of laws may turn into what is called a regulatory taking. That is, the regulation may be so extensive that it denies an owner all effective use of the property. At that point, the Constitution, under the Due Process clause, may call the regulation a form of a regulatory taking. At this point, the taking is treated as a form of eminent domain that demands just compensation for the property that is subject to the overzealous regulation.

As noted above, only states have police powers. What about the federal government? The federal government does not have police power, but it has other ways of effectively getting its way when it comes to passing legislation to protect people. One way is the power to regulate commerce. Congress's commerce power is broad in that it can regulate all aspects of interstate commerce. United States Supreme Court decisions in the last 75 years have construed this commerce authority broadly and therefore under it the environment, discrimination, and labor relations, for example, can be validly regulated. Another way Congress can act is to rely upon Article I, Section 8 of the Constitution. This is the section of the Constitution referred to as the "necessary and proper" or "elastic" clause. The clause reads that Congress shall have the power "[t]o make all laws which shall be necessary and proper for carrying into execution the foregoing powers, and all other powers vested by this Constitution in the government of the United States, or in any department or officer thereof." As first interpreted by Justice John Marshall and the Supreme Court in the landmark *McCulloch v. Maryland*, 17 U.S. 316 (1819) case, this clause gives Congress authority to enact almost any legislation, so long as it is related to or supports the other expressed powers found in the Constitution. For Marshall, he offered a broad reading of the word "necessary."

> Is it true, that this is the sense in which the word "necessary" is always used? Does it always import an absolute physical necessity, so strong, that one thing, to which another may be termed necessary, cannot exist without that other? We think it does not. If reference be had to its use, in the common affairs of the world, or in approved authors, we find that it frequently imports no more than that one thing is convenient, or useful, or essential to another. To employ the means necessary to an end, is generally understood as employing any means calculated to produce the end, and not as being confined to those single means, without which the end would be entirely unattainable.[13]

Congress, then, under its necessary and proper clause, will be given broad authority or slack by the courts in how it will deploy its authority. When examining laws passed by Congress, the courts will generally only subject it to what is called "rational basis scrutiny." That is, so long as Congress has some rational basis to act, the courts will uphold the law. The practical effect of this deference is that so long as no rights are violated, the courts will give any benefit of doubt to Congress when it comes to the constitutionality of legislation it passes. However, when rights are involved, the courts will subject the laws to a more intense or strict scrutiny and place the burden of proof on Congress to show that the law is constitutional. The importance of this level of analysis by the Court when examining legislation, and also of the Necessary and Proper clause, is that Congress is generally given significant deference when it wants to legislate, especially when it comes to economic and property rights today.

A final way that Congress can get things done in the absence of having police power is by using its spending authority to encourage states to act. It does this by conditioning the receipt of federal aid or money upon a state or local government doing something. For example, the federal government was able to convince states to increase their minimum legal drinking ages from 18 to 21 by stipulating that federal highway funds would only be given to them if they made this change. The same was true with laws requiring them to lower their blood-alcohol level limit to .08 in order to receive transportation funding. This use of leveraging federal funds to get states to act has been upheld as constitutional by the Supreme Court. In effect, it gets states to do what the federal government wants "voluntarily" when it otherwise could not force states to act. Overall, given the power of the purse, the Necessary and Proper clause, and the Commerce clause, Congress and the federal government effectively are not hurt by not having a formal police power.

The third major power of state and local governments (particularly when it comes to property) is eminent domain. As generally defined, eminent domain is the power of the government to take private property for a variety of public uses. In the United States, this power is also subject to several stipulations, the most important one being that property owners must be paid just compensation for the property the government acquires. Explaining the origins of this power requires more detail and is subject of the next section.

WHAT IS EMINENT DOMAIN?

According to numerous courts, eminent domain is the authority of the government to take private property for a public use as long as just compensation is paid to the owner for the taking. This authority is available to the federal government by way of the Constitution's Fifth Amendment. Courts have also ruled that state governments hold this power as what they call an inherent attribute of sovereignty. This means that states as sovereign entities have the power to condemn or take private property for a variety of public uses. This power, though, is subject to limitations found in each state's constitution or statutory law. Thus, the power of eminent domain, as with the police power, is a power that states have as states, with their laws and constitutions simply providing definitions on how the power can be limited or employed. Often the most frequent qualifications on eminent domain power in the United States are that the taking must be for a valid public use, and owners must be paid just compensation for any property taken. These are stipulations not easily defined in the United States and not universally recognized around the world. Other countries use powers similar to eminent domain to acquire private property, with names for that authority (legitimate or not) sometimes called nationalization or expropriation.

Where did the concept of eminent domain come from? William Stoebuck, a noted legal historian, traces the use of eminent domain back to the Romans.[14] They used this power for many of the reasons the government takes property today—to build roads or public buildings. They also used it for military and religious purposes. However, when they took property for these purposes, several things were absent in comparison to today. First, no due process was in place. By that, owners could not challenge the taking of their property in court. Second, there was no compensation given to the owners when their property was taken by the Roman republic or empire. Third, there were no stipulations that limited the reasons for why the property could be taken. If the government wanted, they took it—period. To a large extent the reason for this was that there really was no concept of private property that existed then, at least not a concept similar to what many now recognize today.

However, it is back in English common law that the more modern conceptions of eminent domain can be found.[15] To appreciate its origins, it is necessary to say a few and simplified things about feudalism in medieval England. The medieval political legal structure of Europe was once described as public power being held in private hands. By that, at least in early medieval Europe, there was no government in the sense of what exists now. Authority rested in the hands of several private individuals who held power or military supremacy over a specific area. Over time, the geographic reach and control of these leaders emerged, creating eventually what would be considered now to be monarchies and kingdoms. This royal power, at least initially, was no more than the private authority of one person over a large area. The assumption here, too, was that the king actually owned all of the land within his domain. This last point is critical to understanding medieval law and eventually eminent domain.

The king was considered to be the owner of all the property and land within his kingdom. In order to defend the property, he permitted lesser persons such as nobles, knights, and other royalty to inhabit lands, subject to them paying rents or tithes to him. They in turn let others occupy lesser amounts of property, again subject to tithes or rents being paid to them. This hierarchy extended all the way down to slaves or serfs. All of these individuals were permitted to use property ultimately subject to the pleasure of the king. Over time, the rules of occupation became subject to some limits. Important English historical events such as forcing the king to sign the Magna Carta in 1215 began to create rules that eventually have come to be recognized as the common law. These common law rules established concepts such as trespass and nuisance law that we earlier discussed. Out of these common law practices eventually emerged also institutions such as property law, establishing types of ownership rules such as fee simple absolute, life estates, reverters, and remainders.

While the preceding discussion is brief and subject to some qualifications, the important point to take away from it is that even with all these rules of property the assumption or practice that emerged or survived is that ultimately the king or the government held ultimate title to all property within the kingdom. Stoebuck claims that eminent domain originated in medieval feudal law, granting the king supreme power, or eminent domain over all land in the kingdom.[16] Similarly, in their historical analyses of eminent domain, Arthur Lenhoff and J. A. C. Grant trace the origin of the concept to natural law arguments giving the state a natural right to control land to secure "higher" purposes.[17]

A second and more practical purpose for eminent domain lies in the nature of government itself. In part the rationale for government is to solve what economists refer to as market failure when it comes to dealing with collective goods or free rider problems. Market failure refers to situations where the free market is unable to work properly.[18] One situation in which that occurs is with collective goods, such as clean air, water, or public safety. These goods are indivisible, thus making it hard to charge some individuals for these goods and provide it to them at the exclusion of those who do not pay. In some cases, there are free riders, individuals who can receive these goods without having to pay for them. Sellers have no incentive to provide goods to individuals who do not pay for them and people have no incentive to pay for goods they would otherwise receive for free. For example, individuals who listen to public radio or television without contributing are free riders. They get the service for free. To convince them to join, public radio or television stations offer incentives to encourage them to send in money. Governments have a variety of tools to address the free rider problem. Government may need to perform some functions or duties to address situations when the market fails because sellers do not wish to sell or buyers to buy.

In some situations governments may thus need to act to provide goods or services that markets cannot. Moreover, there may be some collective goods that government should provide not simply to address these market failure issues, but also because it would be very economically efficient or convenient to do that. Thus, it would help the economy to provide for roads, bridges, highways, and other basic infrastructure. In some cases, yes, toll roads could be operated and users assessed fees to use them. But it might also be more efficient to socialize these costs and provide them for all to use. Even Adam Smith, author of the 1776 book *Wealth of Nations*, which is considered to be the first major defense of capitalism and the marketplace, recognized an important role for the government in terms of providing for these public works.

> The third and last duty of the sovereign or commonwealth is that of erecting and maintaining those public institutions and those public works, which, though they may be in the highest degree advantageous to a great society, are, however, of such a nature that the profit could never repay the expence to any individual or small number of individuals, and which it therefore cannot be expected that any individual or small number of individuals should erect or maintain. The performance of this duty requires, too, very different degrees of expence in the different periods of society.
>
> After the public institutions and public works necessary for the defence of the society, and for the administration of justice, both of which have already been mentioned, the other works and institutions of this kind are chiefly those for facilitating the commerce of the society, and those for promoting the instruction of the people. The institutions for instruction are of two kinds: those for the education of youth, and those for the instruction of people of all ages.

The consideration of the manner in which the expence of those different sorts of public, works and institutions may be most properly defrayed will divide this third part of the present chapter into three different articles.[19]

In this passage Smith notes both the problem of market failure or public goods when indicating that government needs to provide some services that would be difficult for private individuals to provide at a profit. Second, he recognizes that there is a class of public projects that the government should promote which are useful for commerce and society as a whole. Building roads, bridges, and schools fit into that category. Many of these projects today would be called public works or infrastructure projects that extend from the highways and bridges to waterworks, dams, sewer systems, and perhaps even some forms of telecommunications such as wireless networks. All of these projects can help facilitate commerce and business and are good for society. But his discussion hints at even a larger group of projects that the government may fund, including building schools for education, and maybe even parks for recreation.

The point of this discussion is that there are many public works that are either necessary or useful for the government to undertake because it would be easier for it to undertake those functions than to try to coordinate private individuals to do it. Government thus addresses another problem economists discuss—the collective action dilemma.[20] Specifically, the collective action dilemma is how to get individuals to work together when it might be easier to be a free rider and reap the benefits of a collective good. The decision to undertake a project may be a result of the police power to further the health, education, welfare, or morals of the people. The taxing power may be the way to pay for the project. Finally, the eminent domain power may be necessary to facilitate any of these projects. In order to build roads, bridges, lay cable, erect schools, or lay out parks, the government may need to take private property for these projects.

Additionally, in order to build cemeteries, airports, or other public projects, private property may be needed for these projects. Yes, owners of this property should be compensated for their losses, but some critics contend that eminent domain is not necessary and that the government should simply buy the land on the open market. By that, instead of using eminent domain, the government would simply negotiate with owners to sell. This is what government usually tries to do. But what if one owner wishes to be a holdout and either refuses to sell or demands an unreasonable price for property needed to build a school. Should one person or owner be able to veto the project or blackmail the government (and ultimately the taxpayer) into receiving an unfair price for the property? The answer is no. Eminent domain may be necessary to achieve public goods and prevent holdouts from extorting the government. Of course, how broad the use of eminent domain and the types of purposes it should be used for are a matter of contention. This is the problem of what legitimate public uses eminent domain should be used for, and this is the subject of the debate that the Supreme Court confronted in the *City of New London v. Kelo* case.

PROPERTY RIGHTS AND THE EMERGENCE OF EMINENT DOMAIN LAW IN THE UNITED STATES

Whatever the origin, be it economic purposes as suggested by Adam Smith or evolving out of the common law and the concept of royal power, Stoebuck, Lenhoff, and others agree that eminent domain came to be seen as an essential attribute of sovereignty that could not be alienated or given up. Eminent domain is a necessary power of government to act to address market failures and perform its basic functions. By the time of the writing of the U.S. Constitution and the Fifth Amendment, it was acknowledged even in America that eminent domain was an inherent power of government (as evidenced by colonial use) and not in need of specification. During the Revolutionary War, eminent domain and numerous forms of economic regulation were used by the newly independent states to undertake the war, and even after the war ended eminent domain was regularly used to undertake projects similar to those described by Adam Smith.

Eminent domain is mentioned by John Locke and William Blackstone (the latter an eighteenth-century British jurist whose *Commentaries on the Laws of England* were of tremendous influence on the American founding fathers and the law), among other seventeenth- and eighteenth-century political writers. Locke, while defending an absolute right to property as a political protection against the king, recognized the right of the government to take property as long as it was either with the consent of the individual or of his representative. But Locke did not indicate compensation was due when property was taken.

Errol Meidinger argues that the first recorded uses of eminent domain in America can be traced to a 1639 Massachusetts statute authorizing the taking of land to build roads.[21] This statute did not allow houses, gardens, or orchards to be destroyed and the only compensation that would be given to the owner would be for damage to these items. Simple land acquisition occurred without compensation. In New York, under Dutch law, private property could also be taken without compensation. Other states, including New Jersey and Pennsylvania, had similar statutes. Eminent domain was widely used to acquire land in colonial America, but many scholars agree that neither the principle of just compensation nor a public use limit on acquisition was stipulated in colonial charters or constitutions. Compensation for property taken did not become the rule in the states until the mid-nineteenth century, and it really was not until 1897 that the Supreme Court required states to compensate for property acquisition. Similarly, public use stipulations only slowly emerged after the Revolution and in the nineteenth century.

By the time of the writing of the Constitution in 1787, eminent domain was recognized as a power of states to acquire property for projects such as roads, dams, and schools. Yet just compensation was not a widely accepted practice, despite the fact that Blackstone and parliamentary practice endorsed this concept. William Treanor indicates that colonial constitutions lacked just compensation statutes, giving legislatures broad discretion to determine how land may be best used.[22] Just compensation clauses finally emerged in the 1777 Vermont and 1780 Massachusetts constitutions, and in the 1787 Northwest Ordinance.

James Madison introduced the Fifth Amendment in Congress on June 8, 1789. The amendment as proposed by Madison stated:

> No person shall be subject, except in cases of impeachment, to more than one punishment or one trial for the same offense; nor shall be compelled to be a witness against himself; nor be deprived of life, liberty, or property without due process of law; nor be obliged to relinquish his property; where it may be necessary for public use, without a just compensation.[23]

Although there were debates on other sections of the amendment, no debate on the Takings clause was ever recorded, leaving it somewhat unclear regarding what Madison or the framers had in mind when they adopted it. Eventually, as ratified by the states, the Fifth Amendment read:

> No person shall be held to answer for a capital, or otherwise infamous crime, unless on a presentment or indictment of a Grand Jury, except in cases arising in the land or naval forces, or in the Militia, when in actual service in time of War or public danger; nor shall any person be subject for the same offence to be twice put in jeopardy of life or limb; nor shall be compelled in any criminal case to be a witness against himself, nor be deprived of life, liberty, or property, without due process of law; nor shall private property be taken for public use, without just compensation.

It is the last clause of the Fifth Amendment—"nor shall private property be taken for public use, without just compensation"— that is referred to as the Takings clause. It is here that the federal power of eminent domain is described.

Yet the absence of debate in the drafting of it led to many problems regarding the scope and application of the Takings clause. One question, for example, was whether it or any parts of the Bill of Rights ratified by the states in 1791 should be applied as limitations upon state power. Were states free, absent their own laws, to take private property for any reason and without compensation? This question was posed in the 1833 Supreme Court case *Barron v. Baltimore*, 32 U.S. 243 (1833). In this case the City of Baltimore made some public improvements that resulted in some damage to an owner's wharf which made it unusable. The owner sued the city under the Fifth Amendment, demanding compensation for the loss of his property. While initially winning in the lower courts, he lost before the Supreme Court. There, Chief Justice Marshall ruled that the Fifth Amendment did not apply to the individual states—it was only a limitation upon the federal government. The implication of this decision was that states were free to disregard the Fifth Amendment, and unless there was something in their own state constitutions or laws that limited takings or required compensation, there were no limits on what they could do when taking private property.

Many states thus did engage in extensive use of eminent domain to take property in order to facilitate commerce in the first half of the nineteenth century. Morton Horwitz notes in *The*

Transformation of American Law that the Mills Acts are a good example of how in the nineteenth century eminent domain and property rights clashed.[24] Many states, such as Massachusetts, in order to facilitate the construction of grain mills, required the building of dams that resulted in the flooding of adjacent lands and the disturbing or riparian rights. The Mills Acts permitted this dam construction and flooding but the acts and state court judges, notably Massachusetts Justice Shaw, did not stipulate compensation. Property was damaged, but there was no legal injury. Even though one had lost land to flooding, no legal taking occurred because one did not lose complete use of the property. The property that was lost was considered a legitimate sacrifice for the public good. The Mills Acts were important in the early history of eminent domain because they set a precedent for the transfer of eminent domain to private individuals as long as the actions of the private individuals served a public purpose. Creating a grain mill was deemed a valid public use. The Mills Acts also established the rule that the taking of private property for economic development purposes was a valid public use. The Mills Acts paved the way for the subsequent transfer of eminent domain to other private concerns, such as the railroads, so that other public projects could be secured.

Thus, at least through the first half of the nineteenth century property rights were not necessarily secure against states if the latter wished to use eminent domain. Owners could not rely upon the Fifth Amendment to protect them, and regularly private property was sacrificed in order to promote public projects. All of this activity seemed to go against the rhetoric and belief of John Locke and the framers, who had argued that the protection of property rights was the chief goal of society because their defense was critical to individual liberty. Had nothing changed in the law, it is possible that the ruling of *Barron v. Baltimore* would have remained good law and the state practice of taking property without compensation or other limits might have remained good law. However, something did change, and that was both the economy and the adoption of the Fourteenth Amendment in 1868. The impact of both is described in the next chapter.

debts or obligations associated with the Revolutionary War, was extensively used by the Supreme Court as a tool to protect property rights.[1]

One of the most famous cases from the Marshall era using the Contract clause to defend property rights was *Dartmouth College v. Woodward*, 4 Wheat. 518 (1819). At issue in this case was an effort by the New Hampshire legislature in 1816 to seize the property of Dartmouth College and reorganize the school. The school had been chartered by the British Crown in 1769. While a state court had ruled against the college's trustees, John Marshall and the Supreme Court reversed. The Court found first that the charter was a contract. Second, the Court ruled that the effort to reorganize the school constituted an impairment of the contract. Thus, Marshall ordered the school returned to the control of the trustees. In addition to the *Dartmouth* decision, the Marshall Court issued several other landmark opinions that also used the Contract clause to protect property rights.

Yet once Marshall left the bench and was replaced by Chief Justice Roger Taney, the Contract clause began to fade as an effective tool to defend property rights. In the *Charles River Bridge v. Warren Bridge*, 11 Peters 420 (1837), case, the Court rejected a challenge by the operators of the Charles River toll bridge that the franchise they had received from the Commonwealth of Massachusetts to operate their bridge had been damaged by the chartering of the Warren River Bridge. The Court held that the chartering of the Charles River Bridge never granted them a monopoly against the commonwealth permitting the construction and establishment of other bridges. Thus, even though the Charles River Bridge was financially hurt by the new Warren River Bridge, that harm did not constitute an impairment of contracts under the Constitution. This decision, as well as others under Taney, limited many of the Contract clause decisions under Marshall. Eventually, by the time of the New Deal in the 1930s, decisions such as *Home Building and Loan Assn. v. Blaisdell*, 290 U.S. 398 (1934), brought a death to the Contract clause as a serious tool defending property rights. In that case, the Supreme Court upheld a Minnesota law that issued a halt to foreclosures of mortgages in order to keep people in their homes and farms. The Court ruled that given the emergency the Depression was posing, the temporary nature of the legislature and the moratorium, and the determination by the state of the need to keep people in residences, the Minnesota law was not a violation of the Contract clause. Since the 1930s, the Contract clause has effectively been written out of the Constitution by the Supreme Court.

The point of the above discussion is that, by the Civil War, it looked as if the Constitution would provide little or no protection to property rights. However, several events changed this. First, changes in the economy as a result of industrialization gave a new impetus to the protection of property rights. Specifically, while the Mills Acts took property in order to encourage economic development and industrialization, now these new owners needed their property protected in order to reap the benefits of their investments. Thus, beginning with some state cases in the 1840s and 1850s, state courts began to argue that perhaps there were some limits to what governments could do when it came to affecting property rights.

But the real change for property rights came with adoption of the Fourteenth Amendment in 1868. Specifically, the Due Process clause of this amendment was interpreted to provide some substantive protections for property rights. By that, traditional notions of what the Due Process clause meant dated back to the Magna Carta. Those interpretations stressed that the government had to follow certain rules or procedures before it acted. It had to provide fair hearings or notice before some actions could take place, such as the taking of property away from individuals. But from the 1870s until the late 1930s, the Supreme Court also interpreted the Due Process clause to have a substantive component declaring that there were certain things the government could not do. Among those things the government could not do was interfere with some type of property rights.

It is beyond this book to discuss the history of this era of Supreme Court jurisprudence. But the concept of substantive due process spurred doctrines such as liberty of contract or economic due process. In a host of decisions, the Supreme Court ruled that laws that tried to set minimum wages, maximum working hours, or which otherwise sought to regulate the economy were to be examined with more exacting judicial scrutiny. This heightened scrutiny meant that interference with property rights would not normally be viewed favorably by the courts. The most famous Supreme Court decision of this era was *Lochner v. New York*, 198 U.S. 45 (1905), where a state law regulating the number of hours individuals could work per week in a bakery was declared unconstitutional under the Due Process clause. The case provided a name for this period of law—the *Lochner* era. While some consider the *Lochner* era decisions important for the protection of property rights, many also criticized the Court for overreaching and second-guessing legislatures when it came to regulating the economy in order to protect people. The *Lochner* era came to an end during the New Deal when President Franklin Roosevelt was able to replace enough justices on the Court that they soon came to be more supportive of his programs and efforts to regulate the economy. Today, little of substantive due process still exists for the purposes of defending property rights.

Yet, while the 1868 adoption of the Fourteenth Amendment Due Process clause may have only provided some limited protection for property rights as noted above, it had a more lasting impact. That impact was in terms of how the Due Process clause was fashioned by the Supreme Court to incorporate several provisions of the Bill of Rights to apply to the state. Justice Marshall was probably correct in *Barron v. Baltimore* that the Bill of Rights was not written or intended to place limits on state action. But the constitutional history of eminent domain is intertwined with the Due Process clause. Starting with a series of cases that first involved eminent domain and then later with the First Amendment freedom of speech clauses, the Supreme Court ruled that the Due Process clause incorporated different aspects of the original Bill of Rights to apply as limits on state action. To tell the story about how and why this incorporation took place is the subject of entire courses in law schools, as well as thick books. However, the point that simply needs to be noted here is that, beginning first in *Chicago, B. & Q. R. Co. v. City of Chicago*, 166 U.S. 226 (1897), when the Supreme Court effectively overruled *Barron* in holding that the just compensation requirement of the Fifth Amendment applied to states when they took property, the Takings clause began to become the subject of significant interpretation.

An understanding of eminent domain and the Constitution necessitates that four issues be addressed, driven by the specific language of the Takings clause, which states: "nor shall private property be taken for public use, without just compensation." One is to look at what types of property are implicated by the Takings clause. Specifically, as noted in chapter 2, not all forms of ownership or possession are legally recognized. If an ownership interest is not recognized in the law, then it is also not recognized for the purposes of the Constitution, the Fifth Amendment, and the Takings clause. Thus, the initial threshold question to ask is what types of property are recognized and may be taken by eminent domain.

A second question asks what constitutes a taking. More specifically, when has someone's property been acquired by the government? Answering this question is not so easy. Many might think that a taking is physical occupation of an owner's property by the government. That is correct. But it is also more than that, and it may extend to a host of different types of activities. A third requirement of the Takings clause is that eminent domain may only be used to take private property for a public use. In the last few years, the meaning of "public use" has been the most controversial and subject to debate. This chapter will offer a brief discussion of what the courts have said a valid public use is, with a more extended discussion of that topic reserved for chapter 5. Finally, owners must receive just compensation for the property that has been taken. What are owners to be paid when their property is acquired by eminent domain? Again, this chapter will provide a brief discussion of the topic from a constitutional point of view, leaving for chapter 6 a more detailed discussion of how property is appraised and assessed when it is taken by eminent domain. All four of these requirements have been the subject of significant constitutional adjudication and interpretation. This chapter's cases examine these four issues.

A final note: Unlike earlier chapters, which were more philosophical and policy oriented, this chapter will discuss a lot of case law and opinions issued by the U.S. Supreme Court and other courts. The reason for this is that the discussion here now turns to the power of eminent domain under the Constitution. Since any discussion of the Constitution requires examination of how the courts have interpreted this document, the discussion must examine specific cases and opinions issued that have ruled on what the Takings clause means.

WHAT TYPE OF PROPERTY MAY BE TAKEN BY EMINENT DOMAIN?

One discussion in chapter 2 pointed out that there are many different types of ownership interests or possessory relationships, not all of which are recognized by the law as a form of property. In effect, for property to be considered "property," it generally needs legal recognition. The reason is twofold. First, with legal recognition comes legal protection. By that, if an interest is recognized by the law as property, then one has enforceable rights. One can sue to prevent others from trespassing on it. One can also act to prevent theft or to recover property that has been stolen. One also has the legal right to invest, sell, or otherwise alienate property and give it to another. Legal recognition of a property interest means one has the bundle of rights that can be exercised, subject to the limits defined by the law.

A second and related reason why legal recognition of a possessory interest as property is important is connected to eminent domain. If one has a legal interest in some piece of property and the government takes it by eminent domain, then certain rights exist. The most important of those rights is that any property taken by the government via eminent domain must be paid for. Owners are entitled, under the Takings clause, to just compensation for any property that the government takes from them via eminent domain. Thus to have property rights means, among other things, having a compensable interest. Of course, having a legally recognized and compensable interest also means that the government may have a right to take that property. Recognition of a property interest is thus a dual-edged sword.

But what forms of legally recognized property may the government take via eminent domain? Are there any limits to what type of property that the Takings clause refers to when the eminent domain power is described? The simple answer is no, there are no limits to the types of property that may be acquired. Again, recall from chapter 2 the various distinctions made among the different types of property that exist. Distinctions were made between real and personal property, tangible and intangibles, present and future interests, and types of property based upon greater or lesser interests in the full bundle of rights that might be associated with ownership. One could also add in property, in terms of who owns it, such as individuals, corporations, and governmental units such as a city, town, or village. All of these types of property, as characterized by the different interests or relationships expressed, are forms of property that may be acquired by eminent domain.

At its most basic, real property or real estate, including land and any buildings or structures upon it such as a private home, may be acquired by eminent domain. This means that if the government wants the land upon which your house sits, or the land and the house, it can use eminent domain to acquire it. While recent controversies may question why or for what reason this property may be taken (this is the question about what constitutes a valid public use), there really is no dispute about the ability to take these forms of property. This right to take real property also means that not just residential real estate and homes are subject to acquisition by eminent domain. Commercial property, office buildings, factories, and any other types of real estate (land or buildings) may be taken. Any property held in fee simple absolute is subject to acquisition by eminent domain. But any real property also subject to any lesser property interests can be acquired. This means that property held in terms of leases or tenancy can be acquired by eminent domain. It also means that life estates, remainders, reversions, cooperative and condominium, and all other forms of ownership in real property can be acquired by eminent domain. Furthermore, the right to acquire all of a fee simple absolute also implies a right to acquire any and all or part of the interests associated with this right. To acquire real estate or land, for example, would also include the right to the soil, the minerals in it, oil, gas, gold, diamonds, or anything else located in the land. It would also extend to the airspace rights above property.[2] Finally, eminent domain could be limited in its application. The government could choose to acquire simply the subsoil rights, such as the oil or gas located in property, or it could seek only to acquire the airspace rights or the structures built upon the property. The taking of real property is quite broad.

Personal property may be taken or acquired by eminent domain. Personal property could simply be the household furnishing in someone's home, such as the furniture. But personal property could be even broader. This property could include vehicles, clothing, electronic items, pictures, plants, and just about anything else that a person owns. What if the government wanted to acquire farms? It could seek to use eminent domain to acquire the farm equipment, tools, and perhaps even the cattle or animals that are part of the farm. All of these objects are the potential targets of eminent domain. Whether the government would want to acquire them, of course, is a different question entirely, but in theory the government may want to acquire them.

In addition to thinking about real versus personal property, one can also think about the use of eminent domain in terms of the acquisition of tangible versus intangible property. In *West River Bridge v. Dix*, 6 Howard 507 (1848), the Supreme Court ruled that all forms of property, including contracts, franchises, and even personal property, could be acquired by eminent domain. In the *City of Oakland v. Oakland Raiders*, 646 P.2d 835 (Cal. 1982), the California Supreme Court ruled that a city could, in theory, use its power of eminent domain to condemn and acquire the property of a NFL football team in order to prevent it from moving to another city. This use of eminent domain would permit the taking of individual contracts with athletes. All forms of property, whether personal, real, tangible, or intangible, are subject to being taken by eminent domain.

In effect, here the issue is not necessarily acquiring things, but property relations. The government could acquire liens, mortgages, contracts judgments, franchises, licenses, and intellectual property such as patents and copyrights. Why might the government wish to do this? Assume for example that the government wishes to build a new road and there is a business located in the path where it is supposed to go. Like many businesses, it may have contacts, liens, or patents or copyrights. If the government only had to pay for the tangible assets of the business, such as its land, building, and fixtures, the company might not be receiving the full value for its loss. In some cases the government may seek to acquire not just the physical property of the business. This might be the case where the government is taking over the business. This might be when, for example, the government wants to take over a business, such as to convert a private liquor store to one run by the government, as is common in some parts of the United States. In this circumstance, compensation for the loss of contracts and intellectual property is a legitimate form of just compensation. However, if the government is only acquiring the land, and the business is free to move elsewhere, then it may make no sense to acquire the intangible assets. It just depends on what the government is seeking to acquire.

One issue surrounding the taking of the property of a business addresses the issue of good will. One court defined "good will" as:

> A going business has a value over and above the aggregate value of the tangible property employed in it. Such excess value is nothing

more than the recognition that, used in an established business that has won the favor of its customers, the tangibles may be expected to earn in the future as they have in the past. Owners' privileges of so using them, and their privilege of continuing to deal with customers attracted by the established business, are property of value. This latter privilege is known as good-will.[3]

In many cases, businesses acquire good will with their customers. There is no question that good will is valuable; it is what keeps the same customer coming back through the door or referring new customers to a business. There is no question that it is a valuable commodity. But is it a compensable property interest? No. Courts have said that although good will is valuable, it is not a form of property protected under the Constitution. Some other courts have stated that good will is never taken by the government; it still exists, even if tangible property or location was acquired. Other courts argue that good will is about anticipated future profits and therefore not about a loss of profits that are certain or at hand. Whatever the reason, the rule is that good will is not a form of property protected under the Takings clause. Some states may choose under their own laws or constitutions to protect and compensate for it, but it is not mandated otherwise.

In some cases, other forms of intangibles may be acquired by eminent domain. Earlier subsoil rights were listed as a form of property that could be taken. These rights to minerals or gas or oil are clearly tangible. But there is an old Latin maxim when it comes to property: *"Cujus est solum, ejus est usque ad coelum et ad inferos."* "Who owns the land, owns down to the center of the earth and up to the heavens." The ownership of real property includes the airspace above it. Owning airspace seems intangible, except this type of ownership may be critical in many ways. First, what if airplanes fly too close one's property? When have planes invaded property rights? Second, in many cities the development of airspace is a big issue, such as in New York City. Can the government restrict or regulate the development into the air and limit how high up a building may go? In some cases yes. Issues of this type might affect property interests. Still other types of intangible interests that might be forms of property could include light and air. If the government built something too close to someone else and obstruct sunlight or fresh air, this could turn into a taking.

Finally, when it comes to taking of property, it does not matter who owns it. Property owned by private individuals may be taken by eminent domain. Property owned by joint owners, such as husbands and wives, may be acquired. Property owned by business partnerships, corporations, limited liability companies, nonprofits, and even the government may be acquired by eminent domain. It would be entirely possible, for example, for the federal government to want to acquire property owned by a local government.

Overall, what does the above discussion mean? The Supreme Court and lower federal and state courts have ruled that literally any type of legally recognized type of property may be acquired by eminent domain. This means that homes, businesses, cemeteries, schools, parks, water, wetlands, mountains, intellectual property, and just about anything is property that could be acquired by eminent domain. Surprisingly, the courts have even upheld the use of eminent domain to acquire the property, including players' contracts, of a professional sports team seeking to relocate to another city. The critical two issues to ask when deciding whether the Takings clause applies are: (1) Is the ownership recognized by the law; and (2) who is the legally recognized owner? If the property is legally recognized, then the entity or person deemed the legal owner is entitled to compensation for the loss of the property interest.

WHAT CONSTITUTES A TAKING?

The Takings clause is hardly clear and does not define what constitutes a taking. At the most simple level, when the government takes title to property, then a taking has occurred. As the Supreme Court stated in *Yee v. City of Escondido*, 503 U.S. 519 (1992):

> The Takings Clause of the Fifth Amendment provides: "[N]or shall private property be taken for public use, without just compensation." Most of our cases interpreting the Clause fall within two distinct classes. Where the government authorizes a physical occupation of property (or actually takes title), the Takings Clause generally requires compensation. But where the government merely regulates the use of property, compensation is required only if considerations such as the purpose of the regulation or the extent to which it deprives the owner of the economic use of the property

suggest that the regulation has unfairly singled out the property owner to bear a burden that should be borne by the public as a whole.[4]

In *Yee*, the Court articulated several important points when it came to clarifying the meaning of "take" in the Takings clause. The most important and obvious sense of what constitutes a taking is when the government acquires legal title to property. This type of taking is similar to when a property owner sells his house to another. What occurs at a closing (besides the signing of a ton of papers!) is that one is conveying legal title to another person. One owns the property when legal title to the property has been acquired. Eminent domain at its most basic is taking legal title to property; this is the core notion of a taking.

However, assume that the government does not actually take legal possession of property. Instead, what if the government simply physically invades or occupies an owner's property? Would that constitute a taking? *Yee* suggests that is indeed the case. In *Pumpelly v. Green Bay Company*, 80 U.S. 166 (1871), the Supreme Court ruled that when a government dam flooded the property of an adjacent owner, that flooding constituted a taking. This flooding was a physical invasion or occupation of the property, the Court ruled, and resulted in a taking no different from when legal title had been acquired. According to the Court, there is no difference between taking legal title and physically flooding the property.

> It would be a very curious and unsatisfactory result, if in construing a provision of constitutional law, always understood to have been adopted for protection and security to the rights of the individual as against the government, and which has received the commendation of jurists, statesmen, and commentators as placing the just principles of the common law on that subject beyond the power of ordinary legislation to change or control them, it shall be held that if the government refrains from the absolute conversion of real property to the uses of the public it can destroy its value entirely, can inflict irreparable and permanent injury to any extent, can, in effect, subject it to total destruction without making any compensation, because, in the narrowest sense of that word, it is not *taken* for the public use. Such a construction would pervert the constitutional provision into a restriction upon the rights of the citizen, as those rights stood at the common law, instead of the government, and

make it an authority for invasion of private right under the pretext of the public good, which had no warrant in the laws or practices of our ancestors.[5]

But in *Pumpelly*, the entire property had been flooded. What if less than a total physical occupation of private property takes place by the government or is authorized by the government? Might that not also be a form of a taking? Again, the Court said yes in *Loretto v. Teleprompter Manhattan CATV Corp*, 458 U.S. 419 (1982). At issue in *Loretto* was a law that authorized the installation of cable television in apartment buildings in New York City. The law authorized cable companies to enter private buildings to install cable. The Court found this law was a taking because it constituted a physical entry on to private property.

> When faced with a constitutional challenge to a permanent physical occupation of real property, this Court has invariably found a taking. As early as 1872, in *Pumpelly v. Green Bay Co.*, this Court held that the defendant's construction, pursuant to state authority, of a dam which permanently flooded plaintiff's property constituted a taking. A unanimous Court stated, without qualification, that "where real estate is actually invaded by superinduced additions of water, earth, sand, or other material, or by having any artificial structure placed on it, so as to effectually destroy or impair its usefulness, it is a taking, within the meaning of the Constitution."[6]
> Although this Court's most recent cases have not addressed the precise issue before us, they have emphasized that physical *invasion* cases are special and have not repudiated the rule that any permanent physical *occupation* is a taking. The cases state or imply that a physical invasion is subject to a balancing process, but they do not suggest that a permanent physical occupation would ever be exempt from the Takings Clause.[7]

In *Loretto*, the Court articulated what has come to be called a clear per se rule: Any physical invasion of private property by the government constitutes a taking. One can call this a trespass rule. By that, if the government trespasses on your property, or authorizes another to trespass, that activity constitutes a taking. This is true even if the trespass, as in *Loretto*, is rather minor and included simply the installation of cable for television. Moreover, courts have also ruled that in some cases even pollution by the government, such as noxious odors, or obstruction of light and air, might constitute a taking. Thus in some ways, if the government creates a nuisance that interferes with your enjoyment of property, that might constitute a taking. But not all government trespass is a taking; there are some exceptions. Governments may enter property in emergencies, such as to extinguish a fire, and that would not constitute a taking. Property destroyed by a war does not constitute a taking. Government may also enter property for the purposes of inspecting, and that is not a taking.

Yee also suggests another category of government actions that may constitute a taking. This gets at the difficult issue of regulation and the use of the police power. As noted in chapter 2, the government may use its police power to prevent owners from using their property in a way that constitutes a nuisance to others. What if instead, the government decides to impose some restrictions on how individuals use their property? Can the government do that without it being considered a taking? The answer is that it depends, and resolving the question rests with drawing a line between two government powers—that of eminent domain and the police power.

The police power, as discussed in chapter 2, is the inherent ability or authority of states to regulate the health, safety, welfare, and morals of the people. States have broad police power to protect individuals from numerous problems. In addition, the Supreme Court has ruled that individuals have no right to use their property in a way that causes a nuisance or hurts others. If they do, the government can use its police power to regulate the property to prevent the nuisance. If that regulatory power is used to abate a nuisance, no compensation is due to owners, even if that means that they are denied some use of their property. However, not all regulations are the same, and some may be more extensive than necessary to address a problem. How does one determine when a regulation has become so extensive that it effectively becomes a form of a taking? This is the subject of *Pennsylvania v. Mahon*, 260 U.S. 393 (1922).

The facts of *Mahon* are unique and fascinating. Pennsylvania was an important coal-mining state during the first half of the twentieth century. One of the problems associated with mining is something called subsidence. Subsidence occurs when coal is mined underground, gradually weakening the surface soil above it. This mining might eventually lead to the collapse of the surface or the creation of sinkholes. Subsidence occurs when too

much subsurface coal is removed. One way to address this problem is to place limits on how much coal can be removed from an
area. While this move will help to prevent the collapse of the surface, it also means that those who own the rights to the coal will
be limited in how much they can mine. Quite simply, this means
less coal mined and therefore fewer profits. In an effort to prevent
subsidence, the Commonwealth of Pennsylvania passed the Kohler Act in 1921. The act prevented the mining of anthracite coal in
such way as to cause the subsidence of any structure used as a
human habitation, except in some narrow exceptions. The owners
of the rights to the coal sued, claimed that the act violated their
property rights and they demanded compensation for their losses
as a result of their inability to mine all the coal they wanted.
Pennsylvania courts split on the constitutionality of the Kohler
Act, and the case wound up with the U.S. Supreme Court. Writing for the Court, Justice Holmes struck down the Pennsylvania
law as unconstitutional. Holmes began his opinion by first
stating:

> Government hardly could go on if to some extent values incident to
> property could not be diminished without paying for every such
> change in the general law. As long recognized some values are
> enjoyed under an implied limitation and must yield to the police
> power. But obviously the implied limitation must have its limits or
> the contract and due process clauses are gone. One fact for consid-
> eration in determining such limits is the extent of the diminution.
> When it reaches a certain magnitude, in most if not in all cases
> there must be an exercise of eminent domain and compensation to
> sustain the act. So the question depends upon the particular facts.
> The greatest weight is given to the judgment of the legislature but
> it always is open to interested parties to contend that the legislature
> has gone beyond its constitutional power.[8]

The Justice recognized that many government laws affect property values and it would be impossible to act if it was forced to
compensate for every loss. States such as Pennsylvania need to be
free to use their police power to act to further the public good.
But there are constitutional limits to this ability to act. In the passage above, Holmes suggests those limits are fact-intensive and
whether a regulation is permitted must be determined by the specific circumstances. Holmes then recounts the special circumstances here.

This is the case of a single private house. No doubt there is a public interest even in this, as there is in every purchase and sale and in all that happens within the commonwealth. Some existing rights may be modified even in such a case. But usually in ordinary private affairs the public interest does not warrant much of this kind of interference. A source of damage to such a house is not a public nuisance even if similar damage is inflicted on others in different places. The damage is not common or public.[9]

While Holmes and the Court recognized that legitimacy of using the police power to abate a public nuisance, this did not occur in this instance. Only one house was being protected, and it did not justify the use of the police power. What was occurring here was the protection of a private interest (the homeowner) at the expense of another private interest. This was an invalid use of the police power. The real question, though, is why is not saving one house from subsidence a public good? Here Holmes utters perhaps the most famous line of *Mahon*: "The general rule at least is that while property may be regulated to a certain extent, if regulation goes too far it will be recognized as a taking."[10]

Mahon is a significant opinion on several fronts. First, the decision was not based on the Takings clause. It was decided on the Due Process clause of the Fourteenth Amendment.[11] What the Court was stating was that in some cases, when the police power overregulated property rights, that action could amount to a de facto taking of property without just *compensation*. In effect, at some point the police power will turn into eminent domain if the object of the regulation is too extreme and it is not aimed at abating or addressing a public nuisance. Or, as the Court stated in *Agins v. City of Tiburon*, 447 U.S. 255 (1980), a taking would occur if a regulatory action represented an impermissible use of the police power.[12] The conferring of a private benefit, as indicted in *Mahon*, would be considered a form of eminent domain. This type of taking is called a regulatory taking. Thus, owners who believed that the government was really taking their property, even though the latter was not invoking eminent domain, could sue to recover damages. These types of suits are known as inverse condemnations.

A second major point regarding *Mahon* is about drawing the line between permissible and impermissible regulation. When has a regulation gone too far? Here is where Holmes's opinion has problems. The *Mahon* decision is heralded as significant and important in terms of protecting property rights, but nowhere does the decision offer any guidance regarding what constitutes "too far." Given that vagueness, how has the decision stood the test of time? *Mahon* has been both rejected and refined in the nearly 90 years since it was decided.

One area where *Mahon* has been tested involves land-use regulations, especially zoning. Land-use zoning became popular in the early part of the twentieth century as communities sought to achieve two objectives. One was for planning purposes to maximize the best of land and property. By that, it might be more efficient to use property or land if certain types of functions or usages, such as factories, are all placed in same area where they can share water, sewer, and electrical resources, for example. A second purpose to zoning is to minimize nuisances and protect property values. It may very well be good for a community to have cement factories and single-family homes, but not necessarily next to one another. The pollution and waste from the former may damage or hurt the property values of the latter. Thus, zoning is one way to separate the two different uses as a means of allowing both to coexist without affecting one another.

The constitutional issue with zoning is whether it is a form of policy power regulation that has gone too far to effect a taking. This was the issue raised in *Euclid v. Ambler Realty Co*, 272 U.S. 365 (1926). Zoning regulations limit what owners may do with their property. The Court concluded that zoning regulations are constitutional and generally do not constitute a form of a regulatory taking or inverse condemnation. Zoning seeks to create a public good and, more important, addresses incompatible land uses, a "public bad," or nuisance.

Was the Commonwealth of Pennsylvania really seeking to abate a public nuisance in *Mahon*? Holmes suggested helping one person was not enough to rise to a public nuisance. *Mahon* should be contrasted with *Keystone Bituminous Coal Ass'n v. DeBenedictis*, 480 U.S. 470 (1987), where in a 5-4 opinion, the Court rejected claims that a state law almost identical to the one in *Mahon* constituted a regulatory taking. Here the Court found a public purpose in preventing subsidence, there was no loss of value to property, and more important (unlike in *Mahon* where only one home was protected against the collapse of the surface soil), more structures were protected by the act. The contrast between *Mahon* and *Keystone* perhaps lies in the number of individuals who were benefited by the act, with the latter involving a clear public good that may have been lacking in the former. Thus, *Keystone* appears to reject the holding of *Mahon*, leaving in place the "too far" test. But other cases have sought to clarify the line between regulation and a taking.

For example, in *Hadachek v. Sebastian*, 239 U.S. 394 (1915), at issue was a brick manufacturing plant that was located in Los Angeles. Brick-making is a very dirty endeavor, producing lots of pollution. The plant had operated for years and eventually growth of the city meant that there were homes not very far from the plant. The city passed a law outlawing the making of bricks within the city. Such a law reduced the value of the property from $800,000 to about $60,000. The brickmaker sued, claiming the law amounted to a regulatory taking under *Mahon*. The Supreme Court disagreed. It found that while brick-making is a reasonable business, the city could prohibit it under its police power legislation even though the value of the owner's property had significantly diminished. Moreover, the Court seemed to reject concerns that the adjacent property owners who objected to the plant did so even though the factory was there first and they moved near it.[13] The owner, the Court said, could not claim a vested right to continue to make bricks as times changed. In effect, he bore an unusual sacrifice for the public good.

This concept of assuming a significant burden for furthering the public good was at issue also in *Goldblatt v. Town of Hempstead*, 369 U.S. 590 (1962). Here the town sought to enjoin Goldblatt from operating a gravel pit within its borders because of its impact on the water table in the community. The Court upheld the law. The Court noted:

> Concededly the ordinance completely prohibits a beneficial use to which the property has previously been devoted. However, such a characterization does not tell us whether or not the ordinance is unconstitutional. It is an oft-repeated truism that every regulation necessarily speaks as a prohibition. If this ordinance is otherwise a valid exercise of the town's police powers, the fact that it deprives the property of its most beneficial use does not render it unconstitutional.[14]

According to the Justices, even a significant loss of value is not enough to constitute a taking.

So the issue appears not simply to be a loss of value of one's own property due to a regulation. If that was the case, then valid police power regulations that shut down nuisances could effect a taking because owners lose some value in their property. In *Armstrong v. United States*, 364 U.S. 40 (1960), the Court sought to apply more clarification to the regulatory takings issue. Here it stated:

> The Fifth Amendment's guarantee that private property shall not be taken for a public use without just compensation was designed to bar Government from forcing some people alone to bear public burdens which, in all fairness and justice, should be borne by the public as a whole. A fair interpretation of this constitutional protection entitles these lienholders to just compensation here.[15]

What *Armstrong* seems to suggest is that no one person or entity should be required to exclusively shoulder the burdens of serving the public good. If there is a public good, it should be more evenly distributed upon society. This reasoning, while laudable, did little to clarify the *Mahon* problem. In *Mahon* the Court suggested that the regulatory taking occurred because there was no public benefit. In *Hadachek* and *Goldblatt*, essentially one owner was asked to bear a burden to protect the public. *Armstrong* added another test about how the public burdens were distributed, but it failed to explain what a regulatory taking was. Finally, in *Andrus v. Allard*, 444 U.S. 51 (1979), the Court referred back to property as a bundle of sticks and argued that the loss or denial of use of one stick would not necessarily constitute a regulatory taking. In this case, at issue was a federal environmental law that banned the sale of eagle feathers and artifacts. The law was adopted to protect bald eagles. Traders of these eagle artifacts challenged the law as a regulatory taking. In upholding the law the Court stated: "But the denial of one traditional property right does not always amount to a taking. At least where an owner possesses a full 'bundle' of property rights, the destruction of one 'strand' of the bundle is not a taking, because the aggregate must be viewed in its entirety."[16] Determination as to whether there was a regulatory taking needed to look at the property as a whole, not simply in terms of a loss of one of the sticks.

Another effort to clarifying the issue when a regulation has gone too far came with *Penn Central Company v. New York*, 438

U.S. 104 (1978). In this case, the Court again examined land use or zoning law when it came to the question of a taking. At issue were historic preservation laws that placed a limit on the right of the owner to use the airspace above his property for development purposes. The Penn Central Company sought to develop the airspace above its train terminal and it was denied the right to do so by a city law that limited this type of development. Penn Central claimed this denial amounted to a regulatory taking. The City of New York argued that the promotion of aesthetic goals—historic preservation—was a valid police power function when it came to zoning. Second, the city argued that there was no taking here because one had to look at the overall value of the property when determining whether an owner had suffered a compensable loss. Penn Central claimed that it had suffered a loss because it had been denied a right to use a portion of its property—its airspace rights.

The Court ruled for the City of New York. First, it stated that not all forms of restrictions upon the use of property constitute a taking. Following *Mahon*, a taking occurs only when a regulation goes too far. The Court clarified the concept of what "too far" means.

> Before considering appellants' specific contentions, it will be useful to review the factors that have shaped the jurisprudence of the Fifth Amendment injunction "nor shall private property be taken for public use, without just compensation." The question of what constitutes a "taking" for purposes of the Fifth Amendment has proved to be a problem of considerable difficulty. While this Court has recognized that the "Fifth Amendment's guarantee . . . [is] designed to bar Government from forcing some people alone to bear public burdens which, in all fairness and justice, should be borne by the public as a whole," this Court, quite simply, has been unable to develop any "set formula" for determining when "justice and fairness" require that economic injuries caused by public action be compensated by the government, rather than remain disproportionately concentrated on a few persons.[17]
>
> In engaging in these essentially ad hoc, factual inquiries, the Court's decisions have identified several factors that have particular significance. The economic impact of the regulation on the claimant and, particularly, the extent to which the regulation has interfered with distinct investment-backed expectations are, of course, relevant considerations.

Along with a direct physical taking of property, the Court stated that the loss of investment-backed expectations constituted a taking. This test supposedly gave more clarification to the "too far" language of *Mahon*. The Court here reaffirmed *Euclid*, holding that not all zoning regulations were takings. In some cases, restrictions on airspace development or to promote aesthetic interests would be considered valid police power objectives. A final point in *Penn Central*, which was noted above in *Andrus*: In evaluating whether a taking had occurred, one should look at the impact upon the property as a whole, and not upon specific segments of property.[18] While the dissenters in this case would have found a taking because airspace rights were limited, the majority indicated that a taking must overall evaluate the entire property, not simply look to see if one stick in the bundle of rights was taken. A taking can occur if one loses significant investment-backed expectations in property.

Penn Central supposedly clarified the *Mahon* test. But did it? The investment-backed expectations test did not really answer any questions. Theoretically and in reality, any regulation might cost owners some return on their investment or lead to a damage to some anticipated or existing investments. This test thus would seem to allow for almost anything to count as a taking. Or conversely, the test was so vague that it did no more than add even more confusion to the topic of explaining what "too far" meant. The case really did not provide any help here with defining what a regulatory taking included.

In *First English Evangelical Lutheran Church of Glendale v. County of Los Angeles*, 482 U.S. 304 (1987), the Supreme Court confronted a different issue as it sought to address this issue: What about temporary bans on development? Often local governments impose moratoria on development in order to give themselves time to assess a problem before legislating on it. But here the land owned by the church had been flooded and the City of Los Angeles issued a ban on rebuilding. Was such a temporary ban a taking? The Court established the rule that total temporary bans, such as moratoria, could rise to the level of a compensable taking under some circumstances. This was a significant case. Prior to *First English*, governments could issue moratoria on development of property lasting for years, claiming that they were studying potential changes in zoning laws or comprehensive plans. Or, as in the case of *First English*, prevent owners from redeveloping their land after it had been flooded. Until *First English* the Court ruled that temporary takings, whether they are a total or partial denial of use of property, were not compensable. However, there are limits to this claim that temporary takings are compensable.[19] In *Tahoe-Sierra Preservation Council, Inc. v. Tahoe Regional Planning Agency*, 534 U.S. 1063 (2001), the Supreme Court held that two temporary moratoria on land development that lasted 36 months did not constitute a per se regulatory taking. The Court reasoned that in spite of the total moratoria on development during the temporary period, the property was not taken in its entirety because the property would recover value as soon as the prohibition was lifted.

Penn Central indicated that a loss of one stick in the entire bundle of rights did not necessarily constitute a taking. However, not everyone on the Court agreed with this claim and it was challenged as the makeup of the Justices changed. Both *Nollan v. California Coastal Commission*, 483 U.S. 825 (1987), and *Lucas v. South Carolina Coastal Council*, 505 U.S. 1003 (1992), sought to answer this question. In *Nollan* the Court ruled that a state law granting the public a right-of-way across an owner's private property in order to provide access to the ocean and beach (which was public property) was a form of a taking. Writing for the Court, Justice Scalia invoked a familiar metaphor for property—that it was a bundle of sticks.

> Had California simply required the Nollans to make an easement across their beachfront available to the public on a permanent basis in order to increase public access to the beach, rather than conditioning their permit to rebuild their house on their agreeing to do so, we have no doubt there would have been a taking. To say that the appropriation of a public easement across a landowner's premises does not constitute the taking of a property interest but rather (as Justice BRENNAN contends) "a mere restriction on its use," is to use words in a manner that deprives them of all their ordinary meaning. Indeed, one of the principal uses of the eminent domain power is to assure that the government be able to require conveyance of just such interests, so long as it pays for them. Perhaps because the point is so obvious, we have never been confronted with a controversy that required us to rule upon it, but our cases' analysis of the effect of other governmental action leads to the same conclusion. We have repeatedly held that, as to property reserved by its owner for private use, "the right to exclude [others is] 'one of

the most essential sticks in the bundle of rights that are commonly characterized as property.'"[20]

Property as a bundle of sticks means that ownership is associated with many different rights, including the right to exclude others. Justice Scalia and a majority of the Court believed that a loss of this right to exclude someone from your property rose to a level of a taking.

In *Lucas* the Court looked at coastal regulations that prevented an owner from developing beachfront property due to concerns about flooding. The Court ruled for the owner, with Justice Scalia, writing for the majority, providing important clarification regarding the different conditions determining what constituted a taking. An extended passage from this decision is worth quoting.

> Nevertheless, our decision in *Mahon* offered little insight into when, and under what circumstances, a given regulation would be seen as going "too far" for purposes of the Fifth Amendment. In 70-odd years of succeeding "regulatory takings" jurisprudence, we have generally eschewed any "set formula" for determining how far is too far, preferring to "engag[e] in . . . essentially ad hoc, factual inquiries." We have, however, described at least two discrete categories of regulatory action as compensable without case-specific inquiry into the public interest advanced in support of the restraint. The first encompasses regulations that compel the property owner to suffer a physical "invasion" of his property. In general (at least with regard to permanent invasions), no matter how minute the intrusion, and no matter how weighty the public purpose behind it, we have required compensation. For example, in *Loretto v. Teleprompter Manhattan CATV Corp.*, we determined that New York's law requiring landlords to allow television cable companies to emplace cable facilities in their apartment buildings constituted a taking, even though the facilities occupied at most only 1 ½ cubic feet of the landlords' property.[21]
> The second situation in which we have found categorical treatment appropriate is where regulation denies all economically beneficial or productive use of land. See *Nollan v. California Coastal Comm'n*. As we have said on numerous occasions, the Fifth Amendment is violated when land-use regulation "does not substantially advance legitimate state interests *or denies an owner economically viable use of his land.*"[22]

According to Scalia in *Lucas*, an automatic or per se taking occurs in one of two situations. First, there must be a physical invasion of the property. This is well-established law. Second, if a regulation leads to a total loss of the value of the property, that is a per se taking. If there is not a total loss of value, then there may or may not be a regulatory taking. The facts of the specific case are needed to address this issue. But what about the issue of the government using its police power to prevent harm or abate a nuisance? In *Lucas* one could argue that the Court was seeking to prevent one from building in a flood zone. Is this not a sufficient reason to prevent development? Scalia also sought to address this issue.

> Where the State seeks to sustain regulation that deprives land of all economically beneficial use, we think it may resist compensation only if the logically antecedent inquiry into the nature of the owner's estate shows that the proscribed use interests were not part of his title to begin with. This accords, we think, with our "takings" jurisprudence, which has traditionally been guided by the understandings of our citizens regarding the content of, and the State's power over, the "bundle of rights" that they acquire when they obtain title to property. It seems to us that the property owner necessarily expects the uses of his property to be restricted, from time to time, by various measures newly enacted by the State in legitimate exercise of its police powers; "[a]s long recognized, some values are enjoyed under an implied limitation and must yield to the police power." And in the case of personal property, by reason of the State's traditionally high degree of control over commercial dealings, he ought to be aware of the possibility that new regulation might even render his property economically worthless (at least if the property's only economically productive use is sale or manufacture for sale). In the case of land, however, we think the notion pressed by the Council that title is somehow held subject to the "implied limitation" that the State may subsequently eliminate all economically valuable use is inconsistent with the historical compact recorded in the Takings Clause that has become part of our constitutional culture.[23]

For Scalia, if a land-use regulation seeks to prevent a harm that was not already a restriction on the property at the time of its purchase (not in a property title), then it might also be a taking. Thus, if the owner was aware of a possible restriction on her property at the time of purchase or closing, then there was no loss of investment-backed expectations. The owner's expectations were already and arguably taken into account with the purchase price of the property. Awareness of the nuisance and of the limits on the use of different sticks in the bundle of rights at the time of closing for Scalia and the *Lucas* majority provided more clarification on what a regulatory taking constituted. A regulatory taking that denied all economic value of property is a per se taking unless the nuisance the regulation was seeking to address existed at the time of the sale. If these two conditions were met, no taking occurred. Conversely, in *Palazzolo v. Rhode Island*, 533 U.S. 606, (2001), the Supreme Court seemed to back away from its claims in *Nollan* and *Lucas* and argue that there is no categorical regulatory taking unless the property as a whole is rendered "economically idle" and the owner is deprived of all economically beneficial uses.[24]

Finally, an issue left unanswered by *Nollan* was the degree of justification that a government had to provide if it wished to impose restrictions upon property. *Nollan* involved a common practice of exactions whereby an owner, as a condition of receiving a permit to build or develop property, was required to perform some task, such as give the public access to the property. How far could the government condition development upon these exactions without it rising to a taking? In *Dolan v. City of Tigard*, 512 U.S. 374 (1994), the Justices answered this question. In *Dolan* the Court had to address this issue of exactions. In a decision that many found surprising, the Court suggested that these exactions needed to be examined not under a normal rational-basis standard, but with a more heightened scrutiny that demanded some rough proportionality between the permit and the exaction required. According to Chief Justice Rehnquist in writing for the Court:

> The second part of our analysis requires us to determine whether the degree of the exactions demanded by the city's permit conditions bears the required relationship to the projected impact of petitioner's proposed development.[25]
>
> We think the "reasonable relationship" test adopted by a majority of the state courts is closer to the federal constitutional norm than either of those previously discussed. But we do not adopt it as such, partly because the term "reasonable relationship" seems confusingly similar to the term "rational basis" which describes the minimal level of scrutiny under the Equal Protection Clause of the Fourteenth Amendment. We think a term such as "rough proportionality" best encapsulates what we hold to be the requirement of

the Fifth Amendment. No precise mathematical calculation is required, but the city must make some sort of individualized determination that the required dedication related both in nature and extent to the impact of the proposed development.[26]

Does the majority opinion in *Dolan* represent a revival of property rights and a return to some form of heightened scrutiny for economic rights, and especially for a taking that was characteristic of the *Lochner* era that was mentioned earlier? Some said yes; others depicted the holding as more limited to the special case of exactions. While the Court did not go to the level of strict scrutiny, the "rough proportionality" test here seemed to reintroduce some more heightened analysis to at least one form of government regulation.

Overall, do any rules emerge from these and other cases that offer some guidance regarding what constitutes a taking? Several rules or tests have emerged. A taking occurs

- when the government takes title to property
- when the government physically invades property
- when the government denies all economically beneficial use of property
- if the government uses the police power for an impermissible use
- when a government regulation goes too far
- when a government regulation takes investment-backed expectations
- if the government imposes a temporary ban on the use of property.

These different tests indicate that if the government overregulates property when the regulation is inappropriate or too zealous, or if any physical invasion occurs (flooding, dumping, etc.) then a taking has occurred. These takings are in addition to a taking occurring when the government outright takes legal title to property. If one of the above occurs, then a taking occurs and a next question needs to be asked: Was the taking for a legitimate public use?

WHAT IS A VALID PUBLIC USE?

Once it has been determined that an owner's property is being taken, a third requirement of the Takings clause is that the use of eminent domain must secure a valid public use. Explaining what constitutes a valid public use and how the meaning of that term has evolved over time is the subject of chapter 5. However, a brief overview of the public use history and law will demonstrate that the term has potentially expanded over time, leading up to the scenario in *Kelo* where the Court upheld the taking of a private home for economic development purposes.

The debates in Congress in 1791 when the Takings clause was adopted do not offer any illumination on what they considered a valid public use. However, at the time, colonial and early American uses of eminent domain were confined mainly to the building of roads, schools, and other public buildings. In some cases, eminent domain furthered economic development but generally, while the eminent domain power was established and accepted, little discussion about the meaning of public use occurred. In 1776 only two state constitutions had a public use clause in their constitutions; and it was not until about the 1830s that most states had such a stipulation attached to eminent domain. Because the federal courts did not become very involved with public use and eminent domain questions until the last quarter of the nineteenth century, local state courts were crucial in constructing the public use meaning, subject to local conditions.

As a rule, the federal courts have also given great deference to local determinations of public use. In the twentieth and twenty-first centuries, the Supreme Court has never held a use to be private when a local court had already declared it to be public. There is only one case—*Missouri Pacific Railway Company v. Nebraska*, 164 U.S. 403 (1896)—where the Supreme Court reversed a lower court on this question. Justice Holmes, in *Strickley v. Highland Boy Mining Company*, 200 U.S. 527 (1906), underscored this point, indicating that if eminent domain statutes of a state are constitutional, the Supreme Court would "follow the construction of the state court."[27] As a result of the deference, public use has taken on various meanings.

The term "public use" is vague. Over the last 150 years, courts have ascribed two different meanings to the phrase *public use*. On the one hand, the term has been narrowly defined to mean "used by the public," stipulating that the property taken must actually be used in a way that the public enjoys it. This means that taking property for uses such as building parks, roads, schools, and government buildings all would constitute a valid public use because in all these instances the public at large, or at least the segment that decides to avail itself of the opportunity, can actually use or frequent a park, drive across a bridge, or attend a school. This narrow notion of public use literally means the public uses the property. There is little legal disagreement associated with the legitimacy of using eminent domain and acquiring private property for these "traditional" governmental functions.

But there are also numerous court decisions dating back to the nineteenth century that have adopted a more broad definition of public use. This conception of public use defines the term to be equivalent to or means the same as "public advantage," "promoting the general welfare," the "welfare of the public," the "public good," the "public benefit," and "public utility or necessity." This broad meaning of public use has also been defined or considered to include "actions enlarging resources," "promoting productive power," "conducive to commercial prosperity," and as "furthering an important public policy." While narrow conceptions of the term "public use" have stipulated that the public in some way be given access or use the property taken, broad definitions of the term do not require that the public actually use the property, so long as its acquisition serves the public good. Examples of takings for the narrow public good mean the use of eminent domain for things such as highways, schools, public buildings, and parks. Broad uses mean almost any taking of property is permitted, so long as the private benefit to some specific owner are not primary, but instead are secondary to the value or benefit the public receives from it.

Some might contend that the basic problem with the public-use stipulation justifying eminent domain action has expanded increasingly over time to allow for more and more situations when a taking is permitted. By that, some claim that the meaning of *public use* has shifted from simply being understood in its narrow conception to one becoming ever broader over time. While there may be an element of truth that the meaning has expanded over time, it is also clear that even back in the nineteenth century that the use of eminent domain to take private property from one private owner and give it to another for the purposes of economic development was considered a permissible public use. One clear example of that was with the railroads. Railroad tracks in the United States were often built either with the government condemning land and giving it to the railroad companies to lay rails, or, in some cases, the companies themselves were given the authority to condemn land themselves in order to accomplish the same purpose. Thus, this type of practice, which has caused the most recent controversy, is not a recent phenomenon.

Another criticism of what appears to be the expansion of the public-use doctrine is the belief that somehow the courts have removed themselves from the job of reviewing public-use determinations. The argument is that as the courts have retreated from the *Lochner* era jurisprudence and become less involved in second-guessing legislatures in terms of decisions about protecting property or regulating the economy, they have also become less involved in reviewing eminent domain public-use determinations. Traditionally, courts used to say that the final determination of what is a valid public use is ultimately or finally a matter for the courts to decide. Again, in chapter 5, this issue will be discussed in more detail. For now, it is sufficient to say that there is some evidence that courts have somewhat retreated in terms of their role in reviewing public-use determinations, resulting in giving condemnors more authority to take property for a variety of public uses. Two cases for now highlight that expanded authority given to condemnors, revealing also the scope of what the public-use doctrine means today.

In *Berman v. Parker*, 348 U.S. 26 (1954), the 1954 U.S. Supreme Court decision unanimously upheld the District of Columbia's use of eminent domain to acquire commercial property. In *Berman*, at issue was the taking of a private commercial building as part of a slum clearance project in order to remove urban blight. In effect, this was a community redevelopment project. One objection here was that the specific building in question was not blighted, at least in the eyes of its owner, and he challenged the taking as a violation of the Fifth Amendment because the acquisition was not a valid public use. In rejecting the owner's contentions, the Court first drew a connection between eminent domain and the police power.

> The power of Congress over the District of Columbia includes all the legislative powers which a state may exercise over its affairs. We deal, in other words, with what traditionally has been known as the police power. An attempt to define its reach or trace its outer limits is fruitless, for each case must turn on its own facts. The definition is essentially the product of legislative determinations addressed to the purposes of government, purposes neither abstractly nor historically capable of complete definition. Subject to

specific constitutional limitations, when the legislature has spoken, the public interest has been declared in terms well-nigh conclusive. In such cases the legislature, not the judiciary, is the main guardian of the public needs to be served by social legislation, whether it be Congress legislating concerning the District of Columbia, or the states legislating concerning local affairs. This principle admits of no exception merely because the power of eminent domain is involved. The role of the judiciary in determining whether that power is being exercised for a public purpose is an extremely narrow one.[28]

In *Berman* Justice Douglas, in writing for the Court, first seems to define the limits of the public-use stipulation for eminent domain in terms of the breadth of a state's police power authority. Instead of arguing, as Holmes did in *Mahon*, that at some point the police power could become so expansive that it turned into a taking, here the Court said almost the opposite: the power of eminent domain is perhaps only limited by the range of police power functions possessed by the government. Moreover, the Court here also seemed to reject notions that it was the job of the judiciary to say what a valid public use was. Instead, much in the same way the legislatures should generally be free to decide how best to employ the police powers to protect the health, safety, welfare, and morals of its citizens, they should also be free to do the same when it comes to using eminent domain.

When the Court turned to the issue of what constituted a valid public use, it then adopted a definite board conception of the concept. For Douglas: "[t]he concept of public welfare is broad and inclusive . . . [and] . . . the power of eminent domain is merely the means to the end."[29] The Court was willing to give Congress leeway to decide how, once private property was acquired, to best use that property to serve the public.

[T]he means of executing the project are for Congress and Congress alone to determine, once the public purpose has been established. The public end may be as well or better served through an agency of private enterprise than through a department of government—or so the Congress might conclude. We cannot say that public ownership is the sole method of promoting the public purposes of community redevelopment projects.[30]

Berman v. Parker was a significant decision that both appeared to expand the concept of public use and decrease the role of the courts in reviewing eminent domain decisions. However, the Supreme Court cemented this line of reasoning regarding the scope of the public use definition in *Hawaii Housing Authority v. Midkiff*, 467 U.S. 229 (1984). In *Midkiff*, at issue was the constitutionality of a Land Reform Act enacted by the Hawaii Legislature in 1967. The act sought to reduce the perceived social and economic evils inherent in the then-existing large land estates whose origins were traceable to the feudal chiefs of the pre-statehood Hawaiian Islands. To achieve this purpose, the act created the Hawaii Housing Authority to take title to the real property from the owners of these big estates by eminent domain. They would, of course, compensate for the taking and then sell the property to the tenants. Essentially, this was a land redistribution act. The district court upheld the law under the Fifth Amendment; the Court of appeals reversed, finding that the redistribution did not comply with the public-use requirement. Surprisingly, the Supreme Court unanimously upheld the land redistribution as a valid public use.

The Supreme Court dismissed the Court of Appeals' concern that "[s]ince Hawaiian lessees retain possession of the property for private use throughout the condemnation process, . . . the Act exacted takings for private use."[31]

> The mere fact that property taken outright by eminent domain is transferred in the first instance to private beneficiaries does not condemn that taking as having only a private purpose. The Court long ago rejected any literal requirement that condemned property be put into use for the general public. "It is not essential that the entire community, nor even any considerable portion, . . . directly enjoy or participate in any improvement in order [for it] to constitute a public use. . . . [W]hat in its immediate aspect [is] only a private transaction may . . . be raised by its class or character to a public affair."[32]

Justice O'Connor adopted and expanded the *Berman* claim that public-use determinations were essentially legislative and not judicial in nature.

> The "public use" requirement is thus coterminous with the scope of the sovereign's power. There is, of course, a role for the courts to play in reviewing a legislature's judgment of what constitutes a public use, even when the eminent domain power is equated with the police power. But the Court in *Berman* made it clear that it is "an extremely narrow" one.

The *Midkiff* decision sustained the use of eminent domain as a tool to redistribute private resources within society to accomplish certain widely drawn public purposes, including those that support economic development, even when the property involved is taken from one private party and given to another. This was definitely a very broad conception of public use, anticipating by nearly a generation what the Court would later rule in the *Kelo* opinion.

Tentatively, when asked the question "what is a valid public use?" the Supreme Court (at least up to the issuing of the *City of New London v. Kelo* opinion) had settled on a broad notion of the term that equivocated its meaning with the scope of a state's police power. This means that the Court had endorsed a broad reading of the term, allowing it to be read as permitting almost any taking, so long as it first furthered the public good, advantage, or general welfare. This broad concept of public use also meant a very narrow role for the Court in second-guessing or questioning legislative determinations of the term. Finally, the Court appeared to endorse the taking of private property for economic development purposes, even if it involved the taking from one private individual and giving it to another.

JUST COMPENSATION

"Just compensation" is the fourth and final term of the Takings clause that needs to be discussed if one is to understand the requirements that need to be met for the government or a condemnor to engage in a valid use of eminent domain. Perhaps unlike the other three terms discussed, this is the least controversial and difficult to explain.

Some colonial state constitutions had eminent domain provisions, but not all of them mandated that owners must be compensated for property that had been acquired by the government. Lacking such a state requirement, the question became whether the Fifth Amendment's just compensation clause would require a state to compensate an owner for property taken by the government. As noted earlier, *Barron v. Baltimore* held that neither the Fifth nor the entire Bill of Rights served as a limit upon state behavior. In effect, states did not have to comply with the just compensation clause. States were thus free to take property and not pay owners. During the early nineteenth century, states such as Massachusetts adopted Mills Acts that provided for a flooding of adjacent property without compensation in order to build grist and grain mills. Some scholars have thus argued that economic development in the states was facilitated by the ability to take property and not pay compensation. It forced private individuals to bear the costs of economic development for the community. All this seems contrary to arguments that the Court would eventually make in cases such as *Andrus, Armstrong, Lucas*, and *Nolan*.

In law school, *Barron* is normally read in civil rights/liberties courses as a way to highlight the limited application of the Bill of Rights to the states until the latter part of the nineteenth century when the Fourteenth Amendment Due Process clause was first used to "incorporate" various provisions of the first ten amendments to be limits upon states. However, the case's significance in terms of property rights is also critical. It is one of those rare examples of the Marshall Court not coming to the defense of property rights. Yet *Barron* did not remain the law too long. In*Chicago, B. & Q. R. Co. v. City of Chicago*, 166 U.S. 226 (1897), the Court reversed *Barron*. It also was the first case in which the Supreme Court mandated that the just compensation requirement is binding on states when they acquire property via eminent domain. In this case, the Court stated that the reasons for just compensation were that it would be a "mockery of justice" and a violation of due process not to compensate the owner.[33]

But even before this case, the Court had ruled in cases such as *Pumpelly v. Green Bay & Mississippi Canal Co.*, 80 U.S. 166 (1871), that the just compensation clause was binding upon the federal government, and that whenever it took property it had to compensate the owners for their losses. But what specifically constitutes just compensation?

In *United States v. Reynolds*, 397 U.S. 14 (1970), the Supreme Court declared that just compensation meant:

> The Fifth Amendment provides that private property shall not be taken for public use without just compensation. And 'just compensation' means the full monetary equivalent of the property taken. The owner is to be put in the same position monetarily as he would have occupied if his property had not been taken. In enforcing the constitutional mandate, the Court at an early date adopted the concept of market value: the owner is entitled to the fair market value of the property at the time of the taking.[34]

The Supreme and lower courts have consistently ruled that just compensation is paying the owner the fair-market value for the property acquired, with this value determined in a variety of ways that will be described in chapter 6. But in general, fair-market value is the value of property that would be arrived at when a buyer and seller agree to a price at an "arm's-length" negotiation. Another way to describe just compensation is to ask what a willing buyer would pay a willing seller for a piece of property. In short, just compensation is supposed to leave the owners no worse off than they were before the taking, at least financially. Owners may still feel emotional damages at the loss of property, and businesses may be hurt in terms of loss of customer good will. However, neither of these constitutes compensable forms of property that are protected by the Constitution and, therefore, are not part of the formula when calculating just compensation.

To summarize, then, the Takings clause of the Fifth Amendment has four components referencing what is private property, what is a taking, what is a public use, and what constitutes just compensation. The Supreme Court, along with lower federal and state courts, have issued tens of thousands of decisions seeking to bring clarity to these four terms, with varying levels of success. While at different times in history one of these four parts was more controversial than another, it is the public use provision that seems to be most contentious now. The subject of the next chapter will be to explain why.

CHAPTER FIVE

What Is a Public Use and How Is It Different from a Private Use?

Charles: We're going to resist.
Laura: With guns?
Charles: Yes, Laura.
Laura: I don't understand you. No piece of land is worth losing your life over.
Charles: You're right. You don't understand.
　　　　　　　　　　　　　　—*Little House on the Prairie*

The Fifth Amendment states that private property can only be taken for a "public use." If the government or other condemnors may take private property only for valid public uses, how do we determine if the taking is for a public or private use? The last chapter gave a brief overview of the Takings clause and a few of the cases that have helped define current (at least up until *Kelo*) judicial construction of what "public use" means. This chapter looks at the various tests the courts have formulated to distinguish public from private uses. The emphasis is upon discussing all the various uses that justify the government taking someone's property. What this discussion will show is how flexible the meaning of "public use" is or has become. It has permitted the use of eminent domain for traditional uses such as building schools and roads, to more unusual ones, such as preventing plant closings and runaway sports teams, and encouraging economic development.

Since the adoption of the Takings clause in the Fifth Amendment, along with enactment of similar provisions in state constitutions addressing eminent domain, literally there have been tens of thousands, if not more, court decisions seeking to determine what constitutes a valid public use. It would be impossible to read and review all these decisions in an effort to conclude that they all reach the same conclusion about what constitutes a valid public use. Moreover, there is the impossibility of reconciling decisions of the courts within or among states. Facts vary across cases, as do the laws in many states, making it difficult to say that the courts are deciding the same issues in all these cases. Another source of difficulty lies in the fact that courts were more influenced by established customs of the various states at the time their constitutions were adopted than by a literal interpretation of the words of their eminent-domain clauses. A third problem is that different locations, circumstances, and needs throughout the United States have affected the meaning of "public use."

A final problem is that the word "use" is susceptible to two entirely different meanings; that is, "employment" and "advantage." The last chapter noted these contrasting meanings. It is worth revisiting this issue here again in more detail.

WHAT DOES "PUBLIC USE" MEAN?

This is the $64,000 question. The easiest way to answer this might be to ask what the authors of the Fifth Amendment intended when they drafted and debated the Takings clause. Many constitutional scholars recognize that constitutional language is often vague and that some tools are needed to help clarify what words such as "due process," "equal protection," or "freedom of speech" mean. Chief Justice John Marshall is credited with stating in *Marbury v. Madison*, 5 U.S. 137 (1803), that "It is emphatically the province and duty of the judicial department to say what the law is. Those who apply the rule to particular cases, must of necessity expound and interpret that rule."[1] In uttering this statement, Marshall was declaring that it is the job of the courts to interpret or ascertain the meaning of the Constitution. For some, that meaning is fixed, while others believe that the meaning is somewhat more open, subject to changing circumstances or understandings of the terms in the document.

Those who believe the meaning of the Constitution is fixed often point to the intention of the authors of the Constitution. Ascertaining authors' intent is a well-respected tool of statutory interpretation and many advocate the same when it comes to the Constitution. Unfortunately, intent does not help much here.

James Madison was the original author of the Bill of Rights. In 1789 he introduced what originally were 12 amendments to the Constitution. The Seventh Amendment contained what eventually would be the Takings clause in the Fifth Amendment that was eventually ratified by the states in 1791. Madison's original, which was quoted in chapter 3, is worth repeating here.

> No person shall be held to answer for a capital, or otherwise infamous crime, unless on a presentment or indictment of a Grand Jury, except in cases arising in the land or naval forces, or in the Militia, when in actual service in time of War or public danger; nor shall any person be subject for the same offence to be twice put in jeopardy of life or limb; nor shall be compelled in any criminal case to be a witness against himself, nor be deprived of life, liberty, or property, without due process of law; nor shall private property be taken for public use, without just compensation.[2]

The last clause of this amendment contains the Takings clause. Its language is identical to that found in the final version of the Fifth Amendment. Unfortunately, as noted in chapter 3, there is no recorded debate in Congress on this clause. Scholars are thus left with language but no clear debate regarding either what Madison or Congress thought a valid public use meant or entailed.

Another way perhaps to clarify the meaning of "public use" would be to look to the meaning found in other documents, or look to current practices regarding the use of eminent domain at the time of the writing of the Constitution. Either of these might offer some guidance regarding what Madison or Congress was thinking. For example, maybe one can look to British practice regarding the use of eminent domain to determine what a public use was. However, this is not a good tactic. There was no similar public-use stipulation in British law, and the king could take property literally for any reason. Moreover, the king's powers were clearly different from that given to Congress—they were much broader. After all, England was a monarchy and the

framers were seeking to establish some type of popular government subject to constitutional limits. Finally, one can read the
American Revolutionary War and the Declaration of Independence as a rejection of vast powers by the king.

Another approach is to look to colonial or early statehood practices regarding the use of eminent domain. Maybe state laws provide guidance about what a taking constituted. Again, though,
this approach is limited. On the one hand, during the colonial era
and the Revolutionary War, states confiscated a lot of property.
They did so to fight the British. There was also extensive property
and economic regulation occurring at that time in the interests of
winning the war. If one uses this as a reference point, then "public use" might be read very broadly. But these colonial and war-
time practices also might not be helpful to clarifying what a valid
public use is. Additionally, in the late 1770s, only two states, Vermont and Massachusetts, had public use clauses in their own
constitutions.[3] These two examples might provide guidance
about the meaning of public use when Congress adopted the Takings clause. In these two states, eminent domain was mostly confined to the taking of property to build roads, bridges, and public
buildings. But one could also interpret some of these acts as promoting economic development if one stretches the meaning of
these projects. These state practices might give a clue to what a
public use was. But with only two states having a public-use stipulation, it is difficult to infer that the practices from these states
govern what Congress had in mind when they adopted the Takings clause.

Where does that leave efforts to define what a public use
means? It is time to refer to the two competing notions of public
use described in the last chapter—the narrow and broad
meanings.

TWO MEANINGS TO PUBLIC USE

The "public use" doctrine can be described as an "essentially
contested concept." This suggests that its meaning has been subject to debate over time. Various courts and legislatures have
defined "public use" either from a narrow or a broad perspective. A narrow reading of "public use" indicates "used by the
public." Under this definition, uses such as for bridges, highways, and schools qualify as valid public uses because the public,

or at least some segment of it, can actually physically use the property. Critical here is that more than one person benefits and uses the property. A second, broader definition of "public use" equates the meaning to include the "public advantage," "promoting the public welfare," the "public good," and "public necessity." Here it is not essential that the public actually use the property so long as they benefit from the taking in some way. Again, more than one person must benefit from use of eminent domain. This meaning suggests that almost any project can be construed as a public use, as long as it is shown that it furthers economic development, public welfare, or a better use of local resources.

What is critical to any conception of seeking to determine what constitutes a valid public use is what the term does not permit. The Takings clause does not permit employment of eminent domain for a private use. Efforts to distinguish between a public use and a private benefit have produced various tests. They range, as noted above, from insisting that the public have a right to use the property taken, or that everyone must benefit from the project for the condemnation to be considered valid, to a private acquisition being one where the private benefits are primary and not secondary to the public benefits. Despite these tests, it remains difficult to differentiate between a public and a private use for a few reasons.

The most important factor affecting the meaning of public use is that local customs and conditions have significantly influenced the meaning in both the United States and individual state constitutions. Irrigation of private property in a dry climate, given local weather conditions, the state of the economy, and patterns of land ownership may be considered a valid public use in one community; such irrigation in a wet climate may not be considered a valid public use, but may instead be seen as simply favoring a private interest. Legislatures are clearly influenced by local conditions when determining eminent domain policy, and local courts pay great respect to local determinations of public use. The law on what constituted a valid "public use" was constructed from the bottom up, with local jurisdictions basing determinations upon local conditions and needs. The result was no unified or uniform answer to what constitutes a valid public use. Much in the same way that Justice Marshall in *McCulloch v. Maryland*, 17 U.S. 316 (1819), gave to Congress wide discretion in determining what "necessary and proper" meant in the Constitution when he upheld their creation of a national bank, local judges and courts will also give broad deference to state legislatures and city councils (among other local governments) when they make decisions about what constitutes a valid public use. This deference to legislative determinations is in part what judicial restraint is all about. As a rule, courts should not second-guess Congress or legislatures. Many criticize this practice as a form of judicial activism or legislating from the bench.

The federal courts, too, have offered significant deference to local determinations of public use. In part they did this as a result of *Barron v. Baltimore*, 32 U.S. 243 (1833). In this case the Court ruled that the Bill of Rights, including the Takings clause, did not apply to the states. Thus, federal courts were not involved in formulating or framing the legal issues of eminent domain law, at least at the state level. This meant that until the end of the nineteenth century states were given ample opportunity to construct their own meanings and traditions regarding what constitute valid uses of eminent domain. The 1896 case *Missouri Pacific Railway Company v. Nebraska*, 164 U.S. 403 (1896), was the first and last time the United States Supreme Court overruled a state court determination of what constituted a valid public use. Justice Holmes, in *Strickley v. Highland Boy Mining Company*, 200 U.S. 527 (1906), supported this sentiment, indicating that if eminent domain statutes of a state are constitutional, the Supreme Court would "follow the construction of the state court."[4] Eminent-domain public-use determinations, then, are first largely decentralized, yielding conceptions of public use that are reflective of local conditions. As a result, this deference, along with the absence of federal involvement in eminent-domain cases, produced the multiple conceptions or interpretations over what "public use" meant.

Throughout American history, courts have wavered between the broad and narrow constructions of public use, but in the twentieth century, and most certainly at present, the broad construction of public use has triumphed.[5] This has resulted in legislatures being given wide deference on local determinations of what is a valid public use, with public use eventually given a scope equal to that of the police power in *Hawaii Housing Authority v. Midkiff*, as was pointed out in the previous chapter.

State judges articulated both a broad construction of public use to justify state support of economic development and a narrow meaning to just compensation as a way to have traditional property owners subsidize new commercial interests. Some scholars assert that eminent domain was an important nineteenth-century economic development tool to redistribute economic and political power and wealth. Until the 1830s, then, public use was not a judicial question but generally a legislative one, giving state representatives wide latitude to further economic development. In *Bloodgood v. The Mohawk and Hudson Railroad Company*, 18 Wendall 9 (1837), a New York court used a narrow definition of public use to uphold the taking of private land to build a railroad. Since the railroads were used by the public, it was appropriate for the state to delegate to them that right to take land.[6] *Bloodgood* affirmed the right of a state to transfer to a private party the ability to condemn land that would be turned over to a private party. Such an action constituted a valid public use. The court also stated that the judiciary, and not the legislature, was to decide on the meaning of public use.

The Mills Acts, as noted in the previous chapter, also represent another example of where the government effectively took property to promote a broad public benefit. These acts delegated eminent domain power to millers and gave them the right to build dams and raise water levels for grain mills. As a result of the damming, adjacent lands were flooded and property was de facto taken. In most cases, the Mills Acts authorized the private flooding, stating that a legitimate public use was being furthered. Building dams for grain mills either furthered a private economic good (for the mill owner) that served general economic development needs, and thus was justified under a broad construction of public use; or the grain mills were open to public use and thus justified under a narrow construction. In either case, the Mills Acts gave new meaning to public use by allowing states to use eminent domain as an economic development tool, even when the property taken was not owned by the public.

From the 1840s on, the broad public benefit construction of public use seemed to be eclipsed by the narrow "use by the public" standard. While courts often gave lip service to narrow conceptions of public use, the reality was that a broad reading had already emerged by this point. While some courts were troubled by the private benefits these acts of eminent domain yielded, they ruled that the private benefit was "incidental" to the public benefit. Private interests could profit from eminent domain, but only as long as their profit was not the primary purpose of the taking. Narrow conceptions of public use really did not halt many, if any, takings.

Legal scholars also addressed the public use debate. J. P. Thayer in 1856 offered support for a broad reading of the public-use provision, stating that legislatures may generally determine when to use eminent domain to serve a "public exigency."[7] Courts did have some right to review legislative determinations to protect private property, and that review precluded private transfers of land.

John Lewis's *A Treatise on the Law of Eminent Domain in the United States* was published in 1888, 1900, and 1909.[8] Lewis claimed to survey almost 24,000 eminent domain cases, and concluded that both narrow and broad constructions of public use were used, and neither had complete sway over the judiciary. Lewis found that the case law sustained most takings, including those involving private transfers of land. He also argued that few state constitutions explicitly precluded private takings. This was a sign that the broad meaning had legislative and state constitutional support. Finally, like Thayer, Lewis claimed that the courts generally gave great deference to legislative determinations of public use unless their action was "without reasonable foundation."[9]

Even though the broad meaning of public use appears to be the one endorsed by the courts, neither the broad nor the narrow meaning is able to provide an exhaustive description or rule to explain all eminent-domain public-use holdings. For example, if "public use" means "use by the public," eminent domain may be employed to secure sites for hotels and theaters, which are bound by custom or state statute to serve the public. If, however, "public use" is synonymous with "public advantage," eminent domain might be legitimately employed on behalf of all large industrial enterprises and to regulate the size and distribution of farm holdings. Yet the use of a highway by the public would not in itself be sufficient to justify the exercise of eminent domain unless it appeared that the road was used by enough people to demonstrate that it secured a public advantage.

Whatever may be said in favor of either the narrow or broad constructions of "public use," neither can be accepted as completely controlling without disregarding some of the well-established doctrines or rules of eminent domain. Further efforts at providing a precise definition of "public use" are doomed to fail, and many courts have recognized this and have repudiated efforts to lay down hard and fast rules freezing the definition of this phrase.

Cole v. LaGrange, 113 U.S. 1 (1884), was the first Supreme Court case to deal with the public-use question. *Cole* involved a LaGrange, Missouri, issuance of 25 bonds to the LaGrange Iron and Steel Company to operate a rolling mill. The challenge to the issuance was that the bonds were for private, not public, use and were not sanctioned by the state constitution of Missouri. Justice Gray, writing for the majority overturning the bonding, stated: "[T]he general grant of legislative power in the Constitution of a state does not enable the legislature, in the exercise either of the right of eminent domain, or of the right of taxation, to take private property, without the owner's consent, for any but a public object."[10] The Missouri Constitution, in declaring that takings are only permitted for public use, "clearly presupposes" that private property cannot be taken for private use. Here, the bonds were to the benefit of a private enterprise and therefore the state court was correct in its judgment that this was an unconstitutional private taking.

Cole stood for the proposition that no private takings for private benefit would be permitted. This decision implied that the Supreme Court had given sanction to the narrow reading of public use. It also seemed to pave the way for the Court to be the branch of government to protect property by deciding what a valid public use was. It should come as no surprise that *Cole* was decided around the time the Court was deciding cases such as *Mugler v. Kansas*, 123 U.S. 623 (1887), ushering in the doctrine of substantive due process that was discussed earlier. Transforming public-use decisions into judicial questions was the product of a jurisprudential and constitutional philosophy that was part of the *Lochner* era where the courts questioned the economic regulation of the economy by legislatures.

In *Hairston v. Danville and Western Railway*, 208 U.S. 598 (1908), the Court, citing Lewis's *Treatise on the Law of Eminent Domain in the United States*, ruled that it was the final call when it came to deciding what constituted a valid public use.[11]

The one and only principle in which all the courts seem to agree is that the nature of uses, whether public: or private, is primarily a

judicial question. The determination of this question by the courts
has been influenced in the different States by considerations touch-
ing the resources, the capacity of the soil, and the relative importance of industries to the general public welfare, and the long
established methods and habits of the people.[12]

In *Shoemaker v. United States*, 147 U.S. 282 (1893), the Court held
that a taking for a recreational purpose was a legitimate public
use. In *Fallbrook Irrigation District v. Bradley*, 164 U.S. 112 (1896),
the Court found that the irrigation of private lands constituted a
valid public use because it encouraged the general prosperity of
the area. In this case, the Supreme Court stated that what a valid
public use is depends on local facts and circumstances.

> The legislature, not having itself described the district, has not
> decided that any particular land would or could possibly be bene-
> fitted as described, and therefore it would be necessary to give a
> hearing at some time, to those interested, upon the question of fact,
> whether or not the land of any owner which was intended to be
> included would be benefitted by the irrigation proposed. If such a
> hearing were provided for by the act, the decision of the tribunal
> thereby created would be sufficient. Whether it is provided for will
> be discussed when we come to the question of the proper construc-
> tion of the act itself. If land which can, to a certain extent, be benefi-
> cially used without artificial irrigation, may yet be so much
> improved by it that it will be thereby, and for its original use, sub-
> stantially benefitted, and, in addition to the former use, though not
> in exclusion of it, if it can then be put to other and more remunera-
> tive uses, we think it erroneous to say that the furnishing of artifi-
> cial irrigation to that kind of land cannot be, in a legal sense, a
> public improvement, or the use of the water a public use.[13]

The Court went on to say:

> Assuming for the purpose of this objection that the owner of these
> lands had, by the provisions of the act, and before the lands were
> finally included in the district, an opportunity to be heard before a
> proper tribunal upon the question of benefits, we are of opinion
> that the decision of such a tribunal, in the absence of actual fraud
> and bad faith, would be, so far as this court is concerned, conclu-
> sive upon that question. It cannot be that upon a question of fact, of
> such a nature, this court has the power to review the decision of
> the state tribunal, which has been pronounced under a statute

providing for a hearing upon notice. The erroneous decision of such a question of fact violates no constitutional provision. The circuit court in this case has not assumed to undertake any such review of a question of fact.[14]

Here the Supreme Court stated that it would have to defer to local determinations of public use as a matter of fact. In general, appeals courts defer to lower courts on factual matters, viewing them as better situated to gather evidence, assess credibility of witnesses, and make decisions regarding what facts to admit into court. In some sense, this is what the Court was saying here. Specifically, that it would defer to local determinations of what constituted a valid public use by letting local courts decide, based upon local needs and conditions.

But in this case the Court also appeared to reject a narrow reading of public use.

[T]he use must be regarded as a public use or else it would seem to follow that no general scheme of irrigation can be formed or carried into effect.... The use for which private property is to be taken must be a public one, whether the taking be by the exercise of the right of eminent domain or by that of taxation.... The fact that the use of the water is limited to the landowner is not therefore a fatal objection to this legislation. It is not essential that the entire community or even a considerable portion thereof should directly enjoy or participate in an improvement in order to be considered a public use.[15]

In the early twentieth century there were several cases where the Supreme Court again upheld local determinations of public use, while at the same time appearing to expand the meaning of the concept. In *Clark v. Nash*, 198 U.S. 361 (1905), and *Strickley v. Highland Boy Mining Company*, 200 U.S. 527 (1906), the Supreme Court upheld the taking of land for aerial tramways for mining companies. In *Clark*, the Court declared:

[W]e are always, where it can fairly be done, strongly inclined to hold with the state courts, when they uphold a state statute providing for such condemnation. The validity of such statutes may sometimes depend upon many different facts, the existence of which would make a public use, even by an individual, where, in the absence of such facts, the use would clearly be private.[16]

Similarly, in *Strickley* the Court pronounced:

> In view of the decision of the state court we assume that the con-
> demnation was authorized by the state laws, subject only to the
> question whether those laws, as construed, are consistent with the
> 14th Amendment. Some objections to this view were mentioned,
> but they are not open. If the statutes are constitutional as construed,
> we follow the construction of the state court.[17]

In effect, the Court again said it would defer to local determinations of public use. It did that for a couple of general reasons
that often apply to all lower court decisions, not just in the area
of eminent domain. First, the presumption is that lower courts
can better appreciate local conditions and needs than can federal
courts more distant from the scene. But more important, lower
courts are courts of fact. By that, trial courts determine the facts
and are viewed as being better at gathering this information, such
as making decisions assessing witness credibility, for example,
than are appeals courts, which generally only look to errors in
law. As a rule, appellate courts defer to the lower court in their
determination of facts, leaving for appeal questions of whether
the law was correctly applied. In the case of eminent domain, the
Supreme Court seems to be reiterating this general rule, leaving
up to lower courts the determination of whether something does
in fact promote a valid public use.

Consistently in the twentieth century through World War II, the
Supreme Court deferred to local public-use determinations, the
effect of which was to expand the range of possible uses
considered to be public. The Court rejected the claim that rent-
control laws were a form of a taking without compensation in
Block v. Hirsh, 256 U.S. 135 (1921). It ruled that way in part because
Washington, DC, which had enacted the measure, saw it as a necessary emergency measure after World War I. In *Old Dominion
v. United States*, 269 U.S. 55 (1925), the Court held that the taking of
private land for military purposes was also a legitimate public use.
In *International Paper Company v. United States*, 282 U.S. 399 (1931),
the Court upheld as a valid public use a federal act taking electrical power from the Niagara Falls Power Company and diverting it
for war purposes to other private companies. Summarizing its
views about what constituted a valid public use in these three
cases, the Court in *Old Dominion* declared:

We shall not inquire whether this purpose was or was not so reasonably incidental to the necessarily hurried transactions during the war as to warrant the taking, upon the principle illustrated by *Brown v. United States.* Congress has declared the purpose to be a public use, by implication if not by express words. If we disregard the heading quoted from the latest Act, "Sites for Military Purposes," which we see no reason for doing, and treat "For quartermaster warehouses" as descriptive rather than prospective, still there is nothing shown in the intentions or transactions of subordinates that is sufficient to overcome the declaration by Congress of what it had in mind. Its decision is entitled to deference until it is shown to involve an impossibility. But the military purposes mentioned at least may have been entertained and they clearly were for a public use.[18]

The Court made it clear here that it would defer to local determinations of public use, with such deference effectively expanding the range of permissible applications of eminent domain. This trend continued after the war with the 1954 U.S. Supreme Court case *Berman v. Parker,* which was discussed in a previous chapter. This decision unanimously held that the District of Columbia's use of eminent domain to clear slums and urban blight was a valid public use. The Court again refused to second-guess a determination about what constituted a permissible use of eminent domain, stating:

[t]he concept of public welfare is broad and inclusive ... [and] ... the power of eminent domain is merely the means to the end.[19]

[T]he means of executing the project are for Congress and Congress alone to determine, once the public purpose has been established. The public end may be as well or better served through an agency of private enterprise than through a department of government—; or so the Congress might conclude. We cannot say that public ownership is the sole method of promoting the public purposes of community redevelopment projects.[20]

Berman demonstrated that the broad notion or concept of public use clearly has won.

If the triumph of the broad meaning of public use had not already been confirmed with *Berman,* it definitely was with *Hawaii Housing Authority v. Midkiff,* 467 U.S. 229 (1984). In upholding as a valid public use a land transfer from some private individuals to another person in order to facilitate a more equitable distribution of property ownership in the state, Justice O'Connor wrote:

> The mere fact that property taken outright by eminent domain is transferred in the first instance to private beneficiaries does not condemn that taking as having only a private purpose. The Court long ago rejected any literal requirement that condemned property be put into use for the general public. "It is not essential that the entire community, nor even any considerable portion, ... directly enjoy or participate in any improvement in order [for it] to constitute a public use.... [W]hat in its immediate aspect [is] only a private transaction may ... be raised by its class or character to a public affair."[21]

Contrary to what she would later argue in her *Kelo* dissent, O'Connor did not find that a public use was missing even if the use of eminent domain involved the transfer of property from one private party to another. As with *Berman*, the decision about ownership and how property would be best used rested with the government. Quoting again from *Midkiff*:

> The "public use" requirement is thus coterminous with the scope of the sovereign's power. There is, of course, a role for the courts to play in reviewing a legislature's judgment of what constitutes a public use, even when the eminent domain power is equated with the police power. But the Court in *Berman* made it clear that it is "an extremely narrow" one.[22]

Given decisions such as *Berman* and *Midkiff*, there appeared little question by 1984 that the Supreme Court was endorsing a broad meaning that was attached to the public-use stipulation of the Takings clause. It had arrived at this position as a result of granting deference to local courts to make their own public-use determinations as a product of local conditions and needs. The Court also reached this decision as part of a broader retreat from economic due process and the rejection of *Lochner*-era jurisprudence, and it came to this position by way of deference to Congress to deal with emergencies. Finally, even as far back as the nineteenth century, many of the acts of eminent domain upheld involved economic development issues, or they included the use of government power to transfer property from one private owner to another. Expansion of the public use doctrine was gradual and persistent.

THE PUBLIC-USE DOCTRINE BEYOND THE SUPREME COURT

Repeatedly, the Supreme Court has stated that it would defer to local state court determinations regarding what constituted a valid public use. De facto, this means that local courts have had significant influence deciding what a valid public use is. Three state court decisions typify how they have approached the use of eminent domain.

Poletown Neighborhood Council v. City of Detroit, 304 N.W.2d 455 (Mich. 1981), is one of the most famous cases ever involving the use of eminent domain for economic development purposes. In *Poletown*, the Michigan Supreme Court upheld the City of Detroit's use of its eminent-domain authority to level a city neighborhood, relocate 1,362 households, and acquire more than 150 private businesses in order to accommodate the desire of General Motors Corporation to build a new assembly plant on 465 acres of land. The city designated the Poletown area as blighted and began condemnation proceedings. Several facing condemnation challenged the taking as not constituting a valid public use under the Michigan constitution. They argued that the taking did not serve a valid public purpose but that instead it was for a private purpose and benefit to one entity, General Motors.

The Michigan Supreme Court upheld the taking as a valid public use under the state constitution, contending that the public would be the primary beneficiary, reasoning that "the most important consideration in the case of eminent domain is the necessity of accomplishing some public good which is otherwise impracticable, and the law does not so much regard the means as the need."[23] In *Poletown*, the Court recognized that the needs that would be served by upholding this use of eminent domain included the alleviation of "the severe economic conditions facing the residents of the city and state, [and] the need for new industrial development to revitalize local industries, the economic boost the proposed project would provide."[24]

The *Poletown* decision articulated a broad definition of public use and how a state court determined its role in public-use determinations under its own constitution. In addressing the meaning of the public-use clause in the state constitution, the Court indicated that a "public use changes and with changing economic conditions of society and that the right of the public to receive and enjoy the benefit of the use determines whether the use is public or private."[25] Thus, in order to promote the general economic welfare of the people, the Court approved the municipal taking of private property of some in order to provide land for the future development and expansion of a General Motor's manufacturing facility. As to the judicial role in questioning legislative determinations of public use, the Michigan Supreme Court followed its understanding of *Berman v. Parker* as well as state precedents in equating public use with public benefit and in indicating that "the determination of what constitutes a public purpose is primarily a legislative function."[26] Overall, in summarizing its role in second-guessing the decision to use eminent domain, the Court stated: "The Legislature has determined that governmental action of the type contemplated here meets a public need and serves an essential public purpose. The Court's role after such a determination is made is limited."[27]

Poletown was a controversial lightning-rod decision that upset both political liberals and conservatives.[28] Eventually the Michigan Supreme Court overturned the decision in a 2005 case, setting the stage for many who hoped the U.S. Supreme Court would have followed that ruling when it heard the *Kelo* case. That case, *County of Wayne v. Hathcock*, 471 Mich. 445, 684 N.W.2d 765 (2004), will be discussed later in this book.

Another famous case involving a novel employment of eminent domain was *City of Oakland v. Oakland Raiders*, 32 Cal. 3d 60 (1982). This case upheld the right of a municipality to use eminent-domain power to acquire a business sports franchise contemplating relocation. Here, the City of Oakland was allowed to use its eminent-domain power to seize all real and personal business assets of the Raiders' football franchise. The coliseum that the team played in was leased by the team owners from a public, nonprofit city/county corporation. Upon failure to reach a settlement on an option to renew the lease, the team announced its intention to remove itself to Los Angeles. To prevent this, the City of Oakland commenced an eminent-domain action to acquire all the property rights associated with the team, including players' contracts, team equipment, and television and radio contracts. The franchise owner argued against the city's action on two grounds: (1) that the law of eminent domain did not permit the taking of intangible property not associated with realty (here, the team's network of intangible contractual rights); and (2) that the taking contemplated by the city cannot, as a matter of law, be for any public use within the city's authority. The core of the *Oakland Raiders* decision by the California Supreme Court asked whether the state constitutional requirement that eminent-domain acquisitions must serve a "public use" was met. First, the Court drew upon state precedents and noted that the power of eminent domain was an "inherent attribute of general government" and that "constitutional provisions merely place limits upon its exercise."[29] Among those limiting provisions is a public-use stipulation; yet the Court rejected a narrow reading of this stipulation and held that a "public use is a use which concerns the whole community or promotes the general interest in its relation to any legitimate object of government."[30] Noting that public use has an evolving nature and that the acquisition contemplated here was an unusual application of eminent domain, the Court nonetheless held that "acquisition and, indeed, the operation of a sports franchise may be an appropriate municipal function."[31]

Having established broad constitutional meaning to the state's public-use stipulation in eminent-domain acquisitions, the question turned to whether a city had the power to acquire business property to serve municipal uses. First, the Court noted that "in contrast to the broad powers of general government, however, a municipal corporation has no inherent power of eminent domain and can exercise it only when expressly authorized by law."[32] Explicit statutory provisions would have to support state delegation of eminent-domain authority to municipal corporations if the latter wished to act, and, under California law, such a delegation had occurred via the California Government Code, which provides that "a city may acquire by eminent domain any property necessary to carry out any of its powers and functions."[33] The City of Oakland, then, had authority to acquire the Oakland Raiders' property, including all its intangible property and assets.

Thus, in reversing the trial court's grant of summary judgment in the team's favor, the California Supreme Court rejected both of the team's arguments, concluding that "the acquisition and, indeed, the operation of a sports franchise may be an appropriate municipal function."[34] The court stated, in response to the team's arguments, that "intangible assets are subject to condemnation," and that the subject acquisition could meet the public-use test when it is defined as "a use which concerns the whole community or promotes the general interest in its relation to any legitimate object of government."[35] Perhaps in recognition of the city's argument that "the factual circumstances surrounding the construction of the Oakland Coliseum and the integration of the past use of the stadium with the life of the City of Oakland in general will readily demonstrate the 'public' nature of the use contemplated here,"[36] the Court noted that "[i]t is not essential that the entire community, or even any considerable portion thereof, shall directly enjoy or participate in an improvement in order to constitute a public use." The court accepted the City of Oakland's argument that "the one crucial factor and sole test of public use ... [is that] the use must be for the general benefit of the *public* and not be primarily for private individual gain."[37] Here, while it may appear that, by retaining the team, only the fans and those securing direct economic gain directly profit from this use of eminent domain, the Court accepted the argument that the community as a whole benefits economically and culturally, and in this manner the public-use requirement is served.

While the California Supreme Court did uphold the use of eminent domain here, it is important to note that a federal court eventually invalidated the use of eminent domain to acquire the team on federal constitutional grounds. Specifically, it argued that the use of eminent domain here violated the Commerce clause. It did that by saying that the use of eminent domain was an unconstitutional interference with interstate commerce. While this decision seemed to have ended the possibilities of using eminent domain to prevent a sports franchise from fleeing, it did not invalidate the basic concept that a taking for economic development purposes was an invalid public use.

Finally, a third and more recent case demonstrating how state courts have approached the use of eminent domain is from Minnesota. The Minnesota Supreme Court upheld in *Housing and Redevelopment Authority in and for the City of Richfield*, 641 N.W.2d 885 (Minn. 2002), the taking of real property from one business and giving the land to another private business. In reaching this decision, the Court did not rely upon the state constitution, but instead rendered its opinion based upon a state statute.

In this case, in 1993, the City of Richfield, Minnesota, adopted a redevelopment plan for the Richfield Redevelopment Project Area. In 1999 the comprehensive (or "comp") plan (explained in chapter 6) was modified to include the plaintiff's property. Subsequently, in 2000, the city sought to use tax increment financing to acquire real property owned by Walser Auto Sales and to transfer

it to Best Buy Corporation to encourage the latter to relocate its corporate headquarters within the city. To effect this condemnation,
the city relied on a Minnesota "quick-take" statute (discussed in
chapter 6) and a law that authorized the taking of property for redevelopment purposes in order to remove, prevent, or reduce blight,
blighting factors, or the causes of the blight. Walser objected, contending that its property was not blighted, and challenged the decision in a state district court, which upheld the taking. Plaintiffs
appealed to the Minnesota Court of Appeals.

The court upheld the taking as serving a valid public purpose.
The court first noted how Minnesota law had historically provided a deferential standard of review to what constituted a public use, giving it a broad construction and generally using it and
public purpose interchangeably.[38] Second, it noted how Minnesota law authorized the takings for redevelopment projects to
"acquire blighted areas and other real property for the purpose
of removing, preventing, or reducing blight, blighting factors, or
the causes of blight."[39] Third, in spite of plaintiff's contention that
their property was not blighted, the court noted how the city in
its comp plan sought to redevelop the area, finding its infrastructure to be obsolete. It found the auto sales operation to be incompatible with the city's comp plan and surrounding land uses and
that there was some evidence that the auto sales operation generated excessive noise and hazardous traffic. The district court also
deferred to the city's findings that the proposed project area was
environmentally blighted. The court thus found that the taking of
the property for redevelopment purposes was authorized by the
Minnesota statute in that it met the definition of "blight." Overall, according to the court, the combination of the state statute
authorizing the taking for blight, the 1993 comprehensive plan, as
modified in 1999, and findings of the city persuaded the court
that the taking of the property was for a valid public purpose.

Finally, in addition to challenging the taking as not securing a
valid public purpose use, Walser also argued that the acquisition
of their property was not necessary. The court quickly dismissed
this argument, stating that "absolute necessity" was not required
to support a taking and that instead the proposed taking only
need be *reasonably necessary or convenient* for the furtherance of a
proper purpose."[40]

The state Supreme Court also upheld the ruling in an evenly
split decision (3-3), which meant that the decision of the Court of
Appeals would stand.[41] Thus, the decision to take the property

for redevelopment purposes to abate blight was upheld as a valid public purpose, even though the real property of one private business would be transferred to another.

Taken together, the cases from Michigan, California, and Minnesota demonstrate how state courts have themselves expanded the public-use concept. In fact, several scholars lamented that *Poletown* and *Oakland Raiders* represented the demise of the public-use stipulation or limitation on eminent domain.[42] They have done so by following the cues articulated by the Supreme Court in cases such as *Berman* and *Midkiff*, but they have also done so by following their own state constitutions, laws, and precedents.

Prior to the 2005 *Kelo* decision, then, what constituted a valid public use? No simple or precise definition may be possible, but one could argue that the following criteria helped define the concept. A valid public use:

- is anything that furthers the police power functions of a state in that it enables it to promote the health, safety, welfare, or morals of its people.
- may be determined or influenced by changing local needs and conditions.
- may include the promotion of economic development.
- may include the use of government power to transfer property from one private owner to another.
- may produce private benefits, but only so long as they are secondary to the general benefits they provide to the community.
- is primarily a matter for the legislature or Congress to decide, with the courts giving general deference to their determinations.
- does not mean that property has to be absolutely essential to a project. It merely needs to be convenient or useful.

The above seven points definitely do not provide a simple or elegant definition of *public use*. Instead, they demonstrate that the public-use stipulation of the Fifth Amendment has less of a fixed meaning than some may think. Or at least this is how the Supreme and other state and lower federal courts have approached the concept. *Public use* is an essentially contested concept, and battles over its meaning is exactly what happened in *Kelo*. But prior to that case, one thing was clear, the use of eminent domain to further economic development, even if it meant the taking of private property from one owner and giving it to another, was considered a valid public use.

CHAPTER SIX

The ABCs
of Eminent Domain

Here's the plan. We get the warhead and we hold the world
ransom for ... ONE MILLION DOLLARS! Don't you think
... We hold the world ransom for 100 Billion Dollars!
—Dr. Evil in *Austin Powers*

The government has broad authority to take private property
for a valid public use so long as just compensation is paid to the
owner. This conclusion should have become clear from the discussions in previous chapters. But this restatement of the current
law fails to answer two other important questions. The first is,
should the government take a specific piece of property? Second,
how does the government actually go about taking property that
it wants?

The first question raises a host of pragmatic, planning, political,
and normative questions. In particular, asking whether the government should take a particular piece of property first raises
good questions about whether and why a specific tract of land,
for example, needs to be acquired. Here one can ask a series of
questions about whether it is necessary to build a highway in a
specific place, or tear down housing to build a supermarket, or
raze a neighborhood in order to provide development room for
another private business. In part, the anger generated in *Poletown*
was one that questioned the need essentially to destroy an entire
neighborhood—a viable community—in order to provide space
for GM to expand. Residents in *Poletown* felt that their interests

were being unfairly sacrificed either for the good of the entire city or, even worse, they were being sold out to serve the corporate needs of a big company that had blackmailed Detroit into doing its bidding. This "corporate thuggery" explains part of the resentment and anger about how eminent domain is employed today. It looks to many as if it is the big guy beating up on the little guy.

The question of why a specific piece of property should be acquired is a question about planning. It is about whether there is an alternative way to accomplish the same project without taking a specific piece of land or property. One of the ugly legacies of the 1950s and 1960s was that many highways and economic redevelopment projects appeared to target low-income neighborhoods and communities populated by people of color. These projects often split neighborhoods in two, relocated scores of individuals, or otherwise devised plans that either seemed blind to the impact it was having upon these populations or, even worse, were purposely directed toward them. In either case, asking why a specific piece of property needed to be taken raises some questions about the planning process, the potential political motives, and perhaps a host of other issues and that questioned the reasoning for the taking.

But even beyond these planning and political questions, the "why" question is also an ethical one. It is ultimately about asking a series of questions regarding why, perhaps, condemnors should be permitted to take a single-family house. It is about asking whether specific neighborhoods or people should be asked to sacrifice their property or homes for others. It is perhaps about asking if homes should be given less protection than commercial property. Finally, the ethical question may even extend to asking should eminent domain ever be used to acquire property. This ethical question ultimately turns into a political question that asks important queries about the nature of political society and the power of government. While some may conclude that a limited government that respects freedom should never be permitted to take private property, for reasons that were discussed earlier, it is not so clear that this position can be viably maintained. There may in fact be some projects that clearly need to be done and the only way to build a bridge, school, or other public projects is by employing eminent domain.

But the other question—how the government actually takes property—is also important. Here, one is asking a process question; that is, what legal process must be followed for the government to take property? Clearly it is the case, first, that not just anyone can use eminent domain to take property. In most cases, a private person who tries to take the property of someone else would be committing theft or stealing. Thus, the person taking the property, a condemnor, must be legally empowered to use eminent domain. In most cases, the condemnor is the government. This could be the federal government, or it could be a state or local government such as a city. But a government condemnor could also be its agent. It might be a department of transportation, or perhaps a parks department. In addition, the condemnor could also be an economic development agency of a state or local government. It could also be an airport, or any of a score of other governmental or quasi-governmental units giving the power of eminent domain. While states have inherent authority to condemn, these other units of government do not have the authority to use eminent domain unless given authority by a state government. This means that, lacking statutory authorization, a city or town cannot take property.

But the government is not the only possible condemnor. Governments can also designate private corporations or individuals to be condemnors. In many situations, governments have given eminent-domain authority to public utilities, such as power companies, so that they can build transmission lines for electricity or gas. Railroads, as noted earlier, have been given the power of eminent domain, as have telecommunications companies. All of them have been given this authority so that they can provide functions or services that elected officials have decided are in the public good to provide. However, in some cases, governments may even give eminent-domain authority to private individuals for the same reasons that it may be given to a corporation. Thus, while a condemnor is usually a governmental entity, it need not always be so.

Imagine that a condemnor wants to use eminent domain to acquire property. In particular, imagine that someone wants to condemn or take your home or business with eminent domain. If that were to occur, what must the government (or any condemnor) do in order to take your property? Contrary to what many might think, the decision to take property is not a big surprise to most owners and the process is not usually arbitrary. Instead, several steps must usually be followed or complied with before the government can actually take title to property.

Roughly, there are three basic processes for using eminent domain. The most basic is when the government actually uses eminent domain to take private property. The second invokes what are called "quick-take laws" to expedite the taking process. Quick-take laws allow for property to be condemned even if all the issues surrounding the taking, such as the price for the property, have not been resolved. The third is when an owner either alleges a regulatory taking or when the government has allegedly taken property and the owner sues to seek compensation. This is called an inverse condemnation action. The remainder of this chapter describes these three processes.

THREE WAYS TO TAKE PROPERTY

While there may be one federal government, fifty states, and thousands of local governments as well as many other entities that have the power to take property for public uses, all of these entities take property in similar ways. The basis for this uniformity may be traced in part to the creation of a 1975 *Uniform Eminent Domain Code* drafted by the National Conference of Commissioners of Uniform State Laws.[1] Several organizations in the United States seek to draft model laws or codes that can be used across the entire country. The hope in drafting these model codes is that it will eliminate confusing differences or disparities across city or state borders. The virtue of uniformity is that it will make it easier and less costly to do business across the nation without having to learn new laws or change behavior every time one moves. Uniformity enhances productivity and efficiency. State and local governments have adopted many provisions of the 1975 *Uniform Eminent Domain Code*, thereby creating a basic pattern or sense of uniformity that establishes the three processes for condemnation.

Normal Taking

The first and most basic process is when the government intends to acquire specific property for the purposes of some project, such as the building of a highway or perhaps a new shopping center. This type of condemnation project will be referred to as a "normal taking." A normal taking just does not occur out of nowhere. It is rare that the government just decides at the spur of the moment and without notice to use its eminent-domain power to acquire property for the purposes of building a road or a shopping center. While it is possible that in a real emergency, such as a natural disaster, eminent domain might be deployed rather suddenly, this would definitely be a rare exception to what happens with a normal taking. In most emergency situations, the law already allows the government to enter or seize property and that is not considered an act of eminent domain. For example, if one's house caught on fire and firefighters entered the property to extinguish the blaze, owners could not sue for trespass or claim that a taking had occurred. Moreover, if in nonemergency situations the government did act without notice to the owner to take property, that would be a violation of the law and the owner would have sufficient remedies and defenses to challenge such an action. In brief, the way the government acted here probably would have violated the Due Process clause of the Fourteenth Amendment.

While many might think that the decision to take property is a sudden or perhaps an unexpected or quick decision, the reality is that, by the time the government has decided to use eminent domain to acquire property, numerous actions have already taken place. The actual use of eminent domain is generally a last resort or last step in a process the government uses when it wishes to undertake a public project. For many who criticize the government as pokey, bureaucratic, and slow, it would be odd to think that routine decisions to use eminent domain are hasty! Governments generally cannot move quickly because the Constitution and the laws require a slow deliberate process to protect rights ... at least most of the time.

In the case of a normal taking, there are several steps in the condemnation process.

- Government develops a comprehensive plan for development
- Public hearings held on the comprehensive plan
- Specific plan for development is created
- Hearings on the specific plan is held
- Properties needed for the project are identified
- Properties are appraised
- Condemnor/developer begin efforts with property owners to purchase property
- Relocation assistance for tenants, owners
- If owners sell, then condemnors take title of property

- Government passes resolution/hearing to initiate condemnation process
- Hearing held on public use and condemnation resolution
- Owner notified of intent to condemn and served with papers
- Court hearing for condemnation scheduled
- Pretrial motions, hearings scheduled
- Court hearing and trial
- Court judgment
- Appeals, if any
- Enforcement of judgment, government takes title

Generally, the first step in any condemnation process takes place years earlier, before the government actually moves to acquire a piece of property, at the planning stage. There are two types of plans that a government might undertake as part of planning a project. The first is a comprehensive ("comp") plan, and the second is a plan for a specific project.[2] A comp plan is the most basic type of plan that a government can create when it comes to land use within its borders. Many states have laws that comp plans have to be developed and rewritten every so many years, such as once per decade following the census. A comp plan first performs a survey of how property is currently used in an area. It examines, among other things, the current zoning code, for example. It compares how all the parcels of land in a city are zoned to how they are actually used. Are lots zoned for housing really used for commercial or warehouse space? This is a good question because it seeks to determine if any property has what is called a nonconforming use. A simple survey of how property is currently used is a good way simply to know what people are doing with their property.

Another task of a comp plan is to look at the current demographics of a community. These demographics include information we would want to know about the ages, size of families, birth and death rates, and immigration and emigration patterns. This information is useful in terms of trying to know if the population is increasing or decreasing, where people are moving to, and how living patterns may be changing.

Yet another task of a comp plan is to understand the current state of business in a community—what types of business, commerce, and so on, is taking place. Again, it is useful to inventory this information so that one can learn something about the services available in an area, asking if the community has sufficient grocery stores or other services it may need or want. Finally, the comp plan might also look at other issues such as roads and highways, mass transit and transportation routes, the quality and availability of local government services, health care needs and delivery, the tax base, crime, and perhaps a host of other factors. In a nutshell, the comp plan seeks to take a picture of a community in an effort to understand its strengths and weaknesses.

But the snapshot is more than an idle curiosity. The real goal of a comp plan is to decide where a community wants to go in the future. There is a normative aspect to the comp plan. Good planners will survey their residents and businesses to find out what they want and what they want their community to look like. The real purpose of the comp plan is a needs assessment and chart for the future of a city, town, or a county. It is an effort to answer questions such as: Do we need more housing in the city? Do we need more parks? Is another school needed, or more retail shopping or should we maybe enlarge the tax base by trying to encourage a new factory or business? These are the most general questions that a comp plan tries to address, and the successful plan then tries to make sure that the land use laws for the community reflect the choices that have been made in the comp plan.

Once a comp plan has been developed, it is subject to public debate, hearings, and eventually a vote by a city council or the body adopting it. This plan is often considered a law or an ordinance and in some cases might require more than a simple majority to adopt it. The important point to note is that a good comp plan is subject to long, intense, and open discussion. It permits broad citizen input, and the eventual adoption should not come as a surprise to anyone.

A second major point when it comes to a comp plan is that, once adopted, it does not go onto a shelf or sit in someone's computer. Comp plans are "alive." By that, they are meant to be blueprints for everything else a community does. They should be guides for the economic, housing, and other types of development that a community plans for the next five or ten years. Moreover, comp plans are the cornerstone for many other documents and actions undertaken by the government. Once a comp plan has been adopted it is, for example, the basis for a zoning code. By that, many states require that a zoning ordinance or code reflect the ideas or goals articulated in the comp plan. This means that in terms of a hierarchy, the comp plan is the most important document, and then after that, the zoning ordinance or code must be in accordance with it. Conflicts between the two generally mean that the comp plan prevails. Or, phrased another way, if the zoning ordinance does not comply with the comp plan, the former is illegal.

Combined, the comp plan and the zoning code are really the master plans for economic development and planning for a community. Together they should set out specific goals and a direction for what a community wants to look like in the future. Together they should state, for example, that a community would like to turn some vacant land into a future home for a mall. Or, perhaps together they might state that land currently zoned industrial should be used in the future as a mixed-use residential area with some shopping and maybe some recreational activities. The hope in doing this is that land comped and zoned for a specific use will attract the appropriate investment and interest to make that happen. A local government, such as a city, can also make that possibility more real by doing things such as making infrastructure investments that will facilitate the development they would like to see. These infrastructure investments might be money for roads, water, or sewer lines, or, they might be resources that make it less costly for a developer to build housing or a shopping mall.

Below the level of a comp plan and a zoning ordinance is the creation of a specific plan for a particular project or parcel or parcels of land. This plan too must be in accordance with the comp plan and zoning. If it is not, either the project cannot be done or the comp plan and the zoning must be changed to accommodate or permit this project. But what type of project is in question here? Almost anything. Reference to a specific project means any type of development or public works project proposed by either a private party or by the government or governmental agency. For the former it could be a project to build housing, or maybe a new store, shopping mall, or even perhaps an industrial park or just about anything else that a private party might want to build. For a governmental agency or unit, it could include any of the above; or it might be a road, park, or cemetery; or the agency might want to clear and develop land that will make it possible for a developer to be able to accomplish some project that needs land. The critical issue here is that there is some parcel or several parcels of land within some community and someone wants to develop them. The assumption here will be that the land aimed to be developed is privately owned and it would need to be acquired in order for the project to happen. This is where the government and eminent domain step in.

Any project where eminent domain is involved, or where some type of government action is required, is going to need to be approved by the local government. This may also be true when no government money or action is required. The purpose of the hearings and approvals is to make sure that the project is compatible with applicable zoning and comp plan requirements, that the proposal meets other housing or building code requirements, or that it otherwise complies with all applicable laws that will affect the proposed use and properties in question. The hearings and governmental approval are often also informational. They are in part to inform public officials about a proposed project, and also to provide information to neighbors and other citizens. Finally, these initial hearings may also be necessary if eminent domain is to be used because they may begin the process of helping the government decide if there is a valid public use associated with the project such that it could take property if necessary. Overall, these hearings on a specific project are important in making it possible to develop some property.

At some point during these hearings, the developer and the jurisdiction or government in question will identify specific properties or parcels needed. This may have already occurred in the early design stage when the initial plan for the project was presented. At that point, the government or the developer might have already owned all the property needed for a project, or it might have already identified the land that it needed or wanted, even if neither of them already owned the property in terms of a fee simple absolute. However, in some cases, no specific parcels of land had been designated. In either case, at some point in the project review the property needs will be determined, including ones that need to be acquired from other owners. This property identification will include showing them on a map, but more important, this stage in the process seeks to determine the official legal description for the properties, as well who the owners are. This means asking who has a legal interest in the property.

Owners may have already been involved or contacted during the preliminary planning stage; they may have attended earlier hearings; or they may in fact be a partner or involved already with the project in some way. But at some point, owners need to be officially notified that their property is being considered for some type of development project. With almost any project that involves a public works project or a private development, the starting point begins with seeking the cooperation of the property owners. While the image may be that "big, bad, ugly developers" come into town and force owners to sell their property or threaten them with eminent domain, the reality is that most of the time efforts are first made to negotiate with property owners in order to convince them to sell their property. Almost no one wants a court fight that will drag out for years and cost both sides tens of thousands of dollars or more. The effort will be to convince owners willingly to sell their property.

If owners agree to sell their property, then the issue is price. How much do owners deserve for their property? Constitutionally, the standard is fair market value. This, of course, makes a lot of sense. If an owner plans to sell her property, she would be a fool (or very generous!) to sell her property for less than the fair market value. The very definition of fair market value that courts often use—what a willing buyer would pay a willing seller—is what owner and developer or local government will try to identify. The two will simply negotiate a price that both parties believe is fair. Three ways to decide what the fair price is are often used to guide negotiations.[3]

First, both sides will look to comparable sales of similar property. By that, both sides will look at other properties that are similar in as many respects as possible in order to determine price. This might mean looking at the price that other homes in similar neighborhoods sold for in the last three or six months. This is the same process that realtors often use when trying to price property. A second way to determine a fair market value is the "replacement cost," meaning, what it would cost to replace the home, for example, if it had to be built from scratch today. This is similar to a test used by insurance companies when writing policies. Often property owners will purchase policies for the replacement cost of their homes or businesses. Finally, a third test might be to look at the income stream produced by a specific property. This test is more common with businesses and rental property. Here, one seeks to determine the value of the property as an investment asset. This would be the type of evaluation used most commonly in business negotiations involving the sale of business property.

This preliminary stage when owners and sellers are negotiating the determination of fair market value may be more or less formal. By that, a less formal attempt at determining a price may simply be estimates of value based upon quick estimates of the comparable value, replacement, or income streams. However, in some cases, the appraisal process might be more formal if there is a serious dispute. At this point, outside experts may be brought in to implement a formal appraisal process. Eventually, if the owner and buyer cannot agree on a price and eminent domain is used, a court will hold a hearing regarding what the fair market value is, and formal appraisals will be ordered. Based on those appraisals, a court will fix the fair market value. Later in this chapter, a more detailed discussion of the appraisal process will be developed. For now, it is sufficient to state that if an owner is willing to sell, efforts both formally and informally will be made to reach a fair price.

As part of negotiating fair market value, an owner may also receive relocation costs or assistance. This assistance might include costs associated with looking for a new home or business location, the costs of moving and relocation, and perhaps any other incidental costs. All of this is subject to negotiation. Additionally, if the property has tenants, they too may be awarded compensation to buy out their leases, to pay for relocation, or to address any expenses they may also have. Or in some situations, buyers may condition a sale that requires owners to deliver to them property that is already free of tenants. This means the owners may have to do their own negotiations with their tenants. This might involve buying out their tenants, or they might have what is called a "condemnation clause" in their leases. A condemnation clause would inform tenants that, in the event that the property is taken by eminent domain, the leases would automatically expire within a certain number of days, weeks, or months. These clauses, while not common, are legal and some commercial owners have used them in the past to address the complications that tenants might pose.

If owners and buyers can reach agreement on the sale, then eminent domain is not needed. Instead, what has occurred here is no different from any other purchase of property. A purchase agreement is produced; eventually there is a closing on the property, and the buyer takes possession of the property. For all concerned, this is the best possible option. There are no reliable statistics here, but one could estimate that the vast majority of property acquisitions involving the government are resolved by voluntary sales where no use of eminent domain is employed. But what if there is no agreement between the owner and the buyer? Perhaps the disagreement is over price, or maybe the owner just does not want to sell. What happens then? Here is where the eminent domain process really begins.

Eminent domain is a factor here in at least two ways. First, critics of this authority contend that the threat of eminent domain is a sledgehammer hanging over a property owner. If the government retains the final authority to take property if the owner refuses to voluntarily sell, then some argue that the sale is never undertaken willingly. Yes, in some cases eminent domain is a threat to induce behavior or sales, and in these situations the so-called eminent domain abuse is real. But the percentage of all property transactions involving this abuse is a matter of dispute. Some contend it is significant; however, there is no real evidence to suggest that this is the case. Moreover, even if this abuse occurs, especially when it comes to the value of property, the courts are available to address valuation issues as mandated by the Constitution and state or federal law. Thus, owners will get fair market value for their property. The other abuse—property being taken when it is not for a valid public use—is what many also contend is eminent domain abuse. However, as will be shown in chapter 8, evidence from state courts indicates that they are usually able to distinguish private from public uses and illegitimate and legitimate uses. Hence, while the process is not flawless, claims of eminent domain abuse are greatly exaggerated.

Should owners and buyers be unable to agree on a sale, eminent domain is a last resort. It may be necessary for the government to build a necessary road, bridge, or school. Eminent domain may be needed to prevent some individuals from wrongly holding up a necessary project or blackmailing the government and taxpayers into giving them more money for their property than they deserve. Eminent domain may simply be needed to get an important public job accomplished.

If eminent domain is to be deployed to acquire property, several things need to occur. First, the condemnor is going to have to adopt a resolution that declares a public use and its intent to condemn or take specific properties. At this hearing, several things must occur. First, owners must be given legal notice that their properties are going to be subject to a taking. This is more than perhaps a general notice. In many jurisdictions, owners must receive specific notice served upon them. At the hearing, the condemnor will state its reasons for the condemnation, gather information that will justify the public use, and perhaps even declare the public use. Members of the public, including the owners, will then be given the opportunity to state their reasons for or against the decision to proceed with the condemnation.

At the conclusion of these hearings, the government must finally declare that a public use exists to take certain properties and it must adopt a resolution, ordinance, or law declaring its use and the intent to take the properties via eminent domain. If this happens, again new efforts will be undertaken to negotiate a sale with the owner, but if unsuccessful, the owners will receive notice that their properties are being condemned and taken by a city or other government. This notice is served personally upon the owners.

Effectively, this is the beginning of a legal process that could go to court. Here, the owners can opt to waive a challenge to the taking. If so, they are really consenting to sell their property. If they do not waive, then they are required to answer or respond to the notice of condemnation. What is now occurring is that the eminent domain is moving from a legislative matter to a judicial one governed by rules of civil procedure and eminent domain law. Rules of civil procedure are court rules that determine how parties notify one another of an intent to sue, what court the action will take place in, how to gather evidence, and a host of other issues. These are the rules governing litigation. Generally, once property owners have received formal notice of a condemnation suit, they will have a certain number of days, oftentimes 30, to reply with an answer. The answer needs to respond to the complaint or petition to take their property. The answer can assert that there is no valid public use, it can contest the compensation award, it can challenge the authority of the court to hear the dispute, or the owner can raise other counterclaims.

In many jurisdictions, while the fight over the condemnation takes place, the condemnor may be required to deposit with the court the value of the properties to be taken. This would be the value that the condemnor believes is the fair market value. During this pretrial stage both sides can engage in what is called "discovery." Discovery is the process used to disclose evidence to be used at a trial. This discovery may include requiring the opposing side to produce materials that might be useful in court. This could include materials regarding why the condemnor is taking the property, factors it used to determine the public use, and any other details that might shed light on its decisions. Other parties might also be questioned and other properties might be examined. If the challenge is over whether there is a valid public use and a determination was made, for example, that a specific property was blighted, evidence of blight might be examined.

However, if the issue in the case is over compensation, then opposing sides might bring forward their experts and evidence regarding how they calculated fair market value. At this point, formal appraisals are undertaken and information is produced regarding what the values of the properties in question are. All of this pretrial activity could take months.

At some point, if the condemnor and owner do not settle, there will be a trial. These are civil trials, and seldom are juries used. Instead, they are bench trials before a judge. If the dispute is over questions regarding whether there is a valid public use, the courts have said that they will give significant deference to legislative determinations. This is what Justice O'Connor stated in *Midkiff*. To some extent, the burden is on the property owner to show that there is no valid public use. They might try to show that the taking is for a private use or that there is some other reason to question the condemnation process. If the dispute in the case is overcompensation, then no side carries what is called the burden of proof. Instead, both sides present their evidence about value to the judge and the court ultimately makes the decision regarding fair market value.

Once the trial has concluded, the judge must then render a decision about the validity of the taking or compensation, or both. If no one appeals the decision, the court then issues a judgment; if the condemnor has won, title to the property in dispute is awarded to that entity. The owner is then given a certain amount of time to vacate the property and awarded compensation. If either party disagrees with the court decision, an appeal is possible. If it is the owner appealing, she may wish to stay the court's order so that the change of title does not occur. How long might all this take? It could take months, if not years, depending on the complexity of the legal issues. However, this normal taking, while subject to nuances in different jurisdictions, is the basic process for using eminent domain. It is slow, very public and often costly, but the goal generally is to protect owners.

Quick Takings

But the slowness of the normal process can also create problems. What if there is a genuine need to get a project done, such as build a new road or bridge, and the main issue separating the condemnor and owner is the price. Should a disagreement over price prevent a quick and easy resolution of the issue, especially if the validity of the public use is not in question? In situations like this, many states have created an alternative to the normal taking process. They have created what is called "quick-take legislation." In *King v. State Roads Com'n of State Highway Administration*, 298 Md. 80 (Md., 1983), the Maryland Supreme Court defined quick-take.

> In quick-take cases, the condemning authority takes possession of the property prior to trial upon payment into court of its estimate of the value of the property taken. The condemnee may immediately withdraw the amount of the quick-take deposit and may also recover the amount of any deficiency where the value of the property is later determined at trial to be greater than the amount initially deposited by the condemnor. In addition, the condemnor is required by to "pay interest at the rate of 6 percent per annum on any difference between the amount of money initially paid into court for the use of the defendant and the jury award as stated in the inquisition, from the date the money was paid into court to the date of the inquisition or final judgment, whichever date is later.[4]

In Maryland, the authority for quick-take is described in Article III, Section 40a, of the state constitution.

> The General Assembly shall enact no law authorizing private property to be taken for public use without just compensation, to be agreed upon between the parties, or awarded by a jury, being first paid or tendered to the party entitled to such compensation, but where such property is situated in Baltimore City and is desired by this State or by the Mayor and City Council of Baltimore, the General Assembly may provide that such property may be taken

immediately upon payment therefore to the owner or owners thereof by the State or by the Mayor and City Council of Baltimore, or into court, such amount as the State or the Mayor and City Council of Baltimore, as the case may be, shall estimate to be the fair value of said property, provided such legislation also requires the payment of any further sum that may subsequently be added by a jury.

The entire purpose of the quick-take law, as indicated by the name itself, is to expedite the condemnation process. The *Uniform Eminent Domain Code*, as mentioned above, actually was adopted with a form of quick-take procedure in mind that required payment to the court or the property owner the estimated just compensation, while litigation over the condemnation proceeded.

In the case of a quick-take, the process is almost identical to a normal taking. There will still be the comp plan and zoning code that stand as the basis of the land use laws for a community. There will also be a specific development plan for a project that identifies properties to be used for some purpose. Efforts will be made to negotiate voluntary sales with owners. Everything up to this point is identical to a normal taking. The only difference now is that, if negotiations over the purchase of the property break-down, quick-take laws allow for the condemnor to take legal title to the property, and the court hearing will mainly be confined to determining just compensation. Owners may get compensation in advance and the pretrial and trial activities will revolve around determinations of fair market value. Appraisals are still required and all the other rules of civil procedure apply. Quick-take simply expedites the process of condemnation so that delays do not occur.

Quick-take laws became popular in the 1980s and 1990s as a tool to expedite eminent domain. However, these laws are not always fair to owners. This is the case when the validity of the public use is implicated. In the conclusion, some of the problems with using quick-take will be discussed. However, when it comes to simply addressing compensation issues, quick-take laws make sense.

Inverse Condemnation Process

The third and last type of taking process is inverse condemnation. According to the Supreme Court in *Agins v. City of Tiburon*,

447 U.S. 255 (1980): "Inverse condemnation is 'a shorthand description of the manner in which a landowner recovers just compensation for a taking of his property when condemnation proceedings have not been instituted.'"[5] Inverse condemnation generally occurs in cases of regulatory takings or where the government acts in other ways that de facto result in the taking of property, but where no formal eminent domain action has been initiated. A suit for inverse condemnation allows owners to sue the government to force the payment of compensation for the taking of property.

There are several scenarios where inverse condemnation may be an appropriate tactic for owners to use to protect themselves. The most obvious is where there is a claim of a regulatory taking along the lines discussed or referred to in cases such as *Pennsylvania v. Mahon* (discussed earlier). Perhaps the government has enacted a regulation that is not aimed at abating a nuisance, or perhaps it overregulates. Maybe instead it denies all economically viable use of property or destroys all investment-backed expectations. These would be situations where regulatory takings occur and an owner might bring suit for inverse condemnation to compel compensation. But inverse condemnation may also be appropriate where the government undertakes other actions that effectively render a taking of property. These could be situations where the government issues an excessive temporary moratorium on property development. Another might be where government action blocks access to property, or situations where it floods property. Another scenario might be a claim that a zoning ordinance is excessive and fails to serve or further legitimate state interests. An action for inverse condemnation might also occur when the government simply physically invades private property by illegally authorizing another party to trespass. All these are possible situations where the government has decided not to engage in a formal taking of private property but nonetheless the owner may be able to allege that this is what has happened.

In some states, there might actually be a statute that describes how an owner may bring an inverse condemnation claim. However, courts have ruled that the basis of inverse condemnation claims is found in the Constitution and the Fifth (Takings clause) and Fourteenth amendments (Due Process clause). Usually, inverse condemnation suits are brought as constitutional claims using rules of civil procedure or other legal claims to raise the takings claims. For example, in Minnesota, owners who wish to challenge a government action as a taking by raising an inverse condemnation claim have to bring what is called a "mandamus" claim in court. A mandamus is simply an order from the court directing the government to do something. In the case of inverse condemnation, the order is to compel the government to compensate the owner for his property losses. An inverse condemnation might also seek to compel the formal taking of the property, but in some cases an inverse condemnation proceeding might seek to halt the taking or argue that the action is illegal or unconstitutional. In these cases the owner may be asking the court for an injunction to halt the government activity.

If an inverse condemnation is brought demanding compensation, the owner first needs to demonstrate that a taking has occurred. As discussed in an earlier chapter, several tests have been employed or developed to demonstrate a taking. These tests include asking if a physical invasion of the property has occurred, to looking at whether the regulation advances a legitimate state interest. The owner carries the burden of proof to show that a taking has occurred. If an owner can show a taking, then the topic turns to damages and compensation. Here, owners will need to show that, as a result of the taking, their property was damaged and then they will need to assert a claim for compensation. The standard for damages is compensation for the fair market value of the loss of the property. In a court proceeding for inverse condemnation, all the rules of civil procedure, evidence, and for showing damages and being awarded just compensation are the same as they were in normal and quick-take proceedings. Owners who are unhappy with decisions also are permitted to appeal court judgments or decisions.

DETERMINING COMPENSATION AND
FAIR MARKET VALUE

Normal takings, quick takings, and inverse condemnations are the main three ways that eminent domain action is initiated or used to acquire property. One common thread connecting all three types of actions is the need to compensate owners for their property losses. The constitutional standard is that the owners must receive fair market value for their property losses. A brief sketch at explaining how fair market value is determined was explained earlier in the book. However, some additional detail and explanation is warranted here.

To start with, the valuation of property is not something that just anyone can do. Owners may have a belief about what their property is worth, but such beliefs are often not accurate and, more important, not generally admissible in court as a valid way of determining property values. Instead, determination of just compensation, while ultimately determined by the courts, is often premised upon the expert testimony of appraisers who follow specific standards when seeking to value property.

Individuals who do eminent domain property appraisal are generally licensed at the state level and they are often members of professional appraisal societies. The main organization in the appraisal field is the Appraisal Institute, formed on January 1, 1991, as a result of the merger of the American Institute of Real Estate Appraisers (AIREA) and the Society of Real Estate Appraisers (SREA). The Appraisal Institute generally certifies members to do commercial or residential appraisals. To be a member, one needs a bachelor's degree, creditable experience, and the successful completion of specialized Appraisal Institute courses. In addition, to become members of the Appraisal Institute, appraisers must submit samples of their work product and pass a comprehensive examination that tests their ability to use various valuation techniques.

Beyond being licensed and trained, appraisers must follow specific standards. *The Appraisal of Real Estate*, which has been through a number of editions, is a standard reference book that appraisers use when they do a valuation. Appraisals for federal projects must comply with the uniform standards of professional appraisal practice. Additionally, all appraisals for federally related financial transactions must be made and reported in compliance with the Uniform Standards of Professional Appraisal Practice (USPAP) promulgated by the Appraisal Standards Board (ASB) of the Appraisal Foundation. USPAP comprises 10 Standard Rules that address: the appraisal process, the reporting of real property appraisal, review appraisal, real estate/real property consulting, mass appraisal, personal property appraisal, and business valuation. Finally, to avoid conflicts of interest, an appraiser's compensation may not be linked to the value of the property. In effect, one cannot pay appraisers based on a sliding scale fee tied to the value of the appraisal. This would create incentives to give inflated valuations.

For a property appraisal an owner must first hire an appraiser. Oftentimes the owner and the condemnor may each hire an appraiser or, in some cases, they may agree to hire one person to do the valuation for both of them.

The valuation process begins with appraisers identifying the property to be reviewed and ends when they report a conclusion of its value. This systematic process requires orderly planning, data gathering, analyses, reconciliation, and reporting. The goal is to arrive at a well-supported and documented conclusion of value that will stand up to legal scrutiny.

The basic appraisal process includes several steps. The first step is an accurate identification of the property to be appraised. This identification includes the legal as well as physical description. Legally, one wants to identify all the owners and limits on the property, that is, whether there are any easements or land use restrictions that limit or define some of the ownership interests. Not all owners have a fee simple absolute in their property. There may be other parties with legal interests who need to be identified.

The second step is identifying which property rights are being taken. Remember, property is a bundle of sticks or rights. A taking may occur even if only some of the sticks are being taken. It is critical to know what interests are being acquired in order to ascertain what type of legal interests are at stake.

Third, the date of the taking must be identified in the appraisal. The value of property taken is determined by the date of the condemnation. Property values fluctuate, and timing may be everything. The value of property on January 1, 2007, versus January 1, 2008, or January 1, 2009, could be dramatically different. In fact, given the collapse of real estate prices in the United States during those two years, even a difference of a month or two could make a big difference in the value or fair market price of a piece of property.

Fourth, an appraiser and appraisal report must explain how it defines value. Some states or cities require a specific definition of value. Fifth, the appraisal must identify the assumptions and factors that affect its valuation. An appraisal is often limited by special assumptions or limiting conditions. These assumptions or limits may consist of how value is defined, how comparable properties were identified, or how projected changes in the neighborhood or area affected the appraisal. This information is put in the appraisal as much to inform the reader of the valuation's limitations, as they are put in to protect the appraiser.

When property is taken by eminent domain, one of the most important and critical assumptions is that its value is determined by looking at its highest and best use. This determination of highest and best use is the most critical part of the valuation process. The highest and best use is not necessarily the current use, but one given reasonable assumptions about the market, zoning, and a host of other factors. Often, fights over determining highest and best use are quite nasty and are the source of intense legal disagreement.

Once the above issues or steps have been established, it is now time to do the property valuation. An appraiser generally will use several ways to ascertain value. There are three traditional approaches: sales comparison, cost, and income. Although this portion of the process should be left to the appraiser alone, discussions along the way of the strengths and weaknesses of each approach, and the chosen methodology or techniques applied in the valuation, will allow the lawyer to be better informed about the technical aspects of the valuation. All three approaches to value should be applied in all appraisals. However, depending upon the nature of the property involved and the availability or unavailability of certain information, one or more of the techniques may be omitted. For example, the sales comparison approach will be of little use if there have not been any truly comparable sales in the vicinity within a reasonable time preceding the valuation; the income approach will be inapplicable if the property is not of a type purchased and sold for its income-producing potential; and the cost approach will be inapplicable if the property is vacant and/or is so old that the depreciation estimate is so great that it would render the entire approach unreliable.

The best valuation conclusion will be achieved when there is sufficient information to apply all three approaches. But the simple technique of averaging the value indication arrived at by the three approaches is not acceptable. An appraiser must reconcile a value conclusion from the three approaches by considering the strengths and weaknesses of each and by judging the reliability of the individual approaches in appraising the particular property.

The sales approach is one generally accepted way to ascertaining value. It does that by comparing the condemned property to other similar properties that have recently sold. In the sales comparison approach, market value is estimated by comparing the property being appraised to similar properties that have either recently sold or are under contract for sale. The appraiser compares all differences between the comparable properties and the subject and makes adjustments for differences between them. The assumption with doing the sales comparison approach is that the market value of a property is directly related to the prices paid for comparable properties.

The sales approach is employed to establish value from comparable properties. Several elements and steps are involved, including defining what constitutes similar or comparable properties and then adjusting the different market conditions so that a relevant comparison can be achieved. This may require adjusting for different locations, dates, physical conditions, and a host of other factors. In some cases, the prior sales history of the property being appraised may not be admissible evidence to establish its value.

The cost approach is a well-accepted methodology. It establishes value by ascertaining what it would cost to build or replace a piece of property. The cost approach establishes the value of property by asking how much it would cost to replace or build a similar piece of property. It assumes that a purchaser would not pay more for an improved property than the cost of constructing a similarly located one of equal utility. This method is especially practical when the appraised property has recently been built and represents the highest and best use of the site. The cost approach may be the only approach that provides a reliable indication of value for a unique property used for an unusual purpose. This is not generally the case with residential property. However, a cost approach is less reliable when the building improvements are older and reaching the end of their economic life.

A cost approach can be premised on one of two types of cost: reproduction cost and replacement cost. A reproduction cost is the estimated cost to construct an exact duplicate or replica of the building. This would entail the same design, materials, and quality. Replacement cost, on the other hand, is an estimate of the cost to construct a building of equal utility but not necessarily of equal design, materials, or quality. Cost may be estimated by looking at materials, labor, and land acquisition costs. Oftentimes appraisers will determine all of these by using standards books or guides that provide cost estimates, or they may need to consult industry standards (such as for plumbing) to assist with this.

Finally, the income approach typically provides reliable indications of value for income-producing properties. Courts recognize the income approach, but often restrict estimates of income to actual, rather than speculative, income. They may also require that any rental income must be based on a market rental rate, and that the rental period used is reasonably proximate to the date of the taking. Finally, income must be from legal and not illegal sources.

The steps involved in the income approach are:

- Estimate gross income (EGI)
- Estimate vacancy and collection loss
- Calculate the indicated effective gross income (step 1 minus step 2)
- Estimate expenses
- Subtract expenses from EGI to arrive at the net operating income (NOI)
- Select and apply an appropriate capitalization rate to translate the NOI to an indication of market value

The sales, cost, and income appraisals may produce different value estimates that need to be reconciled. In an appraisal report, the reconciliation section of the appraisal report recaps and reviews the basic applications applied to arrive at each of the three indicated values. The strengths and weaknesses of each approach are analyzed to determine the weight to be given each of the value indications.

The final step in the appraisal process is issuing the report and estimate to the client. An appraisal assignment is not complete until a value is reconciled and a conclusion is communicated to the client. Once the report is issued, then the client may use it in court to help establish an estimate of fair market value. This report will include a signed affidavit by the appraiser indicating how she produced the valuation, and it will include a detailed description of all the assumptions, descriptions, and so on, used to arrive at a final value. At a trial held to establish value, the appraiser may be required to testify. Conversely, condemnors are entitled to cross-examine and present their own experts and estimate of fair market value. Ultimately, it is the task of the judge to decide on fair market value and just compensation for the owner. That determination of value will significantly follow the recommendations of the appraisal reports.

Three final points are in order when describing how fair market value is calculated. First, and this is an issue with businesses, loss of good will is not compensable under the Fifth Amendment.

A business may have established customer loyalty at a specific location or in general built up a good relationship with its customers. Such good will may be golden to a business, but its value is hard to ascertain. Thus, the Fifth Amendment does not provide compensation for loss of good will. However, many states have statutory language that provides compensation for good will. Second, the above valuation process is generally used when there is a permanent taking of a property interest. If, though, a taking is temporary, then it is a little more complicated. Courts will look to identify the time period during which the property will be taken, and perhaps seek to value the loss for that time period. They might also seek to look at the value of the property before and after the taking, and use that as a formula for arriving at just compensation. Temporary and partial takings, while they add a different wrinkle to valuations, ultimately are subject to the same process, standards, and rules as are permanent total takings of property.

Finally, while each state or jurisdiction might have slightly different legal requirements, the process outlined in this chapter should provide rough guidance or a description regarding how the actual condemnation process proceeds. As should be evident, the process is orderly and it actually does give the owner a significant amount of notice and voice in the eminent domain process. Most owners will opt to sell their property when faced with an option to do so, and those who are subject to eminent domain do get a fair value for their property. However, critics will contend that the government has too much of an upper hand; that the laws, especially when it comes to a broad concept of public use, leaves property owners with very little protection of their rights. This is certainly what the residents of Poletown thought when Detroit sought to take their homes or businesses, or what the Kelos thought when New London sought to take their place. Between the time of *Poletown* and *Kelo*, property rights activists mobilized, seeking to challenge what they thought was a threat to ownership rights. They took on what they perceived to be eminent domain abuse. The road to the *Kelo* court case is told beginning in the next chapter.

CHAPTER SEVEN

The Road to *Kelo*: The Property Rights Revolution That Wasn't

Oh, give me a home where the Buffalo roam
Where the Deer and the Antelope play;
Where seldom is heard a discouraging word,
And the sky is not cloudy all day.

—"Home on the Range"

By 1986 property rights had long lost their privileged position under the Constitution and the logic of the *Lochner* era jurisprudence had been dismantled by the New Deal Court. Property could be regulated, according to the logic of the post–*Carolene Products* Court, so long as it was reasonable, with legislatures given wide deference to define reasonableness. Similarly, the Court granted legislatures broad deference to define what constituted a valid public use, and to take private property for a variety of reasons. Both of these assaults bothered conservatives, who felt that property rights were no longer property protected by the Constitution. In addition, the Michigan Supreme Court's decision in 1981 in *Poletown Neighborhood Council v. Detroit*, as well as the Supreme Court's 1984 opinion in *Hawaii Housing Authority v. Midkiff* led many scholars to conclude that the public use clause of the Takings clause no longer had any serious meaning. Richard A. Epstein, in his 1985 *Takings: Private Property and the Power of Eminent Domain*, and Ellen Frankel Paul, in her 1988 *Property Rights and Eminent Domain*, sharply criticized then-recent trends in eminent domain and advocated increased protection for property rights. They were part of a large chorus who sought to reverse what they perceived to be constitutional neglect for property rights, and their battle included reversing many of the decisions made by the Supreme Court since the New Deal, especially as they dealt with property rights.

Political and legal conservatives were generally unhappy with the Supreme Court under the liberal Chief Justice Earl Warren. In addition to his decisions on criminal law, reapportionment, and discrimination law that they did not like, they perceived that the Court under Warren was also unsympathetic to property rights. Additionally, they had hoped that the election of Richard Nixon as president in 1968would change the direction of the Supreme Court to be more sympathetic to their views. Unfortunately for them, Warren's replacement, Warren Burger, did not move the Court as far in the pro-property rights direction as they had hoped. Instead, Burger continued to battle with Warren Court holdover and liberal Justice William Brennan for jurisprudential control of the Supreme Court. The Burger Court clearly did not reverse the direction of the Court when it came to property rights, especially eminent domain, thereby disappointing those supporting ownership rights.

However, President Ronald Reagan's election in 1980 gave, yet again, new promise to conservatives hoping for renewed support for property rights. Initially, though, it looked like they were again to be disappointed. Justice Sandra Day O'Connor, appointed by President Reagan, wrote the unanimous 1984 *Midkiff* opinion that equated public use to the scope of a legislature's police power discretion. This decision and *Poletown* coming during the early part of the Reagan era did not look good to property supporters. However, in 1986, Justice Burger retired and President Reagan elevated Nixon appointee William Rehnquist to be Chief Justice. Rehnquist was a bona fide conservative who had demonstrated that on the Supreme Court. With him as Chief Justice, and the appointment of Antonin Scalia as a new associate Justice, the Supreme Court looked like it might be ready to live up to the expectations of property rights advocates.

The road to the *Kelo v. City of New London* decision begins here. It is with the creation of the Rehnquist Court that one sees what would perhaps be the beginning of a major push to reverse *Midkiff*, maybe *Berman*, and a host of other eminent domain decisions that many viewed as making it too easy to take private property.

THE FIRST PROPERTY RIGHTS TRILOGY

The 1986 term marked the beginning of William Rehnquist's tenure as Chief Justice. For conservatives, his ascension to Chief Justice portended a reversal of many of the Warren era precedents, and a renewed concern and emphasis for the protection of property rights. Three decisions during the 1986–87 term signaled that hopes for a property rights revival under Rehnquist would actually be realized.

Keystone Coal Association v. DeBenedictis

The first case in the trilogy is *Keystone Coal Association v. DeBenedictis*, 480 U.S. 470 (1987). This case involved the Pennsylvania Bituminous Mine Subsidence and Land Conservation Act. Sections 4 and 6 of the act required companies to leave 50 percent of the coal in the ground to preclude flattening and depression of the soil. The act had noted the devastating effects of subsidence to the soil and to structures on the surface, and the 50 percent rule was to allow for enough subsurface soil structure to support surface structures. Keystone Coal Association filed suit claiming that this act, specifically the sections dealing with the 50 percent rule, was an unconstitutional taking without compensation and also a violation of the Contract clause because the act had destroyed its leases with other private persons, which had given the company the rights to mine. The association argued that this case was no different from *Pennsylvania v. Mahon*, where the Court had previously ruled that an earlier version of the Pennsylvania subsidence law effected an unconstitutional taking. In addition, drawing upon *Penn Central Transportation Co. v. New York City*, the owners in *Keystone* argued that the 50 percent requirement denied them substantial investment-backed expectations and it therefore effected a taking.

The majority ruled against the association and distinguished it from *Mahon*. Justice Stevens, writing for a majority that included Justices Brennan, White, Marshall, and Blackmun, first stated that in *Mahon* only one private building was to be saved by the Kohler Act.[1] Thus, according to Stevens, it was questionable even in Holmes's mind whether the law served a substantial public purpose. In this case, many structures, including cemeteries, were involved, and thus a significant public interest was served in saving them.[2]

The second difference concerned the degree of the regulation. In *Mahon*, the act denied all use of the property for mining.[3] The present act still allowed for a 50 percent mining. Stevens noted that, even without the 50 percent rule, companies never extracted all the coal. Much of it was needed to support the mine tunnels. The questions raised, then, were whether the 50 percent rule served a reasonable public purpose, and whether the rule had a substantial impact on the value of the property as a whole. The majority answered yes to the first, noting that two state or public interests supported the act: First, protection of the health and safety of the people of Pennsylvania by the protection of surface land; and second, the legislative finding in the statute that the mining of certain types of coal was commercially impractical because of cost or safety concerns. Because not all of the coal could be extracted, Keystone did not suffer a loss of investment-backed expectations and, therefore, no taking had occurred.[4]

In dissent, Rehnquist, Powell, O'Connor, and Scalia agreed with the association that *Mahon* was controlling.[5] The regulations here and in *Mahon* served public purposes, but both had placed substantial burdens on private property such that a taking had occurred. Even though the law in *Keystone* served a valid public purpose, the dissenters argued that the 50 percent rule denied association members significant "investment-backed expectations" and was not regulation but a regulatory taking and thus an act of eminent domain requiring compensation.[6] The basis of their argument was, first, that one had to look at how the regulation affected a particular segment of the property, not the parcel as a whole. Second, regardless of how much coal would have to remain in the ground, the purchase of the subsurface mining rights affected by the subsistence act does destroy some of the value of the interest. Thus, when the value of the interests of a segmented portion of property is destroyed, a taking has occurred.[7]

Implicit in this dissenting opinion was the foreshadowing of a return to a more heightened judicial scrutiny of legislation affecting property rights. It did that in questioning the legislative findings of fact and purposes in ways not recently common for the Court. A return to strict scrutiny for economic legislation would mean that the line between regulation and eminent domain would be subject to more acute analysis. This is exactly what happened in the next two cases.

Nollan v. California Coastal Commission

Nollan v. California Coastal Commission, 483 U.S. 825 (1987), was a land development case. The Nollans had a contract to purchase beachfront property, tear down the existing structure, and replace it with a three-bedroom house. The Nollans were granted a permit on the condition that they provided a narrow public easement along their property allowing people to walk to the public beach. Similar easements had been required for other houses along the beach. The commission justified the easement as necessary to inform the public that the beach was public because, according to them, a house obstructing the view of the water would lead the public to suspect the beach was private. The Nollans objected to the requirement and brought suit claiming the easement was an uncompensated taking. After a lengthy appeals process that took the Nollans through several administrative and judicial proceedings, they sought review with the U.S. Supreme Court, which accepted their case.

Justice Scalia, writing for a majority that included Rehnquist, White, Powell, and O'Connor, agreed with the Nollans that the forced easement violated the Fifth Amendment.[8] Scalia's majority opinion first pointed out that the right to exclude is one of the most fundamental rights attached to ownership. Second, Scalia then argued that past precedent was clear in that when there was a permanent physical occupation of an owner's property, the Court had concluded that this affected a taking.[9] He then concluded that in demanding the permanent easement across the Nollans' property, the California Coastal Commission was a permanent physical occupation of their property because the public was being given unrestricted access and right to "pass to and fro" across it.[10]

The Court then turned to an examination of any pre-existing public access rights and to the purported goals of the beachfront-access requirement imposed by the Commission. In undertaking this analysis, Scalia effectively used some type of heightened scrutiny, asking what the legitimate objectives of the law and the access rules are, and then demanding that the means advance those interests.[11] First, Scalia found nothing in the California Constitution or case law that indicates that the public has a right to access the beach from private property. He noted how the Commission had never sought to offer this argument to support their decision.

Second, Scalia asked first what constitutes a legitimate governmental interest here, finding that the Commission contended that a wall of houses would create a "psychological barrier" that would prevent or preclude the public from viewing and visiting a coast that they had every right to visit.[12] Scalia responded that the vertical easement would not further this goal because the houses would still preclude a view of the beach and the public access would not rectify that problem. Thus, Scalia asked to see if there is a "nexus" between the easement and the removal of the psychological barrier.[13] Finding none, he both rejected the commissions' arguments that the easement is equivalent to a denial of zoning permit, and drew upon *Armstrong v. United States*, 364 U.S. 40 (1960), to argue that if the Nollans were being asked to assume privately "public burdens which, in all fairness and justice, should be borne by the public as a whole," then their property had been taken.[14]

Scalia thus saw the Nollans being asked by the Commission to give up part of their property for the public good. Scalia did not see how this loss of land would further any aesthetic good. Though the access might or might not have diminished the value of their property, the real question here was one of basic rights of ownership. The building permit was not simply regulation, but "extortion" on the part of the commission to force owners to give away part of their land in return for certain uses.[15] This permit requirement did not serve the objectives of the act, but rather constituted an uncompensated taking.

Brennan's dissent indicated that the majority's decision used significant judicial scrutiny of a legislative purpose and means, stating that the "first problem with this conclusion is that the Court imposes a standard of precision for the exercise of a State's police power that has been discredited for the better part of this century."[16] Scalia's opinion even went so far, according to Brennan, as offering judicial notice of what constituted reasonable regulation to fulfill the stated objects. The majority, not granting latitude to the legislature, had questioned the reasonableness and substance of the statute, and had imposed upon the commission "a precise match between the condition imposed and the specific type of burden on access created by the appellants."[17]

Brennan questioned the majority's use of strict scrutiny, noting its use had not been accepted for 50 years. Brennan contended that the easement here furthered a substantial public purpose; it did not involve a unilateral government action denying use of the property.[18]

The easement requirement took effect only when a building permit was obtained, and even then the permit would require the easement only under certain conditions. No taking had occurred because no preexisting investment-backed expectations were damaged.

First English Evangelical Lutheran Church of Glendale v. The County of Los Angeles

The third case in the 1986–87 property rights trilogy is *First English Evangelical Lutheran Church of Glendale v. The County of Los Angeles*, 482 U.S. 304 (1987). The facts in this dispute are simple. After floods destroyed some of First Lutheran's buildings, the County of Los Angeles declared a temporary and total construction ban on properties in the plane, including that owned by the church. The law stated that "[a] person shall not construct, reconstruct, place or enlarge any building or structure, any portion of which is, or will be, located within the outer boundary lines of the interim flood protection area." Less than a month after the ordinance was passed denying them the right to rebuild, First Lutheran challenged it in court, claiming that it constituted an inverse condemnation that had effectively denied them all use of their property, and which had taken their property without just compensation. They lost efforts to secure declaratory judgments in both in California Superior Court and at the state Court of Appeals, with the California Supreme Court declining to hear the case.

In a majority opinion authored by Rehnquist and including Scalia, White, Brennan, Marshall, and Powell, the temporary but total ban on the use of property was ruled a taking.[19] According to the Court, for the time the ban was in effect, total use of the property was enjoined. During the time the total ban was in place, it precluded the property from being used in its previous way. For the Court, then, the question was whether "the Just Compensation Clause requires the government to pay for 'temporary' regulatory takings."[20]

In ruling for the first time in this case that temporary takings are compensable, Rehnquist first notes that the Fifth Amendment does not preclude the taking of private property; instead, it merely places conditions upon the circumstances under which it is taken.[21] Second, the Court notes how a condemnation of property, even a regulatory taking that goes too far, will require the government to pay the owner for the interest acquired. However, Rehnquist states that past Court decisions have not resolved whether this rule of compensation is required for temporary takings.[22]

In reviewing cases such as *Kimball Laundry Co. v. United States*, 338 U.S. 1 (1949), where the government had temporarily acquired private property during World War II, Rehnquist cited Brennan's dissent in *San Diego Gas & Electric Company v. City of San Diego*, 450 U.S. 621 (1981), that the Constitution does not treat temporary takings as different in kind from permanent ones. Thus, because this was a taking that temporarily denied total use of the church's property, the Fifth Amendment required that they be compensated.[23]

In dissent, Stevens, Blackmun, and O'Connor saw serious implications in requiring compensation for a temporary ban that, given the nature of the area, was reasonable for public protection.[24] The fact that the ban was temporary was important because it was adopted only so long as necessary to protect public health and safety. The minority rejected the majority's contention that, had this ban been permanent, it would have been considered a taking because it was a valid police power regulation necessary to protect the public. Temporary takings thus may fulfill significant public interests and do not have a permanent impact upon the use or investment in the property.[25]

EVALUATING THE FIRST TRILOGY

What do these rulings in the first trilogy say about the Court, property rights, and eminent domain at the start of the Rehnquist Court era? Legal commentaries on these three rulings argued that the Court became even more divided than before on the takings versus regulation issue, specifically as to what protections property has against legislative action. Dennis Coyle argued that *Nollan* and *First Lutheran* represent the (reluctant) revival of property rights.[26] This claim may be somewhat extreme—these decisions do not substantively revive property rights to the status of *Lochner*. The thin substantive protections that the Court seemed to want to extend to property interests in *Nollan* and in *First Lutheran* (and for the minority in *Keystone*) were compensatory rights. They are not the same as substantive due process, which involved widespread judicial review and limitation of the police power to protect private property. As Daniel Farber noted, the Court seemed to be expressing some inclination that regulation has "gone too far" and needs to be trimmed.[27] *Nollan* and *First Lutheran* represented first trimmings, but not a gutting of either the police or eminent domain powers.

In assessing the first property rights trilogy, what else do we learn? First, property interests won two of three cases, with the decisions, such as in *Nollan*, hinting at some increased scrutiny for these type of interests that had not been used since perhaps before the New Deal. Moreover, a breakdown of the votes in the three cases also reveals an interesting pattern (see table 7.1). Whatever revival of property rights that did occur, it did not happen solely with conservative justices. In *First Lutheran*, for example, Brennan and Marshall provided critical votes, and were it not for one of these liberals, the decision would not have been a victory for property rights—especially in light of the fact that O'Connor had voted in the minority. Second, Rehnquist and Scalia voted for property rights in all three cases, suggesting that, as conservatives hoped, they would be reliable defenders of ownership interests. The fact that the Court had not scored a perfect three-for-three victory for property rights, then, was perhaps a consequence of the fact that either conservatives such as O'Connor were not as supportive as previously thought, or that the Court was preparing doctrine for future rulings. Still others, such as James F. Simon in his 1995 *The Center Holds: The Power Struggle Inside the Rehnquist Court*, argued that the conservatives had not taken control and that instead, the moderates and liberals still had the balance of power.[28] Finally, as noted above, with Scalia's

Table 7.1 Individual Justice Voting in the First Property Rights Trilogy, 1986–87 Term

	Keystone	Nollan	First English
Rehnquist	P	P	P
Brennan			P
White		P	P
Marshall			P
Blackmun			
Stevens			
Powell	P	P	P
O'Connor	P	P	
Scalia	P	P	P

P = Voted to support property rights.

opinion in *Nollan* suggesting greater scrutiny for property, perhaps the replacement of one or two Justices would portend the end or altering of the logic of the post–*Carolene Products* era and the placement of new restrictions on the use of eminent domain.

REVERSING *POLETOWN*

The 1981 Michigan Supreme Court decision in *Poletown Neighborhood Council v. Detroit*, upholding as a valid public use the taking of hundreds of tracts of land and turning them over to General Motors for economic development purposes, angered a wide constellation of liberals and conservatives. Consumer activist Ralph Nader, community organizers, and activists saw the decision as an assault on homeowners by corporate America. GM had blackmailed the City of Detroit into providing enormous subsidies and private land in order to serve their profit needs. GM's threat to leave Detroit if it did not get what it wanted pitted the city against its residents. It was just another example of how eminent domain was used to target communities populated by people of color, the poor, and others who were politically powerless or weak. Conversely, for conservatives, *Poletown* represented another assault on the sanctity of private property. Ownership rights were threatened by an activist government with regulatory powers they did not like. *Poletown* was a threat to libertarian free market property rights and it had to be stopped. The question was how?

Post-*Poletown*, several groups began the ideological battle to reverse this case and other eminent domain and property rights decisions they did not like. Individuals and groups that do not like laws or public policies often develop a political mobilization and legal strategy to get what they want. The model for reversing court decisions traces back to the formation of the NAACP—the National Association for the Advancement of Colored People. In 1896 the Supreme Court issued an opinion, *Plessy v. Ferguson*, 163 U.S. 537 (1896), which upheld "separate but equal" as a constitutionally permissible doctrine. This case permitted racial segregation in schools, hotels, and in other places of public accommodation. The NAACP was formed, in part, with the goal of reversing this decision. Over a nearly 50-year period, the NAACP sponsored specific cases and lawsuits, hoping to reverse the decision. It succeeded when, in 1954, its attorney and future

Supreme Court Justice Thurgood Marshall convinced the Supreme Court in *Brown v. Board of Education*, 347 U.S. 483 (1954), to do that. The NAACP legal strategy of sponsoring test cases that had good facts that supported their arguments has been emulated by many other groups since then.

But the NAACP strategy of using the judiciary to achieve legal change does not end with the courts. Many organizations also lobby Congress and legislatures, presidents and governors, and engage in other political activities to further their objectives. Often they also use think-tanks and issue reports and studies that support their arguments or positions. The purpose of these tactics is to create a favorable media and political climate for their positions, with the hope of getting public opinion on their side. One of the groups formed to address property rights was the Institute for Justice.

The Institute for Justice took upon itself the task of addressing what it considered to be eminent domain abuse. In 2003 it issued a report declaring that from 1998 to 2003 there were "10,000 cases where homes, businesses, churches and private land were seized or threatened with seizure over the past five years—not to be used for public use, but instead for private for-profit development." They claimed that the government was strong-arming individuals to either sell their property or face eminent domain and eviction. They sought to dispel notions that the use of eminent domain was a last resort or that owners voluntarily sold their property to the government in most cases. Of course, to strength their claims, the report and their Web page featured profiles of individuals whom they believed were victims of eminent domain abuse. The Institute also litigated and sponsored cases, and one that they supported was *County of Wayne v. Hathcock*, 471 Mich. 445, 684 N.W.2d 765 (2004).

In *County of Wayne v. Hathcock*, the Michigan Supreme Court declared that the taking of property from one private owner and transferring it to another in order to encourage economic development or alleviate unemployment was not a valid public use under Article X, Section 2, of the Michigan Constitution. In reaching this decision, the Michigan Supreme Court overruled its landmark holding in *Poletown Neighborhood Council v. Detroit*. *Hathcock* imposed a significant limit upon the ability of Michigan's state and local governments to use eminent domain as an economic development tool and, potentially, a tool to address business plant closings. Moreover, in reversing *Poletown*, the Michigan Supreme Court also invalidated a major legal precedent cited in many jurisdictions across the United States to support the use of eminent domain for economic development purposes.[29]

At issue in *Hathcock v. the County of Wayne* was a plan by the latter to condemn 19 parcels of private property near the Metropolitan Airport. The parcels were sought in conjunction with the expansion and renovation of the airport. As part of the expansion, several properties would be subject to increased noise and traffic, and the county thus sought to acquire them by voluntary sales. To fund the purchase of the properties, the county received a grant from the Federal Aviation Administration (FAA). This grant stipulated that any property acquired though the noise abatement program would have to be put to productive economic use.

To comply with this FAA requirement, the county and its economic development department decided to create "Pinnacle Project," a 1,300-acre business and technology park that would use these and other parcels that had been acquired south of the airport. Having already acquired more than 1,000 acres for the project and determining that an additional 46 parcels would be needed, the county, pursuant to its authority under Michigan's Uniform Condemnation Procedures Act (UCPA), appraised these properties, resulting in 27 voluntary sales. The owners of the remaining 19 parcels refused to sell, and the county initiated condemnation actions under the UCPA. In a state district court, the owners of the 19 parcels contended that the condemnation violated the Michigan Compiled Laws Section 213.23, as well as Article X, Section 2, of the Michigan Constitution. The district court upheld the taking as a valid public use, and the state Court of Appeals concurred, ruling that the taking was also valid in light of the *Poletown* decision. The Michigan Supreme Court upheld the taking under Section 213.23 (a part of the UCPA), but struck down the taking under the state constitution, and in the process reversed the *Poletown* decision.

Michigan Compiled Laws Section 213.23 generally authorized any public corporation or state agency to condemn private property necessary for a public improvement. The defendants contended that the taking of their property was, in fact, not necessary for the Pinnacle project. They also argued that Wayne County lacked the authority under this statute to take their property. The Michigan Supreme Court disagreed with the defendants on both counts. First, the court asserted that a "careful reading of MCL 213.23 reveal[ed] that this statute is indeed a separate grant of authority" such that it did, in fact, give Wayne County the legal power to condemn private property under certain circumstances.[30] The court also noted that, because Michigan was a home rule state and that its constitution, specifically Article VII, Section 1, gave counties broad powers and immunities, this home rule authority, along with the language of Section 213.23, gave ample power to Wayne County to condemn their property.[31]

Second, the court gave broad deference to Wayne County's determination of the necessity of taking the property. It dismissed arguments that condemnation could not be used unless other means of securing the project were exhausted.[32] Instead, property may be taken so long as it was necessary to advancing one of the specified purposes of the project.

While the court's analysis of Michigan Compiled Laws Section 213.23 was not a surprise, its approach to the constitutional claims and *Poletown* were. The court began by declaring that the primary objective of constitutional interpretation is "to realize the intent of the people by whom and for whom the constitution was ratified."[33] To do that, the court stated that it would apply the plain meaning of the terms used when ratified. When examining Article X, Section 2, the court thus sought to understand what it meant when the Michigan Constitution was ratified in 1963. Thus, what did constitute a "public use" justification for the taking of private property in 1963? Here the Michigan Supreme Court essentially deferred to Justice Ryan's dissent in *Poletown*, arguing that he correctly described the pre-1963 case law regarding the interpretation of Article X, Section 2.

Paraphrasing Justice Ryan, the decision in *Hathcock* stated that a transfer of condemned private property from one owner to another was only permitted in three circumstances:

- First, condemnations in which private land was constitutionally transferred by the condemning authority to a private entity involved "public necessity of the extreme sort otherwise impracticable."
- Second, this Court has found that the transfer of condemned property to a private entity is consistent with the constitution's "public use" requirement when the private entity remains accountable to the public in its use of that property.

- Finally, condemned land may be transferred to a private entity when the selection of the land to be condemned is itself based on public concern.[34]

In the first category, "necessity" in this context refers to those private corporations that generate public benefits and whose existence depends on land that can only be acquired by the government.[35] The class of corporations here includes entities involved in providing canals, highways, and railroads.[36] Entities that meet the accountability test refer to corporations that are generally regulated by the state, such as by the Public Service Commission.[37] Finally, the public concern test is met when land is taken predominantly, for example, to remove housing blight, and the eventual resale of the land was incidental.[38]

It is only under these three instances that condemned private property may be transferred to another private owner under Article X, Section 2, of the 1963 Constitution. Applying these three rules or conceptions of public use to the Pinnacle Project, the *Hathcock* court did not find that any of them applied, and therefore the taking of private property to promote economic development or to alleviate unemployment violated Article X, Section 2.

However, the court went even further than simply declaring the takings in this case to be unconstitutional. All the Justices concurred that under *Poletown's* expansive definition of public use, a taking to promote economic development or alleviate unemployment would have been permissible.[39] Yet, because the *Poletown* holding seemed to be inconsistent with the understanding of what a valid public use was under the 1963 constitution, all of the justices ruled that this 1981 decision was wrong and they therefore overruled that opinion.

Finally, the *Hathcock* court concluded that, because *Poletown* was wrongly decided, they were not making new law in their opinion; and therefore, their decision to overrule that case would be retroactive and it would apply to all cases pending that implicated a challenge to *Poletown*.[40]

Hathcock was a shock and a home run for property rights advocates. It overruled *Poletown* and therefore declared that the acquisition of property to promote economic development or alleviate unemployment was no longer in itself a valid public use in the state of Michigan. The decision appeared to be the first step toward narrowing the scope of eminent domain law and declaring a more narrow reading of what constituted a valid public use. In light of this opinion, the U.S. Supreme Court merely a few weeks later then announced that it would accept an eminent domain economic development takings case from Connecticut that raised similar issues. Property rights advocates hoped that the taking of the case along with the *Hathcock* opinion would be the one-two knockout they had been hoping for. The case the Supreme Court took was *Kelo v. City of New London*, and it was part of a second trilogy of property law cases that the Rehnquist Court would examine.

THE SECOND PROPERTY RIGHTS TRILOGY

In the 2004–5 term, the U.S. Supreme Court confronted its second trilogy of property rights cases. This trilogy, coming nearly a generation after the first one, should have been a more solid victory for owners. Since 1987, several Justices had been replaced—most notably the liberals Brennan and Marshall—and new, supposedly more conservative, Justices such as David Souter and Clarence Thomas were on the bench. In addition, Lewis Powell, who voted for the property owners in all three of the first trilogy cases, was replaced by another supposed conservative in Anthony Kennedy; and Harry Blackmun, who voted against the owners in all three cases, was also replaced. In addition, in cases such as *Dolan v. City of Tigard*, and *Lucas v. South Carolina Coastal Council*, the Rehnquist Court had imposed new protections for owners, suggesting a Court poised to complete a property rights revolution. However, in *Kelo v. City of New London, Lingle v. Chevron, U.S.A. Inc*, and *San Remo Hotel v. San Francisco*, the Court ruled against property interests in all three cases, unambiguously stating that promoting economic development is a valid public use, that the judiciary should not ordinarily second-guess legislative determinations in the area of economic policy, and that there was no exception to the Full Faith and Credit clause that would allow owners to sue in federal court after their claims had been heard at the state level. Legally, these cases represented a major defeat for property rights advocates, but politically *Kelo* was a major victory.

Kelo v. City of New London

Kelo v. City of New London raised the hope of many conservatives that eminent domain authority would be trimmed. In part, hopes were up because *certiorari* was granted on September 28, 2004, less than two months after the Michigan Supreme Court had overturned *Poletown Neighborhood Council v. City of Detroit* in *County of Wayne v. Hathcock* and ruled that the taking of private property for economic development purposes violated the state constitution. In overturning *Poletown*, one case that many had described as the requiem for property rights, that precedent had been dismantled. This raised anticipation that the decision to review *Kelo* would place new limits on eminent domain under the federal Constitution.

In *Kelo v. City of New London*, the U.S. Supreme Court affirmed a decision of the Connecticut Supreme Court which held that the taking of unblighted private property for economic development purposes constituted a valid public use under both the state and federal constitutions. At issue in this case was an attempt by the City of New London, a municipal corporation, and the New London Development Corporation, to use a state law (Chapter 132 of the Connecticut General Statutes) to take unblighted land to build and support economic revitalization of the city's downtown. In its plan, New London divided the development into seven parcels, with some of these parcels including public waterways or museums. However, one parcel, known as Lot 3, would be a 90,000-square-foot technology research and development office space and parking facility for the Pfizer Pharmaceutical Company. Several plaintiffs in Lot 3 challenged the taking of their property, claiming that the condemnation of unblighted land for economic development purposes violated both the state and federal constitutions.

More specifically, they argued that the taking of private property under Chapter 132 and the handing of it over to another private party did not constitute a valid public use, or at last the public benefit was incidental to the private benefits generated. The Connecticut Supreme Court rejected their claims under both the state and federal constitutions.[41] The court ruled that "economic development projects created and implemented pursuant to Chapter 132 that have the public economic benefits of creating new jobs, increasing tax and other revenues, and contributing to urban revitalization, satisfy the public use clauses of the state and federal constitutions."[42] The court stated that Article I, Section 11, of the constitution of Connecticut permitted this type of taking. It reached this conclusion by drawing on several arguments. It cited federal precedents, such as the U.S. Supreme Court's *Hawaii Housing Authority v. Midkiff* and *Berman v. Parker* as federal support for its decision.[43] But more important, it noted how, since 1866, the Connecticut courts had given a flexible meaning and interpretation to the state's public use clause. In state cases it had established a "deferential approach to legislative declarations of public use" that continues to this day.[44] The court declared that the eminent domain "power requires a degree of elasticity to be capable of meeting new conditions and improvements and the ever increasing necessities of society."[45] The court supported its claims by noting how other jurisdictions had reached similar holdings, finding that their state constitutional public use clauses granted broad authority to take private property for economic development purposes.

Finally, the Connecticut Supreme Court addressed assertions that the taking of the plaintiffs' property produced merely an incidental public benefit. The court referenced the trial court's extensive findings of fact regarding how the taking would help the City of New London. It also found that the motive here was not to aid a private business but to encourage economic development for the city and that any benefit to a private party was simply secondary to the overall public good that would be produced.[46]

The Kelos were clearly unhappy with the decision and, with the urging of groups such as the Institute for Justice, they sought Supreme Court review of their case. The U.S. Supreme Court granted *certiorari* to the federal question of whether the taking of private property for economic development purposes, when it involved the transferring of the land from one private owner to another, constituted a valid public use under the Fifth and Fourteenth amendments. Writing for a divided Court, Justice Stevens ruled that the taking did not violate the public use requirement of the Fifth Amendment.

In reaching his holding, Stevens first noted how the case pitted two propositions against one another:

> the sovereign may not take the property of *A* for the sole purpose of transferring it to another private party *B*, even though *A* is paid just compensation. On the other hand, it is equally clear that a State may transfer property from one private party to another if future "use by the public" is the purpose of the taking; the condemnation

of land for a railroad with common-carrier duties is a familiar example.[47]

However, he contended that neither of these rules resolved the case. Instead, drawing upon *Midkiff*, Stevens first reaffirmed the proposition that a taking for a purely private benefit would be unconstitutional. However, in this case, it was not a private taking because the decision to acquire the property was part of a "'carefully considered' development plan" that revealed that neither the real nor hidden motive was to convey a private benefit.[48]

Second, the Court rejected arguments that, because the property would eventually be used and transferred to a private party, it failed the public use requirement because the land would not be used by the public. Stevens stated that the "Court long ago rejected any literal requirement that condemned property be put into use for the general public" and that instead this narrow reading of public use had been rejected in favor of a broader public purpose reading of the public use doctrine.[49] Thus, as Stevens defined the issue, the case turned on whether the taking served a valid public purpose, and he ruled that the Court should adhere to the long-established judicial tradition of deferring to legislative determinations on this matter, as evidenced by its decisions in *Berman v. Parker* and *Hawaii Housing Authority v. Midkiff*.[50] In short, given the broad and flexible meaning attached to the public use stipulation, and past judicial deference to legislative determinations of what is considered a public purpose (use), Stevens and the majority concluded that the taking of private property for economic development purposes was a valid public use.

Finally, Stevens rejected arguments that the Court carve out an economic development exception to the broad public use doctrine that it had created. He rejected this new rule as unworkable, stating that it would be impossible, principally, to distinguish economic development from other valid public purposes.[51] He also rejected assertions that the taking-for-economic-development purposes blurred the distinction between a public and a private taking. Instead, Stevens responded:

> It is further argued that without a bright-line rule nothing would stop a city from transferring citizen A's property to citizen B for the sole reason that citizen B will put the property to a more productive use and thus pay more taxes. Such a one-to-one transfer of

property, executed outside the confines of an integrated development plan, is not presented in this case.[52]

Stevens here offers what the Court might consider to be evidence of a taking for private use, that is, a taking not backed up
by a comprehensive plan. Absent such a plan, it might appear
that the taking was more to convey a private benefit. While with
one, especially a plan replete with legislative findings, it would
provide evidence that the taking was part of a broader public
purpose, and therefore not primarily aimed at conveying a private benefit.

In many ways, *Kelo* really did not make new law in terms of
taking private property for economic development purposes.
Berman, Midkiff, and perhaps even a host of cases going back to
the nineteenth century had already established precedent for
that. As Stevens pointed out, the city could not take private
property for a private benefit for a private party.[53] He also noted
that the more narrow conception of public use had long since
been abandoned, and governments have long had the power to
take for a variety of public welfare purposes, including economic development.[54] *Kelo* really simply reaffirmed a trend already that existed in the law. Overall, *Kelo* seemed to cap a
recent line of jurisprudence, giving governments broad authority
to take private property, even for economic development
purposes.

However, Stevens did not say in *Kelo* that private takings or
that the use of eminent domain for the purposes of a private use
was permitted. Instead, the opinion continued to struggle with
defining what constituted a valid public use. Two points in *Kelo*
are worth underscoring. First, he appealed to a comprehensive or
redevelopment plan as a sign or check to distinguish takings for
public versus private uses. By that, in several locations in the *Kelo*
opinion, Justice Stevens references the existence of a comprehensive plan as critical to upholding a taking. For example, in comparing the taking here to that in *Midkiff*, Stevens states:
"Therefore, as was true of the statute challenged in *Midkiff*, the
City's development plan was not adopted 'to benefit a particular
class of identifiable individuals.'"[55] In reference to *Berman*, he
states: "In *Berman v. Parker*, this Court upheld a redevelopment
plan targeting a blighted area of Washington, D.C., in which most
of the housing for the area's 5,000 inhabitants was beyond

repair."[56] Finally, in discussing the facts in *Kelo*, Stevens concludes:

> The City has carefully formulated an economic development plan that it believes will provide appreciable benefits to the community, including—but by no means limited to—new jobs and increased tax revenue. As with other exercises in urban planning and development, the City is endeavoring to coordinate a variety of commercial, residential, and recreational uses of land, with the hope that they will form a whole greater than the sum of its parts. To effectuate this plan, the City has invoked a state statute that specifically authorizes the use of eminent domain to promote economic development. Given the comprehensive character of the plan, the thorough deliberation that preceded its adoption, and the limited scope of our review, it is appropriate for us, as it was in *Berman*, to resolve the challenges of the individual owners, not on a piecemeal basis, but rather in light of the entire plan. Because that plan unquestionably serves a public purpose, the takings challenged here satisfy the public use requirement of the Fifth Amendment.[57]

The presence of a comp plan to frame the eminent domain decision appears critical to Stevens and the majority in helping to decide what is a legitimate public versus private use. The presumption is that the presence of the plan, along with the hearings associated with them, should offer evidence that the taking was meant to serve a valid public use. Conversely, the absence of a plan is evidence that the taking was for a private use. The definition of a public versus a private use, then, is less about a fixed definition regarding what is a public use and more about the decision-making process fashioned to arrive at a choice.

Second, the majority in *Kelo* made it clear that their holding did not preclude states from imposing greater restrictions on the taking of property for economic development purposes. Specifically, the Court stated:

> We emphasize that nothing in our opinion precludes any State from placing further restrictions on its exercise of the takings power. Indeed, many States already impose "public use" requirements that are stricter than the federal baseline. Some of these requirements have been established as a matter of state constitutional law, while others are expressed in state eminent domain statutes that carefully limit the grounds upon which takings may be exercised.[58]

In effect, while the Fifth and Fourteenth amendments permit the taking of unblighted private property for purely economic development purposes, states, under the own constitutions or by statute, may impose more restrictive conditions upon what constitutes a valid public use. In fact, the Court cited the recently decided *County of Wayne v. Hathcock* as such an example wherein a state did that. This means that *Kelo* did not overrule state decisions that had already placed more restrictions on takings for a public use, if decided on their own constitutional or statutory grounds.

Concurring, Justice Kennedy argued that he agreed that, so long as a taking was rationally related to a public purpose, it should be upheld, whether it is condemnation for economic development purposes or not. However, he also contended that if ''a rational-basis standard of review is appropriate does not, however, alter the fact that transfers intended to confer benefits on particular, favored private entities, and with only incidental or pretextual public benefits, are forbidden by the *Public Use Clause*.''[59] Kennedy noted how pretextual takings which really are meant to benefit a private party have long been forbidden, and that in situations involving these types of takings—especially those involving a transfer of property from one private individual to another—a more heightened standard of review might be needed.[60] However, because the trial judge in this case did not find that the taking was primarily for a private benefit, the heightened scrutiny was not required.

Dissenting, Justice O'Connor, joined by Rehnquist, Scalia, and Thomas, acknowledged that there are three situations in which the Court has upheld the taking of private property under a broad public use doctrine. The first is when the property is transferred to public ownership to construct a hospital, road, or military base.[61] Second, transfers of private property to another private owner are permitted when common carriers such as railroads take possession, because ultimately the public does get to use the property.[62] However, O'Connor also identifies a third category of takings—when property is being used in a harmful manner—as being sanctioned by the Court as a valid public use.[63] In reaching this claim, O'Connor examines both *Berman* and her opinion in *Midkiff*, arguing that in the former, removal of blight; and in the latter, concentrated ownership as skewing the real estate market, were the ''bads'' that the legislatures were seeking to abate, and which the Court was willing to affirm. O'Connor did not see the New London condemnation as one seeking to alleviate some bad that the Kelo property was inflicting upon others. Instead, the Court argued that what the majority opinion had done was to move "from our decisions sanctioning the condemnation of harmful property use, the Court today significantly expands the meaning of public use."[64] Hence, because the taking of the Kelos' property did not fit into one of these three categories, it should not be permitted.

O'Connor's dissent is notable for a couple of other points. First, she does acknowledge the broad deference that generally should be given to legislatures when it comes to making public use decisions.[65] Second, notably absent from her opinion is a clear indication that she wished to increase the level of scrutiny for public use decisions. Granted, O'Connor would carve out three types of takings as permitted public uses, while excluding others, but nowhere does her opinion really suggest heightened scrutiny of legislative motives.

The lone Justice willing to move toward offering property more substantive protection is Thomas. In his solo dissent, he argues for a return to the original meaning of the "public use" clause.[66] For Thomas, public use is not the same as public welfare or purpose, and that property may only be taken to further an expressly enumerated power. Singularly among the Justices, he would not afford deference to legislatures to define what a public use is, and that contrary to what the Court has previously held, *Berman* and *Midkiff* are wrong, and that the Constitution imposes a substantive limit on the power of the government to take private property. In fact, he invokes *Carolene Products'* footnote for logic and the protection it affords to minorities and to those subjected to eminent domain.[67]

Lingle v. Chevron, U.S.A. Inc.

Kelo was the headliner in 2005 for property rights. However, in addition to *Kelo*, the Supreme Court in 2005 also reaffirmed broad legislative authority to make determinations about economic issues related to takings. In *Lingle v. Chevron, U.S.A. Inc.*, 544 U.S. 528 (2005), at issue was a State of Hawaii rent control law that limited the amount that an oil company may charge a lessee-dealer. Chevron contended that the rent control law constituted a taking. It based its argument on *Agins v. Tiburon*, where the Court appeared to have stated that zoning laws that fail to substantially advance a state interest constitute a taking. Here, Chevron argued that the rent control law failed to substantially advance a state goal, and therefore it should be viewed as a form of a compensable taking.

The Court rejected that argument. First it argued that there are only two forms of per se takings that the Court has recognized—when the government permanently physically takes property, or when its actions totally deprive an owner of all economic use of the property.[68] Second, it argued that *Agins* has been misread and that the "substantially advances" language of this case does not constitute a takings test. Instead, owners must show some *"magnitude or character of the burden"* associated with the law on property rights such that it affects a taking.[69] Third, the Court stated that mere interference with property rights does not necessarily constitute a taking; instead, if a taking is alleged, then an independent analysis regarding whether it was for a valid public use is required.

In rejecting the lower court's questioning of the rent cap, Justice O'Connor, in writing for the Court, stated:

> We find the proceedings below remarkable, to say the least, given that we have long eschewed such heightened scrutiny when addressing substantive due process challenges to government regulation. The reasons for deference to legislative judgments about the need for, and likely effectiveness of, regulatory actions are by now well established, and we think they are no less applicable here.[70]

The significance of the *Lingle* opinion is, in pertinent part, that it effectively reaffirms early claims made in *Berman* and *Midkiff* that give governments significant discretion to interpret "public use" broadly, including for economic development purposes, and it also reaffirmed broad judicial deference to legislative decisions regarding economic regulation.

San Remo Hotel v. San Francisco

San Remo Hotel v. San Francisco, 545 U.S. 323 (2005) is the third in the 2004–5 trilogy of property rights cases that the Court decided, and it addressed simple procedural questions growing out of a very complex litigation history. The Sam Remo Hotel was built in San Francisco shortly after the great earthquake of 1906.

Responding to a shortage of affordable rental housing for the elderly, disabled, and other selected populations, the city issued a moratorium in 1979 on the conversion of residential hotel units into tourist units. Two years later, the city enacted the first version of the Hotel Conversion Ordinance (HCO) to regulate all future conversions. The ordinance required that each hotel "file an initial unit usage report containing" the "number of residential and tourist units in the hotel[s]" as of September 23, 1979. In the 1981 version of the HCO, hotel owners could not convert residential units into tourist units unless they obtained a conversion permit. The permits could be obtained only by constructing new residential units, rehabilitating old ones, or paying an "in lieu" fee into the City's Residential Hotel Preservation Fund Account. Jean Iribarren, who was operating the Sam Remo on lease from the owners, submitted an initial usage report for the hotel, which erroneously reported that all of the rooms in the hotel were "residential" units. In fact, the hotel had operated as a tourist establishment for years. Because of that error, along with zoning restrictions in the area, this required the owners and operator to apply for a conditional use permit (CUP) to operate as a tourist hotel. In 1993 the City Planning Commission granted petitioners' requested conversion and conditional use permit, but did so only after imposing several conditions, one of which included the requirement that petitioners pay a $567,000 "in lieu" fee. The owners and operator objected, contending that the fee was unconstitutional as it applied to their hotel.

Petitioners filed in federal court for the first time in 1993, alleging four counts of due process (substantive and procedural) and takings (facial and as-applied) violations under the Fifth and Fourteenth amendments to the U.S. Constitution: one count seeking damages under 42 U.S.C. § 1983, for those violations; and one pendent state-law claim. Following this initial filing, there were numerous subsequent administrative and state and federal court appeals claiming a regulatory taking. Petitioners won and lost some of these appeals. However, a federal district court granted respondents summary judgment. As relevant to this action, the Court found that petitioners' facial takings claim was untimely under the applicable statute of limitations, and that the as-applied takings claim was unripe under *Williamson County Regional Planning Commission v. Hamilton Bank of Johnson City,* 473 U.S. 172 (1985). The *Williamson County* court said that cases could not be reviewed by the courts until administrative bodies such as planning commissions had reached final decisions in matters before them. On appeal to the Court of Appeals for the Ninth Circuit, petitioners took the unusual position that the Court should not decide their federal claims, but instead should abstain because a return to state court could conceivably moot the remaining federal questions. The Court of Appeals granted the request with respect to the facial challenge. By "facial" the court was willing to look at whether the law itself was defective, as opposed to looking at the challenge as "an applied" challenge. The latter assumes the law is valid but it is being enforced unconstitutionally in this specific situation. The court also affirmed the District Court's determination that petitioners' as-applied takings claim was not ripe because they had failed to pursue an inverse condemnation action in state court, and had not yet been denied just compensation as contemplated by *Williamson County*. The Ninth Circuit's opinion also indicated that petitioners were free to raise their federal takings claims in the California courts. If, however, they wanted to "retain [their] right to return to federal court for adjudication of [their] federal claim, [they] must make an appropriate reservation in state court."[71]

The petitioners sought to do exactly that when they reactivated the California case. Here they fought over the standard of review governing their case. Eventually they lost on appeal with the California Supreme Court on the substantive claim that a taking had occurred, with the Court deciding both state and federal issues, despite petitioners' reservation of the federal claims. They then sought to return to federal court to because they felt they had addressed the *Williamson* ripeness issue. The federal court ruled that since the California court had already addressed the takings claim, the full faith and credit statute precluded a rehearing. The decision was affirmed by the Ninth Circuit and the Supreme Court granted *certiorari*.

The issue before the Court was to ask for an exception to the full faith and credit statute so that the federal takings claims could be heard in federal court. Writing for the Court, Justice Stevens ruled that no exception was permitted.[72] He began his analysis by a discussion of the history of the Constitution's Full Faith and Credit clause which requires that "Full Faith and Credit shall be given in each State to the public Acts, Records, and judicial Proceedings of every other State. And the Congress may by general Laws prescribe the Manner in which such Acts, Records and Proceedings shall be proved, and the Effect thereof."[73] In noting how Congress first enacted legislation in 1790 pursuant to this clause, Stevens argued that precluding parties from relitigating issues that have been previously resolved by another court predates the Republic.[74] This rule, however, comes into conflict with the *Williamson* mandate that cases may not be heard in federal court until there is a final state judgment denying compensation. Thus, for the Court, how does one resolve this conflict between full faith and credit versus ripeness?

Stevens resolves this apparent conflict by first responding to the appellants' claim that under *England v. Louisiana Board of Medical Examiners*, 375 U.S. 411 (1964), federal courts should disregard state court decisions of reserved federal claims. In that case, plaintiffs were challenging in federal court the constitutionality of a state chiropractic licensing requirement. The court dismissed the claim, giving the state judiciary opportunity to clarify whether a state education rule actually applied to chiropractors. When the state court did address this issue, it also examined the constitutionality of the law in dispute, leading the federal court to then dismiss the petitioners' claims. According to Stevens, the Supreme Court reversed because *England* stands for the proposition that when the federal courts abstain from deciding an issue so that a state court may resolve a question, litigants may reserve their federal claims when the state and federal claims are distinct from one another.[75] Stevens found that the state and federal issues in *San Remo* were so interconnected and interrelated that *England* did not apply.

Having dismissed the *England* argument, the Court turned to the argument that issue preclusion should not apply when a case is removed to the state courts because of *Williamson*. This claim is also rejected. First, Stevens rejected arguments that in *Santini v. Connecticut Hazardous Waste Management Service*, 251 Conn. 121, 739 A. 2d 680 (1999), which had ruled that parties required to litigate their "state-law takings claims in state court pursuant to *Williamson County* cannot be precluded from having those very claims resolved by a federal court."[76] He stated that the Second Circuit opinion cited no law to support its contention and that the Court, as with the litigants in *San Remo*, simply seemed to assume that they had a right to have their federal takings claims heard in federal court. They do not have that right. Moreover, the Court may not simply create exceptions to the Full Faith and

Credit statute, both because the Court has rejected such exceptions in the past, and because there is no indication that Congress intended for there to be an exception.

Finally, Stevens concludes by arguing that the petitioners over-relied on *Williamson*. By that, *Williamson* did not prevent them from challenging the facial validity of the San Francisco ordinance while at the same time seeking compensation in state court for the takings.[77] These are two distinct issues which could have been litigated at the same time or pursued under the *England* rule.

EXPLAINING THE SECOND TRILOGY AND THE FAILED PROPERTY RIGHTS REVOLUTION

Property rights struck out big legally in the 2004–5 term. They lost all three cases, and more significantly, there were only a total of four votes for owners among the three cases. As shown in tables 7.2 and 7.3, even the most ardent defenders of property interests, such as Scalia and Rehnquist, based upon their support in 1986, only cast one vote each for new limits or remedies in eminent domain action. There also seemed to be little sympathy for heightened scrutiny of property rights claims, with Thomas alone supporting this in *Kelo*. In many ways, 2004–5 was a retreat from the possibilities hinted at in 1986–87. What happened?

What happened, in part, was that even the conservatives who were once thought to be pro-property rights apparently modified their votes. Simply put, the conservatives did not vote as "conservatives." Also, as noted earlier, at least one of the victories (*First*

Table 7.2 Individual Justice Voting in the First Property Rights Trilogy, 2004–5 Term

	Kelo	Lingle	San Remo Hotel
Rehnquist	P		
Stevens			
O'Connor	P		
Kennedy			
Scalia	P		
Souter			
Thomas	P		
Ginsburg			
Breyer			

P = Voted for property rights

Table 7.3 First and Second Trilogy Voting Records

	1986–87 Term			2004–5 Term		
	Keystone	Nollan	First English	Kelo	Lingle	San Remo Hotel
Rehnquist	P	P	P	P		
Stevens						
O'Connor	P	P		P		
Scalia	P	P	P	P		

Lutheran) in 1987 was driven by the liberals. This time, no liberals crossed over. This means that part of the first trilogy victories were driven by a consensus of liberals and conservatives, not simply the latter. In effect, the first trilogy was a victory from the middle and not the extreme right, whereas the second trilogy was a victory for the liberals, or that at least, the conservatives still did not control the Court.

A second explanation is that the conservative justices were never as pro-property rights as some of the zealots had hoped. By that, while Scalia might have hinted at heightened scrutiny in *Nollan* and Thomas the same as in *Kelo*, the Rehnquist court was not really prepared to retrench and return to the *Lochner* era. Its conservatives, then, were conservative, including respect for precedent, and not radicals wishing to return to *Lochner*. A third explanation is that when pushed, the Rehnquist Court and its conservatives may not have been as supportive of property rights as they were of the state or government power, or that they may have favored economic development over property rights.

Finally, maybe one can argue that, yet again, conservatives failed to get a "true believer" on the Court. O'Connor failed to live up to her conservative promise, and Kennedy also. However, to say that Rehnquist, Scalia, or Thomas is conservative because he did not all vote for property owners in all three cases would be odd. Whatever the reasons may be, the property rights revolution failed to go as far as many thought it would travel.

Yet, while property rights lost in court, advocates for ownership rights and opponents seized on *Kelo*, using it as a major political symbol to push their arguments to narrow eminent domain law across the country.

CHAPTER EIGHT

If My Home Is My Castle, Can the Government or Other Thugs Take My Property?

Just after the house was built, along came a wolf.
He knocked at the door of the little pig's house and called,
"Little pig, little pig, let me come in!"
But the little pig answered, "No, no! Not by the hair of my chinny chin chin!"
Then the wolf said, "I'll huff and I'll puff, and I'll blow your house in!"

—"Three Little Pigs"

THE POST-*KELO* REACTION

Property rights advocates lost the legal battle in *Kelo* but they did not lose the war over eminent domain. Instead, one of the most surprising aspects to the *Kelo* decision was the public reaction to it. The Supreme Court's decision upholding the use of eminent domain to take private property from one owner and give it to another in order to promote economic development angered many. The titles of the many articles alone tell the tale of the public reaction.[1]

For example, Timothy Egan's "Ruling Sets Off Tug of War Over Private Property" (noting the efforts in Congress and the states after the *Kelo* opinion to condemn it or limit it with legislation), Michael Corkery and Ryan Chittum's "Eminent-Domain Uproar Imperils Projects" (discussing how the *Kelo* opinion is causing a backlash against many projects involving the use of eminent domain), and Nick Timiraos's "States May Raze Court's Eminent Domain Ruling" (noting the adverse reaction many states had to the *Kelo* opinion and efforts being taken at the state level to place limits on the use of eminent domain for economic development purposes) were three typical headlines after *Kelo*.[2]

Other articles noted possible changes in the law as a result of *Kelo*. For example, Charley Shaw's "Lawmakers Respond to Eminent Domain Ruling" discussed how three lawmakers in Minnesota had already introduced legislation to limit eminent domain takings for economic development purposes. Joi Preciphs's "Eminent-Domain Ruling Knits Rivals" and Jason Hoppin's "High Court's Eminent Domain Ruling Touches a Nerve" noted the backlash and reaction to the *Kelo* opinion, and Adam Karlin's "Property Seizure Backlash" examined the concern among many that the *Kelo* decision has produced homeowner backlash and outrage. There were also op-eds such as "They Paved Paradise," which criticized the *Kelo* decision as rendering homes less safe from condemnation. And then David Kirkpatrick's "Ruling on Property Seizure Rallies Christian Groups" described how some conservative Christian groups are concerned about the condemnation of church property in prime real estate areas because local communities may wish to replace their tax-exempt property with commercial developments. Overall, the media attention and anger was significant.[3]

Summarizing the reaction to *Kelo*, some felt that this decision meant the "public use" stipulation for eminent domain no longer had any meaning and that the Court was now prepared to endorse any taking for any reason, so long as compensation was paid. Did *Kelo* in fact signal the death knell for the "public use" doctrine? If yes, this is not the first time that property rights advocates would have made this claim. Following decisions such as *Hawaii Housing Authority v. Midkiff* and *Poletown Neighborhood Council v. City of Detroit* similar laments were heard. But why the anger over *Kelo*? Several answers are possible.

First, the Kelos were sympathetic plaintiffs. Suzette Kelo was literally the David going against Goliath. She was a 40-year-old nurse who had managed in 1997 to work hard and finally save enough money to buy a house. It was a cottage in the blue-collar neighborhood of New London, Connecticut. The home was no mansion; it was older, modest in size and it needed work. But to Ms. Kelo, like for many others, her home was her castle. Her effort to save her home pitted her against Pfizer Pharmaceuticals and the City of New London who, together, wanted to take her

home in order to build parking and an industrial park for the
drug company. Her battle to save her home was clearly reminiscent of those in Poletown, Michigan, in 1981, who fought unsuc-
cessfully against Detroit and General Motors. But here, unlike
with the residents in Poletown, Ms. Kelo did not stand alone. The
Institute for Justice came to her defense, offering her up as a sympathetic average person facing the threats of big bad government
and big bad business who wanted to screw her out of her home.
But besides property rights advocates, the Kelos were also supported by groups such as the NAACP who saw her battle (even
though she was white) to protect neighborhoods with people of
color that had been targeted by eminent domain. Liberals also
supported her because of her working-class roots and again saw
this as a battle to avenge *Poletown* and its residents against the fat
cats.

Second, unlike with the *Poletown* decision, there were an enormous public relations or media campaign, and political movement accompanying her battle. If the *Poletown* decision was the
beginning of the property rights and ownership movement,
Kelo was the culmination of nearly a quarter of a century of
mobilization.

One of the more important weapons in the eminent domain
propaganda or public relations wars was an April 2003 report by
the Institute for Justice and Castle Coalition entitled *Public Power,
Private Gain: A Five Year, State-By-State Report Examining the Abuse
of Eminent Domain*. Written by Dana Berliner, it asserted that from
January 1, 1998, until December 31, 2002, there were at least
10,282 examples of eminent domain abuse across 41 states in the
United States. Eminent domain abuse was defined as "the number of condemnations for private use or benefit. We break those
down into filed, threatened, total, and development projects with
private benefit condemnations."[4] Among its 10,000-plus examples
of abuse included:

3,722+ properties with condemnations filed for the benefit of private parties
6,560+ properties threatened with condemnation for private parties
4,032+ properties currently living under threat of private use condemnation

Critical to understanding the report are several assumptions
that it made. First, the report definitely takes a narrow definition
or conception of eminent domain, rejecting the line of case law

dating back to at least *Midkiff* and *Berman*, which ruled in favor of a more expansion conception of public use that was equated with a broad meaning of the term that included takings for the purposes of promoting a public benefit, advantage, or general welfare. Second, the report includes both filed condemnations which it alleges were on behalf of private owners, as well as threatened condemnations for that purpose, and pending ones that fit into either category. Threatened condemnations were defined as:

> [T]he number of properties that the government has indicated that it may obtain through eminent domain for the benefit of private parties. It includes authorizations of condemnation, verbal or written threats to condemn and redevelopment plans that call for removing someone's property. We have also included situations where condemnation is proposed and the individual must go to the city and lobby to keep his property.[5]

What is critical to understand here is that the definition of threatened condemnation assumes that any talk or discussion to use eminent domain is automatically placed in this category. Moreover, note how the definition does not include an actual filing of condemnation in court, but it also includes any discussion of it by a governmental body. These are quite broad conceptualizations of eminent domain. Moreover, it assumes that all talk of the use of eminent domain is coercive, and that no owner can freely negotiate when the government contemplates the use of eminent domain. Thus, discounted are any claims that governments seek to buy first and then only use eminent domain as a last resort. By the report's definition, there is no free market transaction to buy. Finally, the report also includes those living under the threat of eminent domain. This means that projects were being debated that included possible discussion of the use of eminent domain. Also critical to the report were several sleights of hand. For example, no discussion of the public versus private benefits was examined. By that, were the beneficiaries of the project primarily the public versus a private party? In the report, the assumption is generally cast that the condemnations are all directed at residential properties, or residential and business properties. However, most of the highlighted case studies profiled in the report emphasized individuals similar to Suzette

Kelo—a single-family homeowner. This is how the 10,000-plus was defined.

However, reexamine the numbers. Assume for the sake of argument that one only looks at actual filings for the use of eminent domain. This number is 3,722. Divide by five (the number of the years in the study yields 744 per year), then divide by 41 (the number of reporting states) and it works out to 18 reported instances of eminent domain abuse per year. This of course still assumes "abuse" means any use of eminent domain for the benefit of a private party. What the report does not document are some additional points. First, it argues that owners do not receive the fair market value for their property by asserting that for the condemnors "the compensation they have to pay is usually less than if they bought the property on the open market."[6] Such a statement ignores the constitutional mandates to pay fair market value for property, and that in many states, other costs, including relocation and business good will, may be compensated.

Second, it ignores some of the benefits that came from the condemnation. The report does do a terrific job discussing how many of the economic development plans associated with the taking failed, but it does not discuss how many of them succeeded and were tremendous additions to the community. Finally, to put the eminent domain abuse claim into perspective, the report does not look at the number of takings that occur every year that are for a valid public purpose (to build a road, hospital, or school, for example), and even its 2,000+ abuses per year pale in comparison to the normal 1,000,000 homeowners who default on their property every year, with those numbers being even significantly higher beginning in 2007 or so when the mortgage market meltdown produced millions of defaults per year. Clearly greedy banks and deceptive and subprime loans were a greater threat to homeowners than is eminent domain.

There are many other problems with the *Public Power, Private Gain* study that question its methodology and conclusions. But it did not matter. First, the media ate up the report. It received wide publicity across the traditional and new media. Second, the report did what all good public relations does—it told a good story that was personalized. It detailed individual cases of abuse across the country, placing faces and names to eminent domain abuse to which average people could relate. Third, and most surprising, the report received almost no critical analysis. There was no major attempt by any party to question its assumptions or arguments or to examine the details of the stories it told. The report was left unrefuted, and the Institute of Justice was able to market its conclusions as it pleased.

The *Kelo* decision only made the arguments by the Institute more salient. Now there was a Supreme Court decision that had in fact represented all that it had deplored in *Public Power, Private Gain*. Ms. Kelo was the single-family, blue-collar homeowner who refused to sell her property. The city wanted to condemn it and give it to a drug company. This was good versus evil, David versus Goliath. Everyone cheers for David even if he loses. Post-*Kelo*, the Institute continues to document eminent domain abuse. It pointed out that the project for which Ms. Kelo's house was taken went bust. Its Web site features more stories like Ms. Kelo's, and the organization continues to issue publications that highlight the problems it sees with eminent domain abuse. It also continues to press its case that eminent domain is abused and that the *Kelo* opinion was unprecedented, again without any other organization responding.

The Castle Coalition's June 2006 *Myth and Realities of Eminent Domain Abuse* documents over a half-dozen eminent domain myths, the first of which is: "In *Kelo*, for the first time in U.S. history, the ordinary private use of property was declared a "public use" for which a government could use its power of eminent domain." The reality is that this assertion is simply wrong. The Court never said that, unless one assumes that any taking other than one that meets the narrow conception of public use is one that serves a private use. To argue that *Kelo* did this is a large stretch of the imagination of the decision. This report again questions the idea that eminent domain is a last resort, again asserting that any project contemplating its use makes it impossible for an owner to negotiate for a fair market price. *Myth and Realities* also discounts the ability of the political process to check eminent domain abuse, and, moreover, it seems to assert that the courts are unable to capture abuses, although the report does not directly make this assertion. Finally, other "myths" document or contend that eminent domain is not needed for economic development projects and that many of the projects using eminent domain did not pan out.[7]

Overall, supporters of eminent domain reform had done a terrific job highlighting Ms. Kelo's story as well as many others. In fact, what the Institute did well was to understand both the law and the media. They understood that the essence of good politics is telling a good story that personalizes some individual's plight. Politicians do that all the time in their speeches, be it talking about Joe the Plumber (as was true in the 2008 presidential campaign), or telling stories about themselves so that they can connect with voters. Suzette Kelo's story was compelling, and it had an element of good versus evil and big versus little guy, or taking on city hall, that plays well. In some ways, Suzette Kelo was the Rocky of the property rights movement. One could not help but cheer for her.

In addition to the good public relations and sponsorship, there did appear to be some momentum toward Kelo's side. The Michigan Supreme Court, as noted previously, had reversed the *Poletown* decision and that created the sense that when the Supreme Court accepted the *Kelo* case for appeal, it too was ready to act. But the decision did not go the way many expected, even if legal scholars were not surprised by the decision.

The actual *Kelo* decision was very different from either the *Berman* or the *Midkiff* rulings. First, the facts in the case revolved around someone losing their single-family home. In *Berman* the plaintiffs (Berman) owned a department store, while in *Midkiff* the challenge to the Hawaiian law was an owner of a large tract of land—essentially a land baron. Neither party makes for a very sympathetic poster child for property rights. Second, in both *Berman* and *Midkiff*, the Supreme Court issued unanimous opinions. *Kelo* was a fractured 5-4 decision along liberal/conservative lines punctuated with two very strong dissents. Moreover, Stevens's majority opinion seemed cold and antiseptic. He recounted the law, expressed little sympathy for the Kelos, and said that states could impose more restrictions on eminent domain if they wished. Not much consolation or comfort for Suzette Kelo.

Justice O'Connor, who had written the majority opinion in *Midkiff*, and who was by now one of the most popular Justices on the Court, wrote in emotional terms expressing concern for the Kelos and their home. She suggested that the decision would threaten the safety of anyone who owned a home when she declared of the majority holding: "Any property may now be taken for the benefit of another private party, but the fallout from this decision will not be random. The beneficiaries are likely to be those citizens with disproportionate influence and power in the political process, including large corporations and development firms."[8] Similarly, Clarence Thomas spoke to how, in the past, eminent domain had targeted racial minorities and the poor.[9] The *Kelo* holding surely would mean this would continue. O'Connor spoke to the homeowners and working class, Thomas to the poor and people of color. Stevens looked like he was the executioner for big business.

But the immediate reporting of the *Kelo* opinion added fuel to the fire that the majority holding was unprecedented. The Associated Press, in reporting on the decision, headlined the story "Cities Can Bulldoze Homes for Development." Similar headlines appeared across the country as newspapers, wire services, cable television, talk radio, and the Web ran news of the *Kelo* opinion. The *Houston Chronicle* editorialized that the decision sanctioned something no different from what the communists did in the Soviet Union and China when they seized private property.[10]

Reaction to *Kelo* was not confined to chat, anger, and resignation. On June 27, 2005, Texas senator John Cornyn introduced legislation, the "Protection of Homes, Small Businesses, and Private Property Act of 2005," to limit the use of eminent domain for economic development. A year later President George W. Bush issued an Executive Order restricting the use of eminent domain "for the purpose of benefitting the general public and not merely for the purpose of advancing the economic interest of private parties to be given ownership or use of the property taken." States and local governments across the country similarly adopted many laws trying to address the *Kelo* decision, following, perhaps Stevens's admonition that they could take action to further limit eminent domain beyond what the Constitution permitted. Within two years of the *Kelo* decision, more than 20 states adopted laws that prohibited takings for economic development reasons or made other changes in the laws to make the use of eminent domain more difficult. Some of these laws required more hearings before a taking could occur, some banned the taking of private homes, some required more evidence before a taking could occur, and others instituted rules to award legal fees to owners if they successfully challenged a taking.

Post-*Kelo*, the Institute for Justice also did an excellent job in shaping the *Kelo* opinion, even several years after it. It declared *Kelo* as symbolic of "eminent domain" abuse. This is a wonderful, pithy phrase that captures the imagination for all types of images of what may be wrong with big government. In addition, it described the *Kelo* opinion as unprecedented, responding to critics who claimed that the decision did not break new legal ground. The Institute continues to add poster children to eminent domain abuse, with on-going stories about the continued abuse of eminent domain and how it continues to hurt individuals. Finally, the battle in *Kelo* was over whether eminent domain could be used for economic development purposes. Property rights groups used that case to target *Poletown* and *Midkiff*. However, had they won in *Kelo* the core ruling of *Berman*—taking property to abate blight—would remain untouched. But since *Kelo* there are indications that groups are also going after the blight abatement justification for eminent domain, seeking to narrow its meaning and scope.[11]

But at the heart of the *Kelo* criticism, there seems to be an argument that eminent domain abuse exists and that property rights are insecure. This suggests in part that the government—especially local government—is running roughshod over homeowners and property owners, and that both are left defenseless. The fear of eminent domain abuse also seems to suggest that the courts are incapable or unwilling to come to the aid of property owners, and that they are unable to smoke out private takings and abuses of eminent domain. But is that really the case? No one can deny that *Poletown* and, to some extent, *Kelo* represented something ugly about eminent domain power. It is probably also true that mistakes and abuses happen. But are courts incapable of discovering and checking these abuses? Is it now the case that the public use stipulation has no meaning? Not necessarily.

REVISITING *KELO*: COMPREHENSIVE PLANS AND EMINENT DOMAIN

It is time to revisit the Stevens majority opinion in *Kelo* again. One of the points he makes in that case is that previous tests at defining what constitutes a valid public use, or efforts to distinguish a public from a private use, have proven futile. Yes, one could categorically state that a taking to further economic development is not a public use. One could also declare that a taking that involves a transfer of property from one private party to another is not a valid public use. There are defensible positions, perhaps. But think about the repercussions of making this type of distinction.

First, consider if the Court in *Kelo* had decided the other way. Yes, it would have been a victory for Ms. Kelo, but it would have also been a victory for judicial activism and legislating from the bench. When Justice O'Connor wrote the *Midkiff* opinion, she essentially said that the courts should not be second-guessing what elected legislatures and officials do when it comes to economic policy. To do otherwise would be to return to the *Lochner*-era of substantive due process where judges substituted their judgments or second-guessed legislatures when it came to making economic policy. Judges are not supposed to do this. Many forget that the majority opinion in *Kelo* was a model of judicial deference and restraint, and that the minority opinion was a decision of judicial activism. Stevens stated what the current status of the law was and then invited states and local governments to make changes as appropriate. The dissenters took it upon themselves to declare what the policy regarding eminent domain should be. If one thing is clear from reading this book, the dissenters got it wrong. Takings for economic development have a long history in the United States, and in many cases the takings do involve giving the land to other private parties for development. This may be bad public policy, but it is not unconstitutional.

Second, it is true that after *Kelo* was decided, the promised benefits from taking her property did not materialize. This is also true with what happened after *Poletown*. However, in many cases, the economic development does work out. It is a reality that some property might be more productively used when redeveloped for a factory, business, or housing project. In tough economic times, it is difficult to argue with a proposition that will generate new jobs, homes for people, and, it is hoped, tax revenues to do other public works projects. Some individuals may be asked to give up their homes but they are compensated for their property. In return, taxpayers, communities, and the public at large may benefit. The benefits may simply be so great that it is hard to say no. In the same way that building a school may be important to a community, so too might be building a new employer who will hire workers.

Third, is it always the case that turning something over to another private party is necessarily a problem that indicates a private taking? In some cases yes, but in others, the building of railroads, factories, malls, and many other important amenities do contribute to the quality of life in a community, and eminent domain may be necessary to achieve them. Simply declaring that transfers to private parties are illegal might be too crude a line to be drawn.

Moreover, banning transfers to private parties will not work for other reasons. First, assume that a local government wishes to engage in the promotion of economic development, but it is barred from acquiring land and transferring it to another private party. There is a simple solution here. The government can continue to own the land and simply rent the property out to private developers or tenants who will operate private businesses. Taxes can be negotiated as part of the fees for rent. In this case, land has not been transferred to a private party. Conversely, what if the ban is on the government promoting economic development? Could this really be prevented? Not likely. From the earliest days of the American republic, public funding for infrastructure has been important to facilitating economic development. Almost every economist supports this type of public investment to help the economy. If one were to ban takings for economic development, then would projects to build roads, bridges, water treatment plants, or industrial parks be banned? Perhaps, but what if one were to say that these types of projects are okay, but not ones that encourage private economic development done by private individuals? In these cases, eminent domain should not be used. There, again, is a problem. First, as Justice Douglas pointed out in his *Berman* opinion, it is not the job of the courts to decide if economic development is better performed with public or private hands. Moreover, it may be cheaper or more efficient to permit the government to acquire property and then let private investment foot the bill for all or some of the economic development. In addition, the way we think about government is increasingly changing. At one time it may have been the case that governmental functions were exclusively performed by the public sector. However, privatization of government services and the increased development of public-private partnerships oftentimes means that nonprofit or for-profit entities are given contracts to perform government services. In such a world where the boundaries among the public, private, and nonprofit sectors are no longer clearly and cleanly discernable, it is often hard to say that the performance of a task by a nongovernmental entity is not a traditional public or governmental use. A nonprofit hospital providing medical care under a governmental contract may be used by the public in the same way that a hospital run by the government would be. Similarly, permitting a government-regulated private utility company to provide electrical needs to a community may be seen by the public in the same way as a municipally owned facility. The point here is that it is not so easy to say what a public or nonpublic function is. Finally, there is a problem of line drawing here. How does one decide whether economic development, of any type, is a legitimate or illegitimate public enterprise?

There is a body of constitutional law from the nineteenth and twentieth centuries that addressed the issue of intergovernmental tax immunities. These cases tried to decide if and when the federal government could tax state government operations. At one time, one test was that traditional governmental operations could not be taxed. The rule sounds simple, but who is to say what a traditional governmental function is? Two hundred years ago, providing K-12 public education was not a traditional governmental function; today, it is. Except for pure market purists who think that, short of providing security and defense, there is no fine line that defines traditional or nontraditional governmental functions. A rule that states that eminent domain cannot be used to transfer private property from one person to another for the purposes of economic development is too crude or inexact of a test. It is a rule that may be impractical in many situations, legally difficult to enforce, and hopeless bad policy in other situations.

Is there a better way to think about how to distinguish a valid public use from an invalid one? Again, let's return to Stevens's opinion, where he suggested that the use of a comp plan can help courts determine when a use is for public versus private purposes. Are the courts incapable of ferreting out private takings? Several examples suggest that this is not the case.

Prior to the U.S. Supreme Court decision in *Kelo*, several state court decisions had independently interpreted their own state constitutions and public use provisions. In some cases, often paralleling the *Berman* and *Midkiff* precedents, state court decisions have evolved to expand upon the public use concept. Conversely, some state courts declined to follow the direction of the Supreme Court and instead interpreted their own constitutions to offer more protections for property rights than were found at the federal level. He also suggested that examination of, or the role of, development plans might be important factors to the courts as they seek to determine if a taking is serving a public or a private purpose.

What might we anticipate in terms of doctrine at the state level as a result of the *Kelo* opinion? Is the public use doctrine really dead this time, and will it be impossible ever to find a taking to be for private use or benefit? What role might comp plans have in distinguishing valid public uses from invalid private takings? Several cases, decided at the state level prior to the Supreme Court decision, might offer some suggestions regarding how the courts might examine comp plans and the public use doctrine in the context of takings used for economic development purposes.

PUBLIC USE AND EMINENT DOMAIN IN STATE COURTS

Nevada

In *City of Las Vegas Downtown Redevelopment Agency v. Pappas*, 119 Nev. 429, 76 P.3d 1 (Nev. 2003), the Nevada Supreme Court upheld the taking of nonblighted commercial property to provide parking facilities for a downtown redevelopment project under both the federal and Nevada constitutions.

The City of Las Vegas created a redevelopment agency, pursuant to state community development law, to address the problems of economic development and blight in the city's urban core. The agency, composed solely of Las Vegas City Council members, was entrusted to determine if redevelopment was needed to address physical, social, or economic blight in the downtown area and, if so, to develop a comprehensive plan to remedy such blight. The agency did conclude that blight existed and that redevelopment was needed. Several years later, a project known as the "Fremont Street Experience" was proposed for a portion of the downtown. The plan called for the creation of a pedestrian plaza along Fremont Street and the building of a five-story parking complex that also included retail and office space. To finance this proposal, the agency utilized a consortium of casinos that would provide the capital for the project and then run the garage and share in its revenues. Three of the 32 properties set to be acquired for the parking lot were owned by the Pappas, and when approached about selling their property, they refused, setting into motion agency condemnation of their land. The Pappas raised several challenges to the taking in district court, including claims that the agency acted in bad faith and that it lacked the authority to take their property. The agency cross-filed, and summary judgment was requested by both parties. The district court dismissed many of the owners' claims and the agency's counterclaims and, among other reasons, concluded that Pappas's property could be acquired for the parking facility because it promoted a valid public use under the federal and state constitution.

In addressing whether it indeed served a valid public use, the Nevada Supreme Court first noted that the United States and Nevada constitutions have parallel eminent domain stipulations.[12] The Court then noted that, while the U.S. Supreme Court had given broad construction to the term "public use," Nevada courts, too, had also given similar broad reading to their own language, concluding that the term could be read to include public advantage, benefit, and utility. In addition, they noted that other states with public use clauses similar to that found in the Nevada Constitution had reached the same conclusion.[13]

Second, the Nevada Supreme Court also rejected the notion that public use required that the public own the condemned property, arguing instead that the rights of owners are protected when they receive just compensation for any interests taken.[14] Thus, the more narrow conception of public use—requiring use or ownership by the public—was not mandated by the Nevada Constitution.

Finally, the Court noted how, in enacting its Community Redevelopment law, the state legislature had defined the eradication of blight to be an important public purpose. The issue is then how the specific development plan serves that purpose, and not whether the land condemned is publicly owned, which is critical to determining whether the use of eminent domain served a valid public use.[15] What this meant was that the Court was unwilling to second-guess agency determinations of blight or necessity for the taking. First, citing *Berman v. Parker*, the Nevada Supreme Court indicated how federal law since that case afforded broad discretion to legislatures to define blight, and that, like in other states, it too was going to defer to the agency's decision and judgment regarding whether the blight had been abated. Second, the Court also refused to question the necessity of the property taken, stating that "it is up to the legislative body [...] to determine how to accomplish the public purpose" and the "courts may not substitute their own judgment" regarding what should be condemned to secure the public purpose.[16]

Overall, what the Nevada Supreme Court did in upholding that taking was to take many of its legal cues from the U.S. Supreme Court, and from decisions in other states, in seeking to clarify the meaning of "public use" in its own constitution. It equivocated public use with public utility or advantage, rejected claims that public ownership was a necessary component of this doctrine, and ruled that it would give broad deference to agency determinations of what constituted a valid public purpose, whether blight existed, and what property should be acquired.

Illinois

The Illinois Supreme Court ruled in *Southwestern Illinois Development Authority v. National City Environmental, L.L.C*, 199 Ill.2d 225, 768 N.E.2d 1 (2002), that the taking of private property from one business in order to allow another to expand was not a valid public use. In this case, though, the court did not categorically rule out the use of eminent domain for economic development purposes; instead, it ruled that this taking did not secure a public purpose.

The Southwestern Illinois Development Authority (SWIDA) was created in 1987 with the legislative mandate to "promote development within the geographic confines of Madison and St. Clair counties."[17] Among the powers that the legislature conveyed to SWIDA was the authority to use eminent domain to acquire properties located in those counties in order to promote economic development and expansion.

In 1996 SWIDA issued bonds to assist Gateway International Motorsports Corporation (Gateway) develop racetrack facilities. Subsequently, in 1998, Gateway sought additional land, then occupied by National City Environmental, L.L.C., and the St. Louis Auto Shredding Company (collectively NCE) in order to expand its parking facilities. Initially, Gateway sought to negotiate with NCE for the purchase of its property; when that failed, Gateway requested that SWIDA use its quick-take eminent domain authority to acquire the land and transfer it to them so that the latter could expand. However, before SWIDA could use its quick-take powers, Gateway had to complete an application stating the reasons it wanted the land. In this application, Gateway also indicated that it would pay for all of the expenses SWIDA incurred. County board approval was also required before

SWIDA could use its quick-take powers, and the St. Clair County Board adopted a resolution requesting that the condemnation proceed. In its resolution, it also indicated that the acquisition would increase racetrack attendance, address parking needs, and enhance the public health, welfare, safety, and tax revenue of the southwestern Illinois area. Subsequently, SWIDA also adopted a resolution to use its quick-take powers, again citing many factors the county had in undertaking this condemnation.

NCE challenged the condemnation at a quick-take hearing in a circuit court, claiming that the taking was for a private use and that the land sought was excessive, given the need. Specifically, they alleged that the taking violated both the Fifth Amendment to the United States Constitution, and Article I, Section 15, of the Illinois Constitution, both of which mandated that private property may only be taken for a public use. The Circuit Court upheld the taking, the Court of Appeals reversed, and the case was appealed to the Illinois Supreme Court.

The court upheld the taking, relying on testimony by St. Clair County and SWIDA that the condemnation was needed to relieve blight, promote economic development, and to abate a traffic public safety problem in the area that had arisen as a result of the construction and expansion of the Gateway race facility.[18] The judge also relied upon testimony from Gateway officials who stated that the taking for parking would be cheaper than building a parking ramp and that the new land would help their company expand. The state appellate court reversed, holding that SWIDA had exceeded its constitutional authority. The case was appealed to the Illinois Supreme Court, which upheld the appellate court.

The Illinois Supreme Court saw the issue in this case to be whether this specific taking served a valid public use. The court first stated that the Illinois Constitution limited the use of eminent domain to situations which served a valid public use.[19] The taking of private property and the eventual transfer to another private party did not necessarily contravene the public use mandate. The court also acknowledged that the U.S. Supreme Court had appeared to equivocate public purpose and public use in *Midkiff*, but that the two were not necessarily the same under the Illinois Constitution.[20] Even though the Illinois Court noted that the term "public use" had been applied flexibly, ultimately the judiciary in Illinois was the final arbiter of what the term meant and that "this flexibility does not equate to unfettered ability to exercise takings beyond constitutional boundaries. 'A purely private taking could not withstand the scrutiny of the public use requirement; it would serve no legitimate purpose of government and would thus be void.'"[21] For a taking to be for a valid public use, the "public must be to some extent entitled to use or enjoy the property, not as a mere favor or by permission of the owner, but by right."[22] Yet the Court noted that it was not easy to draw the line between what was a public purpose versus a private benefit lacking a "legitimate public purpose to support it."[23]

In this case, the Court acknowledged that the taking of the NCE property would serve an important public purpose in mitigating blight or public safety problems. It also recognized how, in previous case law, it had found economic development to be a valid public purpose. However, the Court characterized this condemnation as "private venture designed to result not in a public use, but in private profits."[24] Critical to reaching this conclusion, the Court noted the absence of a study, commission, or plans to study the parking problem. Second, SWIDA seemed simply willing to acquire whatever Gateway wanted. Third, SWIDA, despite its public purpose claims to the contrary, according to the Court, simply acted as the "default broker of land for Gateway's proposed parking plan" when Gateway's efforts to purchase the NCE property failed.[25] Overall, the Court stated that these factors pointed to the conclusion that no independent public use or purpose had been found for the project. Thus, given the facts in this case, the Court found it to be a taking for a private benefit that violated both the United States and Illinois constitutions.

Southwestern Illinois Development Authority is a limited holding. It does not necessarily stand for the proposition that a taking to promote economic development would not constitute a public use. Nor does the case stand for the rule that states a taking of land from one private party and giving it to another is invalid under the state public use doctrine. Instead, it holds that there must be an independent public use, distinct and primary from any private use. Critical to the decision in *Southwestern Illinois Development Authority* was the Court's observation that at no point did SWIDA undertake an independent study of the Gateway parking problem or otherwise consider alternatives beyond the acquisition proposed by Gateway. Had it done so, presumably, the Court might have come to a different conclusion.

Arizona

In *Bailey v. Myers*, 206 Ariz. 224, 76 P.3d 898 (Ariz. Ct. App. 2003) the Arizona Court of Appeals ruled that the taking of private property for retail redevelopment was not a valid public use under the state constitution.

The Baileys had operated a business on their property in Mesa, Arizona, since 1946. In 1996 the Mesa City Council adopted a resolution calling for the creation of the Mesa Town Center Redevelopment Area, which originally did not include the Baileys' property. Subsequently, another private business owner approached the Mesa City Council with a desire and plan to expand his hardware store to include the property owned by the Baileys. The council then amended its redevelopment plan to include the Baileys' property. A condemnation order was then issued for the Baileys' property, and the council sought immediate possession of it. The Baileys objected, claiming the taking violated the Arizona Constitution, specifically Article II, Section 17. The trial court upheld the taking, granted the order for immediate possession, but stayed the order while the case was appealed to the Arizona Court of Appeals. The Court of Appeals ruled that the taking was for a private and not a public use, thereby overturning the trial court order.[26]

Critical to the holding of the court was the specific wording of the Arizona Constitution and its eminent domain–public use clause. Article II, Section 17, states:

> Private property shall not be taken for private use, except for private ways of necessity, and for drains, flumes, or ditches, on or across the lands of others for mining, agricultural, domestic, or sanitary purposes. No private property shall be taken or damaged for public or private use without just compensation having first been made ... which compensation shall be ascertained by a jury, unless a jury be waived.... *Whenever an attempt is made to take private property for a use alleged to be public, the question whether the contemplated use be really public shall be a judicial question, and determined as such without regard to any legislative assertion that the use is public.*[27]

Specifically, the court noted, Article II, Section 17 explicitly states that determinations of what constitutes a valid use are judicial questions not requiring deference to any legislative determinations. This meant that, unlike the U.S. Constitution, which is silent on the issue of who has authority to determine public use decisions—thereby freeing the Court up in cases such as *Kelo* and *Midkiff* to rule that this was a legislative determination—the Arizona Constitution gives to its judiciary the task of making this determination.[28]

The Appellate Court criticized the trial court for failing to undertake an independent and serious review of the taking under the Constitution to determine if the condemnation was "really public."[29] In undertaking this review on its own, the Court of Appeals relied upon past precedent to make several distinctions. First, citing *City of Phoenix v. Superior Court*, it noted how the question of what constituted a valid public use differed from questioning the necessity of the taking. In the *City of Phoenix* case the Arizona Supreme Court stated that, while determinations of the necessity of a taking demanded a "deferential standard of review" for legislative determinations of this matter, a lesser standard of deference was to be afforded under Article II, Section 17.[30] Second, the Appeals Court, again relying upon *City of Phoenix*, rejected claims that the mere taking of property and transferring it to another private party made the use of eminent domain for private benefit. Instead, it noted how, in *City of Phoenix*, the Arizona Supreme Court had permitted the taking and transferring of private property from a private person to a business if the property was a slum or blighted.[31]

Third, the Court of Appeals argued that the *City of Phoenix* case did not stand for the proposition that "any property within a designated slum or blighted area is automatically subject to being taken for redevelopment without the constitutionally required judicial determination that the property is being taken for a use that is 'really public.'"[32] In fact, the court noted how in the case of the Baileys' property there were no specific findings that the property was blighted. Fourth, the court rejected appeal or precedent in *Midkiff* and *Berman* to guide their reading of the state constitution, noting how those opinions were not controlling in their construction of Article II, Section 17.[33] Finally, the court, noting the parallel between its constitution and that of the State of Washington, cited precedent from the Washington Supreme Court contending that a "beneficial use is not necessarily a public use."[34]

Overall, the Court of Appeals made the above distinctions in an effort to construct what it felt the Arizona Constitution demanded of the state judiciary when making its own independent determinations of what constituted a valid public use:

> [W]e hold that when a proposed taking for a redevelopment project will result in private commercial ownership and operation, the Arizona Constitution requires that the anticipated public benefits must substantially outweigh the private character of the end use so that it may truly be said that the taking is for a use that is "really public." The constitutional requirement of "public use" is only satisfied when the public benefits and characteristics of the intended use substantially predominate over the private nature of that use.[35]

To undertake this weighing, the court noted how many factors—including but not limited to questions about who will own the property, how it will be used, paid for or financed, who benefits from the project and whether there are any public health issues implicated—would have to be considered. In considering these factors, the court stated that the City of Mesa had not proved its burden that the taking was for a public use, noting how it was not for a traditional use such as a street or sidewalk, or that it was necessary for health or safety reasons. Instead, because the taking was for the creation of a privately owned commercial project, this condemnation furthered a private interest and therefore did not constitute a valid public use.[36]

LESSONS LEARNED?

Public use decisions from Nevada, Illinois, and Arizona rendered by courts in these states under their own constitutions reveal an interesting pattern regarding other jurisdictions, and may address the taking of private property for economic development in light of the U.S. Supreme Court's *Kelo* opinion.

First is the importance attached to findings of fact and the development of comp plans in determining whether the taking was for public or private purpose. By that, in the cases upholding the taking, a comp plan was in place and the taking was considered in light of how it advanced the plan or how the findings in it supported the condemnation. In the cases where the taking was found to be for private benefit, there was no comp plan (Illinois) to support the taking, and the plan in Arizona was deficient on several grounds. Only in Nevada was the taking upheld and the comp plan critical to the court ruling that the taking was for public benefit. Thus, all of these cases anticipated one of the major points or distinctions made by Justice Stevens in *Kelo* when he indicated that the presence or absence of a comp plan would be critical to determining whether the taking was for private or public benefit.

Second, it is still possible to invalidate a taking in jurisdictions with broad public use doctrines, even if comp plans are in place. In Arizona, the existence of the plan did not salvage the taking. In part, this was because of the constitutional provision giving the court independent authority to make public use decisions. However, the facts of the case were also important: There was an original comp plan that did not include the property that was in dispute in this case. Instead, the plan was amended, almost at the request of another private business that wanted the property. The facts here looked suspicious to the court, considering this and the traditional factors considered in order to make public use determinations. Here, perhaps had the property originally been part of the plan, the court might have looked upon the condemnation differently because one could have argued that its inclusion and taking were part of a broader design to further a public good. Instead, it looked more opportunistic on the part of a specific business that wished to expand.

Of course the Illinois case shows what happens when no real plan was executed. Granted, there were findings of fact, yet no real comp plan was developed and no real finding to support a real public purpose existed. It is in Nevada, then, where a plan existed, and where the property to be acquired was originally part of it, that the condemnation was upheld. The facts here suggest that this was not a private taking, and the comp plan was decisive in showing that.

In the three cases here, the specifics of the comp plan, or its absence, along with the specific facts of the condemnation, were critical factors affecting where a public use existed. None of these cases revealed a categorical or bright-line rule that takings for economic development purposes were always or never permitted; instead it depends on the circumstances surrounding each taking.

Kelo was deemed a major loss to property rights advocates who saw in this decision the final demise of the public use limitation on the use of eminent domain. They hoped that the Court would have issued a bright-line ruling invalidating takings for economic development purposes, yet instead what they got was a message that that would not be the case.

Kelo did not sound the demise of the public use provision. Instead, it suggested a new test for distinguishing valid public uses from private takings, centering on the role that comprehensive plans could have in clarifying the differences between the two. Drawing upon pre-*Kelo* state cases, it is clear that even with the presence of a development plan, not all takings will be upheld, showing that in fact there is still some life to the public use doctrine. Whether the new test hinted at in *Kelo* is viable, or whether it will fail the way previous tests have, however, needs yet to be seen.

However, these examples do suggest that the courts are not incapable of sorting out when a taking is for a private or public use. Yes, in some situations power grabs do exist, and the political process does not adequately protect individual ownership rights. Stevens's opinion, then, in arguing that public use decisions ultimately must be grounded in comp plans and the planning process, suggest an important direction toward eminent domain abuses. Exactly what the abuses really are, and ways to remedy them, are the subject of the final chapter.

CHAPTER NINE

Conclusion: Fixing Eminent Domain Abuse

Property does not have rights. People have rights.
—Justice Potter Stewart

Does eminent domain abuse exist? In all fairness, the work of the Institute for Justice, while flawed and perhaps exaggerated, did raise some disturbing questions about the use of eminent domain. Two points are worth noting. First, in some cases eminent domain is used at the behest of large corporations or wealthy interests at the expense of the poor or people of color. The Castle Coalition and Institute for Justice somewhat ignore these two groups and place more of their emphasis upon how middle-class and small businesses are targeted. These are two different groups that may be treated very differently. Targeting people of color has a different racial impact or animus than condemning business property, and going after the poor is different from going after the middle class. In either case, what makes projects such as those referenced in *Poletown* so distasteful is how groups already poor and disadvantaged are then asked to sell their homes or businesses to help GM or Pfizer. Even worse, what the Institute for Justice passes over are all the tenants and nonproperty owners who are evicted before actual condemnation takes place, and they lose out on any potential relocation benefits or assistance. The point is that, while the Castle Coalition and Institute for Justice seek to highlight the losers and beneficiaries in eminent domain abuse, they ignore the real losers who are not even on the map as part of the constituencies they wish to defend. Individuals affected by eminent domain but who otherwise have no property interests recognized by the law are the real losers. Their interest is in protecting property rights, not the rights of individuals per se.

But having said this, the strength of the work of the Castle Coalition and Institute for Justice is to point out what Justice Thomas discussed in his *Kelo* dissent: that there is a historic pattern of "urban removal" that bears down on some groups at the expense of others. Rarely does one see a high end, white neighborhood targeted by eminent domain, much in the same way that rarely are the affluent at a loss to protect themselves politically or in the criminal justice process. Eminent domain, to the extent that it leaves some groups at a disadvantage in the political or legal process that involves condemnation, really is concentrated among select groups who are disadvantaged in many ways in American society.

Second, the original *Public Power, Private Gain* report highlighted what is perhaps a real problem. These are quick-take laws. Quick-take laws were introduced in the 1970s as a way to expedite the eminent domain process. They allowed a condemnor to immediately take possession of property, deposit the compensation with the court, and then allow the owner to go to court to contest the damage award. Quick-take laws are fine if the owner otherwise wants to sell and the only issue is over the determination of fair market value. However, what if the owner wishes to challenge the taking as an invalid public use? In this case, quick-take laws are deficient and clearly do not protect the interests of the owner.

One example of this is the case of *Rhode Island Economic Development Corp. v. The Parking Co., L.P.*, 892 A.2d 87 (R.I., 2006).[1] In this case The Parking Company (TPC) operated a successful parking facility at an airport that was in competition with another facility operated by the Rhode Island Airport Corporation (RIAC), a public corporation organized as a wholly owned subsidiary of the Rhode Island Economic Development Corporation (EDC). TPC had entered into a long-term contractual agreement with RIAC to operate its facility. In fact, TPC was very profitable due to the fact that it provided valet parking for its customers. For a variety of reasons, RIAC's revenue on its parking ramp declined and it sought to renegotiate a new agreement with TPC.

When the negotiations broke down, RIAC had the EDC deploy its power of eminent domain to quick-take the interior of TPC's parking facility. In effect, since the EDC could not renegotiate the lease it had with TPC, it decided simply to quick-take the facility. Since it was a quick-take, there was no hearing on whether the condemnation served a valid public use. TPC challenged the action, and eventually the Rhode Island Supreme Court sided with them.

The Parking Company had made two basic arguments. First, it argued that the quick-take law itself violated the Rhode Island Constitution in that it did not allow for a public use hearing prior to the actual taking. The court rejected this argument as a facial challenge. Instead, it ruled that, as applied, the quick-take in this circumstance was unconstitutional. It did so not because it deemed a predeprivation hearing was required, but instead because it found that the taking failed to serve a valid public use. Specifically, the court declared:

> In condemning TPC's property interest in Garage B, EDC altered the balance of bargaining power in its favor and was able to achieve in Superior Court the concessions it was unable to obtain from TPC. We are satisfied that these circumstances do not establish a public purpose for the taking, but rather are similar to the arbitrary and bad-faith taking of private property that we condemned in *Capital Properties, Inc.*, 749 A.2d at 1087, upon a finding that the City of Providence exercised its condemnation authority in a bad faith and retaliatory manner after a drawn-out dispute with a downtown developer. See also *Union Station Associates v. Rossi*, 862 A.2d 185, 187 (R.I.2004). (In this companion case to *Capital Properties, Inc.*, Court noted, "at times the actions of the city during this saga could aptly be described as municipal thuggery.") Furthermore, such hasty maneuvering bears little resemblance to the comprehensive and thorough economic development plan that was undertaken and upheld by the United States Supreme Court in *Kelo v. City of New London*, 545 U.S. 469, 125 S.Ct. 2655, 162 L.Ed.2d 439 (2005).[2]

In this case, the court first noted that the purpose of the taking was to use eminent domain to get out from a contract that the EDC did not like. It used eminent domain as a threat. Second, the court noted that, unlike in *Kelo* in which the presence of a comp plan was supposed to provide a check on the taking, there was no such plan here. Instead, the court saw little more here than a private grab by the EDC for TPC's parking facility and profits. It was simply a case of bad faith and thuggery. Thus, none of this served a valid public use and the taking was declared illegal. Eventually, in a later decision involving these two parties, the Supreme Court would require the EDC to disgorge all of its profits that it reaped during the time it had illegally controlled TPC's property.

Here is a case that really did involve eminent domain abuse. While the target was not poor and defenseless, it nonetheless had to fight hard to secure its remedies and win. It did win, but only because of the resources it had to challenge the EDC. Others might not have been so similarly successful. The court here did not find that the quick-take law was unconstitutional, only that the taking here did not serve a valid public use. This case, though, along with claims by the Institute for Justice and the Castle Coalition, does raise concerns about quick-take laws and assertions that predeprivation hearings are not required. By that, it does seem unfair to use quick-take laws and deprive owners of their property when the latter are challenging the validity of the taking as not serving a valid public use. Owners deprived of their property under quick-take laws who eventually prevail on a public use challenge may win merely a pyrrhic victory—they get compensation for their losses. This is hardly a satisfactory remedy. It is akin to awarding damages to victims of faulty consumer products, such as tainted toys or food products, when the manufacturer knew of the defect. After-the-fact compensation is not sufficient to protect rights. In these situations when owners challenge whether the taking served a valid public use, quick-take laws should not be permitted.

CORPORATE THUGGERY AND EMINENT DOMAIN

Chapter 8 examined the role that comp plans could have in addressing some of the problems or abuses associated with eminent domain. Comp plans were highlighted by Justice Stevens's *Kelo* opinion as a way to sort out takings for private versus public uses. He seemed to suggest that development and implementation of a comp plan prior to property acquisitions is a necessary, but not sufficient, condition to preventing private takings and protecting ownership rights. The American Planning Association

(APA), in a 2004 report, also underscored the powerful role that comp plans could have in clarifying what constitutes a legitimate public use.

The report adopted as its first policy:

APA and its Chapters support the adoption of state legislation requiring that a redevelopment area may be established only if the local government agency performing redevelopment has adopted a local comprehensive plan and the redevelopment area plan conforms to the comprehensive plan insofar as the plan applies to the redevelopment project, and intergovernmental cooperation to ensure that actions of single purpose agencies are not inconsistent with local adopted redevelopment plans.[3]

In elaborating upon this policy, the APA report described why comp plans were important:

A local comprehensive plan based on an understanding of the wide range of social, economic, and environmental issues and conditions that affect a community will provide a sound framework for rational decisions regarding long-term physical development. Like specific plans and neighborhood plans, a plan for a redevelopment area should be consistent with the overall plan for the jurisdiction. Redevelopment should also be recognized as a tool that local government can use to implement its comprehensive plan. Requiring a redevelopment area plan to be consistent with the comprehensive plan as a prerequisite to redevelopment ensures that the selection of redevelopment approaches and resources will help to implement and not conflict with the comprehensive plan's goals and objectives for the entire community.[4]

According to the APA, a planning process that seeks to incorporate broad citizen input, addresses social equity issues, and seeks to minimize impacts on communities of color, which damages traditional social fabrics, is one that can go a long way toward addressing some of the abuses found in redevelopment projects such as in *Poletown* and *Kelo*.

But a good planning process, while a necessary step in addressing eminent domain abuse, is not a sufficient one. What *Kelo* also highlighted was a second problem in many of the famous cases involving alleged abuses of eminent domain—the use of eminent domain by a condemnor to serve powerful corporate interests. This is the real core of what eminent domain abuse is about. In the *Kelo* case, the criticism was that private property was being taken simply to serve the corporate interests or plans of Pfizer Pharmaceutical Company. The City of New London, Connecticut, in an economically desperate situation, needed to accommodate Pfizer in the development of this economic development project or else it would lose this company, as well as its jobs and tax revenue, to some other community. Similarly, back in the early 1980s when the City of Detroit was economically reeling from the job losses and the hemorrhaging of the automobile industry, it capitulated to the demands of General Motors to use its eminent domain authority to provide land for a new assembly plant, or face the prospect of the auto giant going elsewhere to expand. As a result, in *Poletown Neighborhood Council v. City of Detroit*, the Michigan Supreme Court upheld the City of Detroit's use of its eminent domain authority to level a city neighborhood, relocate 1,362 households, and acquire more than 150 private businesses in order to accommodate the desire of General Motors Corporation to build a new assembly plant on 465 acres of land. On top of this land acquisition, the City of Detroit also provided more than $200 million in tax breaks and other subsidies to GM to support this project, only to find the promised creation of 6,000 new jobs to be illusionary.

Kelo, Poletown, and even the *Southwestern Illinois Development Authority* case discussed in the previous chapter highlight the unsolved problem of eminent domain—how to prevent corporate thuggery.[5] What are the checks to prevent powerful corporate interests from blackmailing politicians into using takings power to further their private interests? While enactment of a valid comprehensive plan may eliminate many private takings, *Kelo* does nothing to prevent future GMs, Pfizers, and other developers from forcing changes in them in order to accommodate their economic expansion needs.

Political economist Charles Lindblom once described the marketplace as prison.[6] Governmental entities and the political decision-making process are islands embedded within a larger economic sea that leaves, in the hands of private economic players, the power to make business investment decisions. Developers can use this tool—invest or withhold investment and flee from a jurisdiction—if they do not secure the benefits they desire from a community. Such a threat has been successful in corporations extracting tax credits and breaks for business relocation decisions, even though the empirical evidence suggests that such incentives are minor factors affecting the siting of facilities. Similarly, sports teams use the threat of relocation along with fan-base loyalty to wrestle new, publicly financed stadiums from cities and other local governments.

The point here is that there is a well-trod path of eminent domain being used on behalf of powerful interests to secure their needs, with the occasions of *Midkiff* takings (the breaking-up of land monopolies to benefit tenants) being the exception to the rule. What perhaps infuriated the Kelos and other families in Connecticut so much was not simply that their property was being taken, but that they felt they were being ganged up on by developers, a corporate giant, and the city. For the Kelos, as well as the many others across the country who see developers and city officials working together to push them out of their homes, the problem is that democracy has broken down and there is no way they see that the political process is going to listen to them or respect their voice.

What needs to be addressed, post-*Kelo*, is not simply the eminent domain process, but the substantive power inequities in the political arena that make it possible for corporate and wealthy interests to be able to use the condemnation to their advantage. Perhaps better judicial review of the eminent domain process, such as in *Southwestern Illinois Development Authority*, might smoke out some of the power inequities when they grossly reveal that there is no valid public use, but the real solutions may lie elsewhere. Paul Boudreaux, in a 2005 *Denver Law Review* article, suggested that the problem with many eminent domain actions is that groups or individuals facing a taking lack appropriate representation in the political process.[7] By that, these groups do not have elected representatives advocating on their behalf, defending their interests at the various stages of the planning process. Many groups—the poor, people of color—do not have the resources to get involved, or do not have representatives who will adequately look out for them while a comp plan is being developed, or while a specific project is being proposed or examined, or even during the stage when a city council, for example, is doing its public use hearing. Their interests are sacrificed to that of the community. It is here that the real abuse of eminent domain occurs. When the public good is calculated, their interests are outweighed by interests of the rest of the community. This is definitely the case when a broad conception of public use is employed, but nothing says that a narrow construction of the public use to mean "used by the public" will not also produce these abuses. It is just as easy to sacrifice the interests of the poor and people of color to build schools as it is to build a shopping mall. Restricting the permissible uses for which private property may be taken does not eliminate the abuse of eminent domain; only a restructuring of the political process to give traditionally marginalized groups more political leverage will solve that. Finally, groups that are often politically powerless are generally equally weak in the judicial process. Thus, giving them more legal options to sue also does little, especially for those who do not even have legally cognizable property interests.

Structurally, how can one strengthen the power of these groups in the political process to address eminent domain abuse? The reforms may include campaign finance reforms that limit corporate and individual contributions and lobbyist influence. It could also include fairer legislative districting to ensure that these groups receive adequate representation of their interests. Even more radical, tax policies that discourage concentrated wealth, along with renewed antitrust regulation aimed at addressing the political power that flows from economic monopolies, might also be ways to affect the power inequalities in the political process.

Whatever the solution may be, the private takings problem after *Kelo* will not be solved with new laws simply demanding enhanced judicial scrutiny of public use decisions, by banning takings for economic development reasons, or by raising the burden the government must carry to condemn private property. The needed reforms go deeper, asking how democratic societies allocate power and reach decisions. Future *Kelos* will not be avoided unless one looks behind the law to see what real changes need to be made to assure that democracy is not sacrificed to corporate thuggery.

However, assume that these broader structural reforms are not possible. Are there other possible reforms that should be instituted? After *Kelo*, a host of laws was enacted supposedly to address eminent domain abuse. Some of these laws declared takings for economic development to be illegal. Other laws increased the evidentiary burdens necessary to do a taking, or required more hearings or notices, or allowed for increased compensation or the awarding of attorneys' fees if one successfully challenges a taking action.

What impact have all of the post-*Kelo* laws had on eminent domain usage across the United States? It is too soon to tell. *Kelo* was decided in June 2005. Some states enacted laws quickly after the decision that banned taking for economic development purposes, prevented private land transfers, or imposed additional evidential or process requirements before the taking of property. Others made changes to the law months or years afterwards. The exact impact of these laws as of 2009 is yet to be determined.

Yet, even prior to *Kelo*, many states had already changed their laws in response to the property rights movement. In 2008, the Georgetown Environmental Law and Policy Institute issued a report called *The Track Record on Takings Legislation*.[8] This report examined the experiences of two states—Florida and Oregon—which had changed some of their compensation requirements for owners facing eminent domain. The Georgetown study is highly critical of these changes.

First, the study contends that the changes have not led to more protections for the Davids facing the Goliaths. Instead, the distributional pattern of benefits has gone disproportionally to special and wealthy interests who have used the new laws to delay public projects in order to exact increased compensation for their property. The report asserts that many of the supposed protections to community interests, presumably homeowners, did not materialize. Third, the laws have actually increased litigation costs, as well as costs to the public. Finally, the Georgetown report argues that these new compensation requirements undermined local democracy. They did so by giving a few owners the right to potentially halt a public project, to preempt public debate in a legislative setting by removing it to a judicial one, or by making it difficult for local governments to regulate and legislate for the best interests of the community. Overall, the Georgetown study contends that there are costs associated with pre-*Kelo* legislation which make it more difficult to affect a taking. These costs did not necessarily address the abuses alleged by its advocates, and instead they have only reinforced the basic issue with some of the problems of eminent domain articulated by the Institute for Justice. Specifically, they have served to provide a windfall for already-wealthy interests at the expense of the public, while doing little to protect those affected by eminent domain who do not have compensable interests, or who are otherwise already politically impotent in the political and legal process.

There is no question that, as future analysis of the post-*Kelo* legislation is undertaken, one will find that many of the outcomes already described by the Georgetown study will come to light. Some of the legislation simply did not address the problems some of the *Kelo* critics articulated. In Texas, for example, changes in the eminent domain law exempted takings to build a new football stadium for the Dallas Cowboys. Other abuses of these laws will no doubt show similar exemptions. In addition, changes in the law shift costs. If some interests are now going to receive increased legal protections, then someone has to bear these costs. Banning the use of eminent domain for economic development purposes will lead either to increased costs to the taxpayer to acquire property or it will mean that some projects will not get done.

What has been surprising is that local and state governments have not had their stories or poster children to support their claims. They have not pointed out that the changes in the law will cost taxpayers more money, or that jobs or other community development programs that generate public revenues or private income may be lost. These are just some of the costs associated with these changes in the law. For every Suzette Kelo, there is a Jane Doe who may not have a job, or a John Doe who is paying more taxes, as a result of the post-*Kelo* changes.

Recognizing all of the above, what might legitimate reforms of eminent domain law include to address the abuses that are found in its use? Short of the structural political changes noted a couple of pages ago, several changes can be recommended. First, as Justice Stevens indicated, the use of eminent domain needs to be contextualized within the comprehensive planning process. This means that communities need to strengthen the development of the comp plan within their communities and also enhance the public participation in terms of crafting it. Often the public, or at least the poor and perhaps people of color, may ignore or overlook the importance of getting involved in the construction of the comp plan process. They should not. More effort needs to be undertaken to emphasize the importance of their engagement in this process. Planners and other public officials must do more to solicit their input and participation, seeking their views or their ideas for what they would like their communities or neighborhoods to look like. The stronger the comp plan process and the document that it produces, the better it will inform individuals about what might happen to their property. Information on possible land uses and planning should prevent many abuses.

Second, either local or state law should safeguard the comp plan process by making such documents mandatory, and also by insisting that all other planning documents, such as zoning codes and site plans, conform to it. Placing it at the apex of the land use process is an important guard against hasty changes driven by special interests. With that, many communities already make it difficult to amend a comp plan, once adopted. Often they require a qualified majority, such as a two-thirds vote, before it can be amended. This is also a good legal protection against hasty decisions that can lead to eminent domain abuse. Additionally, perhaps another approach is to ban spot zoning or make it more difficult to change comp plans in haste. Perhaps there should be a waiting period between the time a comp plan can be amended and then a specific project approved for development in an area affected by the change. This "cooling off" period might prevent hasty decisions from being made at the behest of political pressure by some developer.

Another set of reforms looks at the process of making a public use decision. If in fact one of the concerns is that eminent domain targets the poor and people of color, or at least the neighborhoods where they reside, then additional respect or protection of the interests of these parties is needed. One common tool used for protecting the environment and endangered species is the production of an environmental impact statement (EIS). These are generally, but not always, mandated when government-funded or -assisted projects are developed. A variation of an EIS to look at how particular projects impact certain types of neighborhoods or communities might be appropriate. They could detail their impact on the poor or people of color. The results of this impact statement would have to be addressed in public use hearings and specific development projects. Possibly, one could also mandate that negative impacts have to be addressed before a project commences or is executed. This might require detailing how the rights of specific individuals are being addressed, or it might even require a qualified majority of representatives who must vote and find a valid public use before eminent domain could be used or the development project itself could be undertaken. Such a review might be more costly, but the additional protection of rights justifies the costs.

Another reform turns to the use of quick-take laws. As the Rhode Island *The Parking Company* case suggests, quick-take laws are not appropriate tools when property owners are challenging the validity of a public use. While the court in that case was unwilling to rule the quick-take law unconstitutional, there is a good argument to be made that these laws do not provide sufficient due process to owners when public use decisions are being challenged. Either the courts should declare quick-take laws unconstitutional except when owners consent to the takings but disagree on the price for their property, or state and local governments should change their laws to reflect this. A new model Uniform Eminent Domain Code should be produced that makes this change in quick-take laws.

But another problem highlighted by the Institute for Justice and the Castle Coalition is that some of the projects involving eminent domain to promote economic development have failed. That is certainly the case. The *Poletown*/GM project was a disaster, as was the *Kelo*/Pfizer one. It is entirely possible that they were ill-conceived economic development ideas right from the start, and the use or absence of eminent domain did not change that. Bad or faulty economic development projects should be avoided. Addressing why governments made bad public policy is another topic entirely. However, it is enough to point out that a high percentage of private economic development and business startups and ventures also fail. Whether governments' track records here are any better than the private sector is an interesting question. However, the track record on whether to use eminent domain is different from the issue of abuse.

Critics might respond that increasing the costs of eminent domain, or that the poor track record in securing successful projects, does not directly address the issue of eminent domain abuse. Yes, protecting property rights may increase costs to taxpayers or prevent the government from doing certain things, but that is the purpose of the Constitution and Bill of Rights. In the same way that one should not do a cost/benefit analysis to decide if one has a right to free speech or freedom of religion (although the Supreme Court seems to be applying such logic now when it comes to protecting individuals against illegal searches and seizures), perhaps one should not do that when it comes to property rights. Two responses are in order.

First, as former Supreme Court Justice Potter Stewart once stated, "Property does not have rights; people do."[9] My chair,

sofa, car, or home does not have rights. Changes in eminent domain law should not confer rights to things, but rights and protections to individuals. Any successful reforms to eminent
domain law should be aimed at protecting the rights of individuals, not property. The question, as noted above, to be asked is
whether individuals have adequate protections in the political
process. It is first a question about political power and decision-
making. After that, one needs to ask if the type of decision in
question is one that the political process through majority rule
should be making, or whether this is the type of decision that
cannot be trusted to be made here. If it is the latter, then the
courts may be the appropriate place to locate the decision, either
for review or as the final arbiter. Thus, while city councils or
legislatures are the appropriate bodies to make public use decisions as part of their responsibility of looking out for the general
welfare of their communities, courts should not totally abandon
their role and become lap dogs in deference to public use decisions
made in the political arena. Courts should remain open to allega-
tions of due process violations, concerns about discrimination, and
other challenges that property owners and perhaps other parties
affected by eminent domain may wish to raise. As cases discussed
in the last chapter, such as *Southwestern Illinois Development Authority*, indicated, abuses may occur and the courts are not incapable of
rooting them out. Judicial review must remain an option for an
eminent domain decision in order to protect individual rights.

However, the political process does make a lot of silly or
foolish choices; yet foolishness is not a legal issue. As Supreme
Court Justice Felix Frankfurter once stated in *Bridges v. State of
California*, 314 U.S. 252 (1941):

> We are not invested with the jurisdiction to pass upon the expedi-
> ency, wisdom, or justice of the laws of the states as declared by
> their courts, but only to determine their conformity with the Fed-
> eral Constitution and the paramount laws enacted pursuant to it.
> Under the guise of interpreting the Constitution we must take care
> that we do not import into the discussion our own personal views
> of what would be wise, just, and fitting rules of government to be
> adopted by a free people, and confound them with constitutional
> limitations.[10]

The constitutionality of the law is different from its wisdom.
The New Deal supposedly ended the days when the courts

should or could question the wisdom of economic policy. The Court wisely stated that allowing judges to second-guess elected representatives regarding economic policy was antidemocratic. It is a form of judicial activism or legislating from the bench. The same point applies to the use of eminent domain and *Kelo*. As a rule, judges should not question the wisdom of policy being constructed by legislatures, mayors, and city councils. They were elected by the people to help improve the welfare of their communities. It is true that, in some cases, they make bad policy and everything should be done to try to prevent policy failures. But government can be a critical player in the economy, providing infrastructure investment and other resources to improve the quality of life in a community. Unless one is a market purist, free markets are not perfect. They are subject to market failures and a host of other problems (as the economic meltdown of 2008–9 demonstrates). Government may need to act. It may make mistakes, but so does the free market; however, ultimately it is not the job of the courts to correct mistakes unless individual rights are at stake. At this point the courts should enter, and this is also true when it comes to eminent domain.

In the end, individual rights and eminent domain can be reconciled. Reports of eminent domain abuse may be greatly exaggerated, but they do occasionally occur. These abuses can and should be addressed, and changes to the comprehensive planning process, quick-take laws, and more careful and realistic assessment regarding what a specific project can accomplish are better and more surgically precise ways to correct eminent domain than the crude sledgehammers and overheated rhetoric that currently frame debates over what constitutes a valid public use.

Cases

Notes

CHAPTER 1

1. Dwight H. Merriam and Mary Massaron, *Eminent Domain Use and Abuse: Kelo in Context* (Chicago: American Bar Association, 2006).

2. Carla T. Main, *Bulldozed: "Kelo," Eminent Domain, and the Lust for Land* (New York: Encounter Books, 2007); Jeff Benedict, *Little Pink House: A True Story of Defiance and Courage* (New York: Grand Central Publishing, 2009).

3. David A. Schultz, *Property, Power, and American Democracy* (New Brunswick, NJ: Transaction Press, 1992).

4. One of the best accounts of the events and controversy surrounding the *Poletown* case is found in Jeanie Wylie, *Poletown: Community Betrayed* (Urbana: University of Illinois Press, 1990).

5. David Schultz, "Comprehensive Plans, Corporate Thuggery, and the Problem of Private Takings," *Government, Law and Policy Journal* 9 (Spring 2007): 6–12.

6. Charles E. Lindblom, "The Market as a Prison," *Journal of Politics* 44 (May 1982): 324–36.

CHAPTER 2

1. Numa Denis Fustel De Coulanges, *The Ancient City: A Study of the Religion, Laws, and Institutions of Greece and Rome* (Baltimore: Johns Hopkins University Press, 1980).

2. John Locke, "The Second Treatise of Government," in *Two Treatises of Government* (New York: New American Library, 1963), pars. 46 and 49 (generally, standard references to the Second Treatise refer to the

paragraph numbers and not page numbers), states the classic view of the land in North America when the British and Europeans arrived. He describes North American lands as not being anyone's property and therefore simply used in common by all. Such unclaimed land could then be occupied and claimed for the British Crown, making it the property of the king or queen. Of course such a view of North America ignores any rights of Native Americans that one might have asserted that they had in the land.

3. For a general discussion on how the rules of property ownership have changed over time or vary over cultures, the following four books offer good basic overviews: Alan Ryan, *Property* (Minneapolis: University of Minnesota Press, 1987); Andrew Reeve, *Property* (Atlantic Heights, NJ: Humanities Press, 1986); Alan Ryan, *Property and Political Theory* (New York: Basil Blackwell, 1984); and Margaret Davies, *Property: Meanings, Histories, Theories* (New York: Routledge-Cavendish, 2007).

4. David Hume, *A Treatise of Human Nature* (New York: Oxford University Press, 1980).

5. A good overview of the social contract tradition can be found in Ernest Barker, *Social Contract: Essays by Locke, Hume, and Rousseau* (New York: Oxford University Press, 1977). He points out that the use of contractual metaphors to justify political authority was based in part upon the analogy from law regarding how individuals enter into contracts and then are legally obligated to obey them.

6. David Hume, *Moral and Political Philosophy* (New York: Hafner Press, 1948), 362–63.

7. Ibid., 358–59.

8. Hume, *Treatise of Human Nature*, 490–91.

9. Pierre-Joseph Proudhon, *What Is Property?* (New York: Cambridge University Press 1994).

10. Jean-Jacques Rousseau, "Discourse on the Origin and Foundations of Inequality," in *The First and Second Discourses*, trans. Roger D. Masters (New York: St. Martin's Press, 1964), 141–42.

11. Jean-Jacques Rousseau, "Discourse on the Origin and Foundations of Inequality," in *The Social Contract and Discourses*, trans. G. D. H. Cole (New York: J. M. Dent and Sons, 1978), 79.

12. Jean-Jacques Rousseau, "The Social Contract," in *The Social Contract and Discourses*, trans. Cole, 165.

13. Karl Marx, "Manifesto of the Communist Party," in *The Marx-Engels Rreader*, ed. Robert C. Tucker (New York: W. W. Norton, 1978), 484. Here Marx states: "In this sense, the theory of the Communists may be summed up in a single sentence: Abolition of private property." Vladimir Lenin, "The State and Revolution," in *The Lenin Anthology*, ed. Robert C. Tucker (New York: W. W. Norton, 1975), offers the best statement of Lenin's views on property.

14. Locke, "Second Treatise," pars. 4–21.

15. Ibid., par. 27.

16. Ibid., par. 28.

17. Ibid.

18. In fact, some political theorists and writers see in Locke's labor theory of value and property the basic ideas for a free-market economy based upon the selling of labor for wages. One political theorist who argues this is C. B. Macpherson, *The Political Theory of Possessive Individualism* (New York: Oxford University Press, 1975). A contrasting view that depicts Locke's theory of ownership as grounded in religious reasons can be found in John Tully, *A Discourse on Property: John Locke and His Adversaries* (Cambridge: Cambridge University Press, 1980).

19. Locke, "Second Treatise," pars. 27, 46, 48. With the introduction of money property is not limited to a short duration of some types of goods that could spoil. Instead, Locke describes money as a form of property that not only eliminates the problem of goods spoiling but also makes possible a vast increase in the amount property one can own. Thus, money as a form of property makes it possible to accumulate wealth and then to exchange that money for other items that are desired.

20. Robert Nozick, *Anarchy, State, and Utopia* (New York: Basic Books, 1974), 151.

21. Locke, "Second Treatise," pars. 6, 7, 21, 127.

22. Ibid., par. 87.

23. An enormous amount of literature examines the impact of John Locke's theory on property in the United States. Among the many books and articles that look to his impact are the following: G. E. Aylmer, "The Meaning and Definition of 'Property' in Seventeenth Century England," *Past and Present* 86 (1980): 93–95; David Fellman, "The European Background of Early American Ideas Concerning Property," *Temple University Law Quarterly* 23 (1940): 497–516; Walter H. Hamilton, "Property According to Locke," *Yale Law Journal* 41 (1932): 864–80; Paschal Larkin, *Property in the Eighteenth Century with Special Reference to England and Locke* (London: Cork University Press, 1930); Richard McKeon, "The Development of the Concept of Property in Political Philosophy: A Study in the Background of the Constitution," *Ethics* 4 (1938): 297–366; Elizabeth V. Mensch, "The Colonial Origins of Liberal Property Rights," *Buffalo Law Review* 31 (1982): 635–735; Jennifer Nedelsky, *Private Property and the Limits of American Constitutionalism* (Chicago: University of Chicago Press, 1990); David Schultz, *Property, Power, and American Democracy* (New Brunswick, NJ: Transaction Press, 1992); David Schultz, "Political Theory and Legal History: Conflicting Depictions of Property in the American Political Founding," *American Journal of Legal History* 37

(1993): 464–95; and David Schultz, "The Locke Republican Debate and the Paradox of Property Rights in Early American Jurisprudence," *Western New England College Law Review* 13 (1991): 155–88.

24. Many historians have noted the influence of John Locke upon the American framers. Perhaps the most famous book arguing this is Louis Hartz, *The Liberal Tradition in America* (New York: Harcourt Brace Jovanovich, 1954). Hartz's theory is that American politics and history is basically Lockean-inspired and that there is a basic consensus surrounding John Locke's Liberal values, which stress individual liberty, political equality, and a commitment to limited government. Other books debating the relative Lockean influence on American include the following: Richard Ashcraft, *Revolutionary Politics and Locke's Two Treatises of Government* (Princeton, NJ: Princeton University Press, 1986); Bernard Bailyn, *The Ideological Origins of the American* Revolution (Cambridge: Harvard University Press, 1965); John P. Diggins, *The Lost Soul of American Politics* (Chicago: University of Chicago Press, 1986); Steven M. Dworetz, *The Unvarnished Doctrine: Locke, Liberalism, and the American Revolution* (Durham, NC: Duke University Press, 1990); Michael Liensch, *New Order of the Ages: Time, the Constitution, and the Making of Modern Political Thought* (Princeton, NJ: Princeton University Press, 1988); Wilson Cary McWilliams, *The Idea of Fraternity in* America (Berkeley: University of California Press, 1974); and Gordon Wood, *The Creation of the American Republic: 1776–1787* (New York: Norton, 1972).

25. Milton Friedman, *Capitalism and Freedom* (Chicago: University of Chicago Press, 2002).

26. Alan Ryan's *Property and Political Theory*, esp. pp. 91–118, provides a good overview of the utilitarian theory of property as being based on maximizing the social good and happiness for all.

27. G. W. F. Hegel, *Philosophy of Right*, trans. T. M. Knox (New York: Oxford University Press, 1967), pars. 45, 46, 217–18.

28. Margaret Jane Radin, *Reinterpreting Property* (Chicago: University of Chicago Press, 2006).

29. For a discussion of these influences see Fellman, "European Background of Early American Ideas Concerning Property"; Schultz, "Political Theory and Legal History."

30. Locke, "Second Treatise," par. 138.

31. J. G. A. Pocock, *The Machiavellian Moment: Florentine Political Thought and the Atlantic Republic Tradition* (Princeton, NJ: Princeton University Press, 1975).

32. James Harrington, "Oceana" in *The Political Works of James Harrington*, ed. J. G. A. Pocock (Cambridge: Cambridge University Press, 1977), 167.

33. Pocock, *Machiavellian Moment*, 209.

34. Ibid., 144.

35. William Blackstone, *Commentaries on the Laws of England*, 4 vols. (Chicago: University of Chicago Press, 1979), 2:1.

36. Ibid., 1:120, 124, 134. For an extended discussion of this topic on the different political or philosophical traditions that influenced the founders' views on property please see my article "Political Theory and Legal History."

37. G. Hunt, ed., *The Writings of James Madison* (New York: Putnam, 1906), 6:101; J. Cooke, *Alexander Hamilton: A Biography* (New York: Scribner's, 1982), 78, and A. Hamilton, in *Federalist Paper* no. 85, in James Madison, Alexander Hamilton, and John Jay, *The Federalist Papers* (New York: Modern Library, 1937), 568; Thomas Jefferson, letter to James Madison, October 28, 1785, in *Thomas Jefferson: Writings*, ed. Merrill D. Peterson (New York: Library of America, 1984), 842; McKeon, "Development of the Concept of Property in Political Philosophy," 353, 356–57; Liensch, *New Order of the Ages*, 93.

38. Samuel Bryan, "*Letters of Centinel*," October 1787, in *Anti-Federalists versus Federalists: Selected Documents*, ed. John D. Lewis (Scranton, PA: Chandler Publishing (1967), 141.

39. Frank Bourgin, *The Great Challenge: The Myth of Laissez-Faire in the Early Republic* (New York: HarperCollins, 1989), 38.

40. Arthur M. Schlesinger Jr., *The Cycles of American History* (New York: Mariner Books, 1999), 220.

41. Bourgin, *Great Challenge*, 23.

42. Morton J. Horwitz, *The Transformation of American Law: 1780–1860* (Cambridge: Harvard University Press, 1977), 260–64.

43. Wesley Newcomb Hohfeld, "Some Fundamental Legal Conceptions as Applied in Judicial Reasoning," *Yale Law Journal* 23 (1913): 16–53.

44. Jeremy Bentham, *The Principles of Morals and Legislation* (New York: Hafner Publishing, 1948), 247–50.

45. A. M. Honore, "Ownership," in *Oxford Essays in Jurisprudence*, ed. A. G. Guest (Oxford: Oxford University Press, 1961), 107–47.

46. One typical and very good example of a standard law school property law book is Jon W. Bruce and James W. Ely Jr., *Cases and Materials on Modern Property* Law (St. Paul, MN: West Publishing, 1994). Some of the discussion that follows parallels some of the points made in this book and in later editions of it.

47. In volume 2 of Blackstone's *Commentaries* he provides a classic categorization of types of property that have forever been repeated in every property book and law school class. The classification discussed here roughly follows the same format.

CHAPTER 3

1. For a good discussion on how British common law translated over into the United States see William Nelson, *Americanization of the Common Law* (Cambridge: Harvard University Press, 1979).

2. For a discussion of the different characteristics of classical Greek political thought take a look at Donald G. Tannenbaum and David Schultz, *Inventors of Ideas: An Introduction to Western Political Thought* (New York: Wadsworth Publishers, 2003), chap. 3.

3. Plato, *The Republic of Plato*, trans. Francis MacDonald Cornford (New York: Oxford University Press, 1968), 55–59.

4. Tannenbaum and Schultz, *Inventors of Ideas*, chap. 6.

5. Thomas Hobbes, *Leviathan* (New York: Collier Books, 1962), 100, 130–32.

6. Rousseau, *Second Discourse*, 105–11, 141. Here Rousseau asks readers not to confuse the person whom they see around them (and corrupted by social conventions) as the same person in the state of nature.

7. Locke, *Second Treatise*, 159.

8. Locke, *Second Treatise*, pars. 6, 86–88, 90, 105. Here Locke emphasizes that government has no more authority over individuals than is given to it by the people. The people consent to be ruled and it is this consent, plus their natural rights, that limits what government may do. In Locke's writings then one finds the origins of ideas such as majority rule, consent of the governed, and constitutionalism or limited government.

9. Richard Hofstadter, *The American Political Tradition and the Men Who Made It* (New York: Vintage Books, 1989), 5

10. *Federalist Papers*, no. 10, 55, 56.

11. Ibid., no. 51, 337.

12. Charles A. Beard, *An Economic Interpretation of the Constitution of the United States* (New York: Macmillan, 1964). Charles Beard's claim that the Constitution was an antidemocratic and pro-economic or -capitalist document produced by those who had economic interests hurt by the Articles of Confederation government remains eternally controversial. There are also some who question the scholarship and cogency of his claims. However, despite any criticisms, his central assertion that protection of property interests lies at the heart of the Constitution is one that few have disputed.

13. *McCulloch v. Maryland*, 17 U.S. 316 (1819), 413.

14. William B. Stoebuck, "A General Theory of Eminent Domain," *Washington Law Review* 47 (1972): 553–608.

15. Among some of the sources discussing the origins or eminent domain and property rights in Europe include Lawrence C. Becker, *Property Rights: Philosophical Foundations* (London: Routledge and Kegan

Paul, 1977), and David Fellman, "The European Background of Early American Ideas Concerning Property," *Temple University Law Quarterly* 23 (1940): 497–516.

16. Stoebuck, "General Theory of Eminent Domain," 555–60.

17. Arthur Lenhoff, "Development of the Concept of Eminent Domain," *Columbia Law Review* (1942): 596–620; J. A. C. Grant, "The 'Higher Law' Background of the Law of Eminent Domain," *Wisconsin Law Review* 6 (1930–31): 67–89.

18. David L. Weimer and Aidan R. Vining, *Policy Analysis: Concepts and Practice* (Upper Saddle River, NJ: Prentice-Hall, 2005), 54–55.

19. Adam Smith, *An Inquiry Into the Nature and Causes of the Wealth of Nations* (New York: P. F. Collier and Son, 1937), 452–53.

20. The classic statement on the collective action problem is found in Mancur Olson's *The Logic of Collective Action* (Cambridge: Harvard University Press, 1976).

21. Errol E. Meidinger, "The 'Public Uses' of Eminent Domain: History and Policy," *Environmental Law* 11 (1980): 2.

22. William Michael Treanor, "The Origins and Original Significance of the Just Compensation Clause of the Fifth Amendment," *Yale Law Journal* 94 (1985): 694–716.

23. Bernard Schwartz, *The Great Rights of Mankind: A History of the American Bill of Rights* (New York: Oxford University Press, 1977), 231–46.

24. Morton J. Horwitz, *The Transformation of American Law: 1780–1860* (Cambridge: Harvard University Press, 1977), 260–64.

CHAPTER 4

1. Two good books that document the history of property rights before the Supreme Court are Edward S. Corwin, *Liberty Against Government, The Rise, Flowering, and Decline of a Famous Juridicial Concept* (Baton Rouge: Louisiana State University Press, 1948), and James W. Ely Jr., *The Guardian of Every Other Right: A Constitutional History of Property Rights* (New York: Oxford University Press, 2007).

2. A good discussion on how the traditional notion of property rights extending into the sky was challenged with the invention of the airplane is found in Stuart Banner's *Who Owns the Sky?: The Struggle to Control Airspace from the Wright Brothers On* (Cambridge: Harvard University Press, 2008).

3. *Heberle Crystal Springs Brewing Co. v. Clarke*, 30 F.2d 219, 222 (2nd Cir. 1929).

4. *Yee v. City of Escondido*, 503 U.S. 519, 522 (1992).

5. *Pumpelly v. Green Bay Company*, 80 U.S. 166, 177–78 (1871).

6. *Loretto v. Teleprompter Manhattan CATV Corp.*, 458 U.S. 419, 427 (1982).

7. *Loretto*, 458 U.S. at 432.

8. *Pennsylvania v. Mahon*, 260 U.S. 393, 413 (1922).

9. *Mahon*, 260 U.S. 393.

10. *Mahon*, 260 U.S. at 415.

11. For a general discussion on how the takings and police powers contrast, see Joseph L. Sax, "Takings and the Police Power," *Yale Law Journal* 74 (1964): 36–76.

12. *Agins v. City of Tiburon*, 447 U.S. 255, 262 (1980).

13. *Hadachek v. Sebastian*, 239 U.S. 394, 414 (1915).

14. *Goldblatt v. Town of Hempstead*, 369 U.S. 590, 592 (1962).

15. *Armstrong v. United States*, 364 U.S. 40, 48 (1960).

16. *Andrus v. Allard*, 444 U.S. 51, 65–66 (1979).

17. *Penn Central Company v. New York*, 438 U.S. 104, 123 (1978).

18. *Penn Central Company*, 438 U.S. at 130–31.

19. As a result of this case the question became at what point does a temporary delay in development constitute a taking? What is the delay is a week? A month? One year? See David Schultz, "The Price Is Right! Property Valuation and Damage Awards for Temporary Takings," *Hamline Law Review* 22 (1998): 281–302, for an effort to try to sort out these questions.

20. *Nollan v. California Coastal Commission*, 483 U.S. 825, 831 (1987).

21. *Lucas v. South Carolina Coastal Council*, 505 U.S. 1003, 1015 (1992).

22. *Lucas*, 505 U.S. at 1015–16.

23. *Lucas*, 505 U.S. at 1027.

24. *Palazzolo v. Rhode Island*, 533 U.S. 606, 632 (2001).

25. *Dolan v City of Tigard*, 512 U.S. 374, 388 (1994).

26. *Dolan*, 512 U.S. at 391.

27. *Strickley v. Highland Boy Mining Company*, 200 U.S. 527, 530 (1905).

28. *Berman v. Parker*, 348 U.S. 26, 31–32 (1956).

29. *Berman*, 348 U.S. at 33.

30. *Berman*, 348 U.S. at 33.

31. *Hawaii Housing Authority v. Midkiff*, 467 U.S. 229, 243 (1984).

32. *Midkiff*, 467 U.S. at 243–44.

33. *Chicago B. & Q. R. Co. v. City of Chicago*, 166 U.S. 226, 236 (1897).

34. *United States v. Reynolds*, 397 U.S. 14, 15–16 (1970).

CHAPTER 5

1. *Marbury v. Madison*, 5 U.S. 137, 177 (1803).

2. Bernard Schwartz, *The Great Rights of Mankind: A History of the American Bill of Rights* (New York: Oxford University Press, 1977), 231–46.

3. Both William Michael Treanor in "The Origins and Original Significance of the Just Compensation Clause of the Fifth Amendment," *Yale Law Journal* 94 (1985): 694–716, and Errol E. Meidinger in "The 'Public Uses' of Eminent Domain: History and Policy," *Environmental Law* 11 (1980): 1–66, provide useful and engaging discussions seeking to establish the original meanings and understandings of the Takings clause.

4. *Strickley v. Highland Boy Mining Company*, 200 U.S. 527, 530 (1905).

5. For various views on the history of eminent domain and the evolution of the public use doctrine see Leslie Bender, "The Takings Clause: Principle or Politics?" *Buffalo Law Review* 34 (1985): 735–832; Lawrence Berger, "The Public Use Requirement in Eminent Domain," *Oregon Law Review* 57 (1978): 203–46; Susan Crabbtree, "Public Use in Eminent Domain: Are There Limits After *Oakland Raiders* and *Poletown*?" *California Western Law Review* 20 (1983): 82–108; Martin J. King, "Rex Non Potest Peccare??? The Decline and Fall of the Public Use Limitation on Eminent Domain," *Dickinson Law Review* 76 (1972): 266–81; Suzanne LaBerge, "The Public Use Requirement in Eminent Domain: A Constantly Evolving Doctrine," *Stetson Law Review* 14 (1985): 649–64; Mark C. Landry, "The Public Use Requirement in Eminent Domain—A Requiem," *Tulane Law Review* 60 (1985): 419–35; Errol E. Meidinger, "The 'Public Uses' of Eminent Domain: History and Policy," *Environmental Law* 11 (1980): 1–66; Philip Nichols Jr., "The Meaning of Public Use in the Law of Eminent Domain," *Boston University Law Review* 20 (1940): 615–41; Harry Scheiber, "The Road to Munn: Eminent Domain and the Concept of Public Purpose in the State Courts," in *Law and American History*, ed. Donald Fleming and Bernard Bailyn (Boston: Little, Brown, 1971), 615–41.

6. In fact, it may come as a surprise to many that the government often delegates eminent domain authority to private parties such as corporations or individuals so that they can take property to fulfill a variety of public functions. Often these private parties are public utilities such as power companies, but in some cases other corporations, such as railroads, have been given this authority. James W. Ely Jr., in *Railroads and American Law* (Lawrence: University Press of Kansas, 2001), provides a fascinating and detailed account of this topic.

7. J. B. Thayer, "The Right of Eminent Domain," *The Monthly Law Reporter* (September 1856): 241–63.

8. John A. Lewis, *Treatise on the Law of Eminent Domain in the United States* (Chicago: Callaghan, 1909).

9. Ibid., 497.

10. *Cole v. LaGrange*, 113 U.S. 1, 3 (1884).

11. *Hairston v. Danville and Western Railway*, 208 U.S. 598, 606 (1908).

12. *Hairston*, 208 U.S. at 606.

13. *Fallbrook Irrigation District v. Bradley*, 164 U.S. 112, 167 (1896).

14. *Bradley*, 164 U.S. at 167–68.

15. *Bradley*, 164 U.S. at 167.

16. *Clark v. Nash*, 198 U.S. 361, 368 (1905).

17. *Strickley v. Highland Boy Mining Company*, 200 U.S. 527, 530 (1906).

18. *Old Dominion v. United States*, 269 U.S. 55, 66 (1925).

19. *Berman v. Parker*, 348 U.S. 26, 33 (1956).

20. *Berman*, 348 U.S. at 33.

21. *Hawaii Housing Authority v. Midkiff*, 467 U.S. 229, 243–44 (1984).

22. *Midkiff*, 467 U.S. at 240.

23. *Poletown Neighborhood Council v. City of Detroit*, 304 N.W.2d 455, 459 (Mich. 1981).

24. *Poletown Neighborhood Council*, 304 N.W.2d at 459.

25. *Poletown Neighborhood Council*, 304 N.W.2d at 457.

26. *Poletown Neighborhood Council*, 304 N.W.2d at 458.

27. *Poletown Neighborhood Council*, 304 N.W.2d at 458.

28. For two views on the decision see Jeanie Wylie, *Poletown: Community Betrayed* (Urbana: University of Illinois Press, 1990), and Joseph Auerbach, "The Poletown Dilemma," *Harvard Business Review* (May–June 1985): 93–99.

29. *City of Oakland v. Oakland Raiders*, 32 Cal. 3d 60, 63–65 (1982).

30. *Oakland Raiders*, 32 Cal. 3d at 69.

31. *City of Oakland v. Oakland Raiders*, 32 Cal. 3d 72 (1982).

32. *City of Oakland v. Oakland Raiders*, 32 Cal. 3d 60, 64 (1982).

33. *Oakland Raiders*, 32 Cal. 3d at 65.

34. *Oakland Raiders*, 32 Cal. 3d at 72.

35. *Oakland Raiders*, 32 Cal. 3d at 68.

36. *Oakland Raiders*, 32 Cal. 3d at 75.

37. *Oakland Raiders*, 32 Cal. 3d at 69.

38. *Housing and Redevelopment Auth. v. Walser Auto Sales*, 630 N.W.2d 662, 668 (Minn. Ct. App. 2001).

39. *Walser Auto Sales*, 630 N.W.2d at 669.

40. *Walser Auto Sales*, 630 N.W.2d at 670. The italics were in the original opinion.

41. *Housing and Redevelopment Authority in and for the City of Richfield v. Walser Auto Sales*, 641 N.W.2d 885 (Minn. 2002).

42. Ellen Frankel Paul, *Property Rights and Eminent Domain* (New Brunswick, NJ: Transaction Publishers, 1988); Emily Lewis, "Corporate Prerogative, 'Public Use' and Neighborhood Plight: *Poletown Neighborhood City Council v. City of Detroit*," *Detroit College of Law Review* 4 (1982): 907–29; Donald Large, "The Supreme Court and the Takings Clause: The Search for a Better Rule," *Environmental Law* 18 (1987): 3–54; Landry, "The Public Use Requirement in Eminent Domain"; Richard A. Epstein, *Takings: Private Property and the Power of Eminent Domain*

(Cambridge: Harvard University Press, 1985); Thomas C. Coyne, *"Hawaii Housing Authority v. Midkiff*: A Final Requiem for the Public Use Limitation on Eminent Domain," *Notre Dame Law Review* 60 (1985): 388–404; Crabbtree, "Public Use in Eminent Domain."

CHAPTER 6

1. National Conference of Commissioners of Uniform State Laws, *Uniform Eminent Domain Code: With Prefatory Notes and Comments* (Chicago, 1975).

2. Charles Hoch, *The Practice of Local Government Planning* (Washington, DC: ICMA, 2000), provides a good overview on government land use planning, including a discussion of comprehensive plans.

3. A detailed discussion on the various methods to do appraisals and the steps in the process can be found in Appraisal Institute, *The Appraisal of Real Estate* (Chicago: Appraisal Institute, 2008). The institute is perhaps the leading professional organization dedicated to performing real estate evaluations and their book is the most comprehensive handbook outlining the different methods of assessing value.

4. *King v. State Roads Com'n of State Highway Administration* 298 Md. 80, 85–86 (Md. 1983).

5. *Agins v. City of Tiburon*, 447 U.S. 255, 258, footnote 2 (1980).

CHAPTER 7

1. *Keystone Coal Association v. DeBenedictis*, 480 U.S. 470, 483 (1987).

2. *Keystone Coal Association*, 480 U.S. 470 at 504–5.

3. *Keystone Coal Association*, 480 U.S. at 499.

4. *Keystone Coal Association*, 480 U.S. at 499.

5. *Keystone Coal Association*, 480 U.S. at 506–7.

6. *Keystone Coal Association*, 480 U.S. at 515–16.

7. *Keystone Coal Association*, 480 U.S. at 520.

8. *Nollan v. California Coastal Commission*, 483 U.S. 825, 841–42 (1987).

9. *Nollan*, 483 U.S. at 831–32.

10. *Nollan*, 483 U.S. at 832.

11. *Nollan*, 483 U.S. at 834–35.

12. *Nollan*, 483 U.S. at 828–29, 835.

13. *Nollan*, 483 U.S. at 837.

14. *Nollan*, 483 U.S. at 835, footnote 4.

15. *Nollan*, 483 U.S. at 837.

16. *Nollan*, 483 U.S. at 842.

17. *Nollan*, 483 U.S. at 849.

18. *Nollan*, 483 U.S. at 863.

19. *First English Evangelical Lutheran Church of Glendale v. The County of Los Angeles*, 482 U.S. 304, 310–11 (1987).

20. *First English*, 482 U.S. at 313.

21. *First English*, 482 U.S. at 314.

22. *First English*, 482 U.S. at 318.

23. *First English*, 482 U.S. at 322.

24. *First English*, 482 U.S. at 325–26.

25. *First English*, 482 U.S. at 323.

26. Dennis J. Coyle, "The Reluctant Revival of Landowner Rights," unpublished paper presented at the 1987 American Political Science Association annual convention, Chicago, September, 1987.

27. Daniel A. Farber, "Taking Liberties," *New Republic* (June 27, 1988): 19.

28. James F. Simon, *The Center Holds: The Power Struggle Inside the Rehnquist Court* (New York: Touchstone, 1999).

29. See *Gen. Bldg. Contractors, L.L.C. v. Bd. of Shawnee County Commr's.*, 66 P.3d 873, 881 (Kan. 2003) (ruling that counties can take property with eminent domain for the purpose of acquir[ing] property for industrial or economic development purposes); *Minneapolis Cmty. Dev. Agency v. Opus Nw., L.L.C.*, 582 N.W.2d 596, 599 (Minn. Ct. App. 1998) (reviewing Minnesota's broad interpretation of public use including acquisition of private property for use by a different private entity); *City of Jamestown v. Leevers Supermarket, Inc.*, 552 N.W.2d 365, 372 (N.D. 1996) (noting that the trend following Poletown is to allow broad legislative discretion to use powers of eminent domain for a variety of economic development purposes). But see *City of Midwest City v. House of Realty, Inc.*, 100 P.3d 678, 680 (Okla. 2004) (ruling that the city, which claimed that the taking of private property was necessary for economic development purposes, did not possess powers to condemn properties for the purpose of economic redevelopment and blight removal).

30. *County of Wayne v. Hathcock*, 684 N.W.2d 765, 774 (2004).

31. *Hathcock*, 684 N.W.2d at 775, 778.

32. *Hathcock*, 684 N.W.2d at 778.

33. *Hathcock*, 684 N.W.2d at 779.

34. *Hathcock*, 684 N.W.2d at 781–83.

35. *Hathcock*, 684 N.W.2d at 781.

36. *Hathcock*, 684 N.W.2d at 781.

37. *Hathcock*, 684 N.W.2d at 782.

38. *Hathcock*, 684 N.W.2d at 783.

39. *Hathcock*, 684 N.W.2d at 787.

40. *Hathcock*, 684 N.W.2d at 798.

41. *Kelo v. City of New London*, 843 A.2d 500 (Conn. 2004).

42. *Kelo*, 843 A.2d at 520.

43. *Kelo*, 843 A.2d at 520.

44. *Kelo*, 843 A.2d at 523.
45. *Kelo*, 843 A.2d at 551.
46. *Kelo*, 843 A.2d at 540.
47. *Kelo v. City of New London*, 545 U.S. 469, 477 (2005).
48. *Kelo*, 545 U.S. at 478.
49. *Kelo*, 545 U.S. at 478–79.
50. *Kelo*, 545 U.S. at 480–81.
51. *Kelo*, 545 U.S. at 483–84.
52. *Kelo*, 545 U.S. at 486–87.
53. *Kelo*, 545 U.S. at 477–78.
54. *Kelo*, 545 U.S. at 483–84.
55. *Kelo*, 545 U.S. at 489.
56. *Kelo*, 545 U.S. at 489.
57. *Kelo*, 545 U.S. at 488.
58. *Kelo*, 545 U.S. at 483.
59. *Kelo*, 545 U.S. at 490.
60. *Kelo*, 545 U.S. at 491.
61. *Kelo*, 545 U.S. at 497–98.
62. *Kelo*, 545 U.S. at 498.
63. *Kelo*, 545 U.S. at 498.
64. *Kelo*, 545 U.S. at 501.
65. *Kelo*, 545 U.S. at 499.
66. *Kelo*, 545 U.S. at 505–7.
67. *Kelo*, 545 U.S. at 521–22.
68. *Lingle v. Chevron, U.S.A. Inc.*, 544 U.S. 528, 537–38 (2005).
69. *Lingle*, 544 U.S. at 543.
70. *Lingle*, 544 U.S. at 545.
71. *San Remo Hotel v. San* Francisco, 545 U.S. 323, 330–31 (2005).
72. *San Remo Hotel*, 545 U.S. at 347.
73. *San Remo Hotel*, 545 U.S. at 336.
74. *San Remo Hotel*, 545 U.S. at 336–37.
75. *San Remo Hotel*, 545 U.S. at 340–41.
76. *San Remo Hotel*, 545 U.S. at 342.
77. *San Remo Hotel*, 545 U.S. at 345–46.

CHAPTER 8

1. Post-*Kelo* several books also aptly capture the anger towards the decision with titles such as: Jeff Benedict, *Little Pink House: A True Story of Defiance and Courage* (New York: Grand Central Publishing, 2009); Richard A. Epstein, *Supreme Neglect: How to Revive Constitutional Protection for Private Property* (New York: Oxford University Press, 2008); Carla T. Main, *Bulldozed: "Kelo," Eminent Domain, and the Lust for Land* (New York: Encounter Books, 2007); and Dwight H. Merriam and Mary

Massaron, *Eminent Domain Use and Abuse: Kelo in Context* (Chicago: American Bar Association, 2006).

2. Timothy Egan, "Ruling Sets Off Tug of War over Private Property," *New York Times*, July 30, 2005, A1; Michael Corkery and Ryan Chittum, "Eminent-Domain Uproar Imperils Projects," *Wall Street Journal*, August 3, 2005, B1; Nick Timiraos, "States May Raze Court's Eminent Domain Ruling," *St. Paul Legal-Ledger*, July 18, 2005, 3.

3. Charley Shaw, "Lawmakers Respond to Eminent Domain Ruling," *St. Paul Legal-Ledger*, July 18, 2005, 1; Joi Preciphs, "Eminent-Domain Ruling Knits Rivals," *Wall Street Journal*, July 8, 2005, A4; Jason Hoppin, "High Court's Eminent Domain Ruling Touches a Nerve," *St. Paul Pioneer Press*, July 24, 2005, B1; Adam Karlin, "Property Seizure Backlash," *Christian Science Monitor*, July 6, 2006, 1"They Paved Paradise," *Wall Street Journal*, June 30, 2005, A12; David Kirkpatrick, "Ruling on Property Seizure Rallies Christian Groups," *New York Times*, July 11, 2005, A16.

4. Dana Berliner, *Public Power, Private Gain: A Five Year, State-By-State Report Examining the Abuse of Eminent Domain* (Arlington, VA: Castle Coalition, 2003), 2, 8.

5. Ibid., 8.

6. Ibid., 4.

7. Castle Coalition, *Myth and Realities of Eminent Domain Abuse* (Arlington, VA: Castle Coalition, 2006), 1, 4, 6, 9, 11.

8. *Kelo v. City of New London*, 545 U.S. 469, 505 (2005).

9. *Kelo*, 545 U.S. at 522.

10. Carla, T. Main, *Bulldozed: "Kelo," Eminent Domain, and the Lust for Land* (New York: Encounter Books, 2007), 174, 175.

11. Nathan Koppel, "There Goes the Neighborhood: A Fight over Defining Blight," *Wall Street Journal*, April 30, 2009, A11.

12. *City of Las Vegas Downtown Redevelopment Agency v. Pappas*, 76 P.3d 1, 10 (Nev. 2003).

13. *Pappas*, 76 P.3d at 10.

14. *Pappas*, 76 P.3d at 11.

15. *Pappas*, 76 P.3d at 11.

16. *Pappas*, 76 P.3d at 15.

17. *Southwestern Illinois Development Authority v. National City Environmental, L.L.C*, 768 N.E.2d 1, 3 (2002).

18. *National City Environmental*, 768 N.E.2d at 5.

19. *National City Environmental*, 768 N.E.2d at 6–7.

20. *National City Environmental*, 768 N.E.2d at 8–9.

21. *National City Environmental*, 768 N.E.2d at 9.

22. *National City Environmental*, 768 N.E.2d at 9.

23. *National City Environmental*, 768 N.E.2d at 9.

24. *National City Environmental*, 768 N.E.2d at 9.

25. *National City Environmental*, 768 N.E.2d at 10.

26. *Bailey v. Myers*, 76 P.3d 898, 904–5 (Ariz. Ct. App. 2003).

27. *Bailey*, 76 P.3d at 900. The italics are in the original court opinion.

28. *Bailey*, 76 P.3d at 901.

29. *Bailey*, 76 P.3d at 901.

30. *Bailey*, 76 P.3d at 902.

31. *Bailey*, 76 P.3d at 902.

32. *Bailey*, 76 P.3d at 902.

33. *Bailey*, 76 P.3d at 903.

34. *Bailey*, 76 P.3d at 903–4.

35. *Bailey*, 76 P.3d at 904.

36. *Bailey*, 76 P.3d at 904.

CHAPTER 9

1. As a disclaimer, this author advised TPC in this case.

2. *Rhode Island Economic Development Corp. v. The Parking Co., L.P.,* 892 A.2d 87, 106 (R.I., 2006).

3. American Planning Association, *Policy Guide on Redevelopment* (Chicago: American Planning Association, 2004).

4. Ibid.

5. Some would argue that the use of eminent domain as a tool to combat corporate threats of leaving a community is one way to address corporate thuggery. See David Schultz and David Jann, "The Use of Eminent Domain and Contractually Implied Property Rights to Affect Business and Plant Closings," *William Mitchell Law Review* 16 (1990): 383–427, and Gregory Buckley, "Eminent Domain: The Ability of a Community to Retain an Industry in the Face of an Attempted Shutdown or Relocation," *Ohio Northern University Law Review* 12 (1985): 231–55.

6. Charles E. Lindblom, "The Market as a Prison," *Journal of Politics* 44 (May 1982): 324–36.

7. Paul Boudreaux, *"Eminent* Domain, Property Rights, and the Solution of Representation Reinforcement," *Denver University Law Review* 83 (2005): 24–25.

8. Georgetown Environmental Law and Policy Institute, *The Track Record on Takings Legislation: Lessons from Democracy's Laboratories* (Georgetown, VA: Georgetown Environmental Law and Policy Institute, 2008).

9. *Lynch v. Household Finance Company*, 405 U.S. 538, 551 (1972).

10. *Bridges v. State of California*, 314 U.S. 252, 281 (1941).

Bibliography

Alexander, Gregory S. *The Global Debate Over Constitutional Property*. Chicago: University of Chicago Press, 2006.

American Planning Association. *Policy Guide on Redevelopment*. Chicago: American Planning Association, 2004.

Appraisal Institute. *The Appraisal of Real Estate*. Chicago: Appraisal Institute, 2008.

Ashcraft, Richard. *Revolutionary Politics and Locke's Two Treatises of Government*. Princeton, NJ: Princeton University Press, 1986.

Auerbach, Joseph. "The Poletown Dilemma." *Harvard Business Review* (May–June 1985): 93–99.

Aylmer, G. E. "The Meaning and Definition of 'Property' in Seventeenth Century England." *Past and Present* 86 (1980): 93–95.

Bailyn, Bernard. *The Ideological Origins of the American Revolution*. Cambridge: Harvard University Press, 1965.

Baker, C. Edwin. "Property and Its Relation to Constitutionally Protected Liberty." *University of Pennsylvania Law Review* 134 (1986): 741–816.

Banner, Stuart. *Who Owns the Sky?: The Struggle to Control Airspace from the Wright Brothers On*. Cambridge: Harvard University Press, 2008.

Barker, Ernest. *Social Contract: Essays by Locke, Hume, and Rousseau*. New York: Oxford University Press, 1977.

Beard, Charles A. *An Economic Interpretation of the Constitution of the United States*. New York: Macmillan, 1964.

Becker, Lawrence C. *Property Rights: Philosophical Foundations*. London: Routledge and Kegan Paul, 1977.

Bender, Leslie. "The Takings Clause: Principle or Politics?" *Buffalo Law Review* 34 (1985): 735–832.

Benedict, Jeff. *Little Pink House: A True Story of Defiance and Courage.* New York: Grand Central Publishing, 2009.

Bentham, Jeremy. *A Theory of Legislation.* New York: Hafner Publishing, 1948.

Berger, Lawrence. "The Public Use Requirement in Eminent Domain." *Oregon Law Review* 57 (1978): 203–46.

Berliner, Dana. *Public Power, Private Gain: A Five Year, State-by-State Report Examining the Abuse of Eminent Domain.* Arlington, VA: Castle Coalition, 2003.

Blackstone, William. *Commentaries on the Laws of England.* 4 vols. Chicago: University of Chicago Press, 1979.

Boudreaux, Paul. "Eminent Domain, Property Rights, and the Solution of Representation Reinforcement." *Denver University Law Review* 83 (2005): 1–54.

Bourgin, Frank. The *Great Challenge: The Myth of Laissez-Faire in the Early Republic.* New York: HarperCollins, 1989.

Bruce, Jon W., and James W. Ely Jr. *Cases and Materials on Modern Property Law.* St. Paul, MN: West Publishing, 1994.

Brune, Russell. "Containing the Effect of *Hawaii Housing Authority v. Midkiff* on Takings for Private Industry." *Cornell Law Review* 71 (1986): 428–52.

Buckley, Gregory. "Eminent Domain: The Ability of a Community to Retain an Industry in the Face of an Attempted Shutdown or Relocation." *Ohio Northern University Law Review* 12 (1985): 231–55.

Castle Coalition. *Myth and Realities of Eminent Domain Abuse.* Arlington, VA: Castle Coalition, 2006.

Cooke, J. *Alexander Hamilton: A Biography.* New York: Scribner's, 1982.

Corkery, Michael, and Ryan Chittum. "Eminent-Domain Uproar Imperils Projects." *Wall Street Journal,* August 3, 2005, B1

Corwin, Edward S., *Liberty Against Government, The Rise, Flowering, and Decline of a Famous Juridicial Concept.* Baton Rouge: Louisiana State University Press, 1948.

Coyle, Dennis J. "The Reluctant Revival of Landowner Rights." Unpublished paper presented at the 1987 American Political Science annual convention, Chicago, September 1987.

Coyne, Thomas C. "*Hawaii Housing Authority v. Midkiff:* A Final Requiem for the Public Use Limitation on Eminent Domain." *Notre Dame Law Review* 60 (1985): 388–404.

Crabbtree, Susan. "Public Use in Eminent Domain: Are There Limits After *Oakland Raiders* and *Poletown?*" *California Western Law Review* 20 (1983): 82–108.

Davies, Margaret. *Property: Meanings, Histories, Theories.* New York: Routledge-Cavendish, 2007.

Davis, Sue. *Justice Rehnquist and the Constitution*. Princeton, NJ: Princeton University Press, 1989.

De Coulanges, Numa Denis Fustel. *The Ancient City: A Study of the Religion, Laws, and Institutions of Greece and Rome*. Baltimore: Johns Hopkins University Press, 1980.

Diggins, John P. *The Lost Soul of American Politics*. Chicago: University of Chicago Press, 1986.

DiUbaldo, Robert W. "A Second Take: Re-examining Our Regulatory Takings Jurisprudence Post- Tahoe." *Fordham Urban Law Journal* 30 (2003): 1949–77.

Dworetz, Steven M. *The Unvarnished Doctrine: Locke, Liberalism, and the American Revolution*. Durham, NC: Duke University Press, 1990.

Eagle, Steven J. "Some Permanent Problems with the Supreme Court's Temporary Regulatory Takings Jurisprudence." *University of Hawaii Law Review* 25 (2003): 325–52.

Egan, Timothy. "Ruling Sets Off Tug of War over Private Property." *New York Times*, July 30, 2005.

Ely, James W., Jr. *The Guardian of Every Other Right: A Constitutional History of Property Rights*. New York: Oxford University Press, 2007.

———. *Railroads and American Law*. Lawrence: University Press of Kansas, 2001.

Epstein, Richard A. *Supreme Neglect: How to Revive Constitutional Protection for Private Property*. New York: Oxford University Press, 2008.

———. *Takings: Private Property and the Power of Eminent Domain*. Cambridge: Harvard University Press, 1985.

Farber, Daniel A. "'Taking' Liberties." *The New Republic*, June 27, 1988, 19–22.

Fellman, David. "The European Background of Early American Ideas Concerning Property." *Temple University Law Quarterly* 23 (1940): 497–516.

Friedman, Milton. *Capitalism and Freedom*. Chicago: University of Chicago Press, 2002.

Georgetown Environmental Law and Policy Institute. *The Track Record on Takings Legislation: Lessons from Democracy's Laboratories*. Georgetown, VA: Georgetown Environmental Law and Policy Institute, 2008.

Grant, J. A. C. "The 'Higher Law' Background of the Law of Eminent Domain." *Wisconsin Law Review* 6 (1930–31): 67–89.

Hamilton, Walter H. "Property According to Locke." *Yale Law Journal* 41 (1932): 864–80.

Harrington, James. "Oceana." In *The Political Works of James Harrington*, ed. J. G. A. Pocock. Cambridge: Cambridge University Press, 1977.

Hartz, Louis. *The Liberal Tradition in America*. New York: Harcourt Brace Jovanovich, 1954.

Hegel, G. W. F. *The Philosophy of Right*. Translated by T. M. Knox. New York: Oxford University Press, 1967.

Hill, G. Richard. *Regulatory Taking: The Limits of Land Use Controls*. Chicago: American Bar Association, 1993.

Hobbes, Thomas. *Leviathan*. New York: Collier Books, 1962.

Hoch, Charles. *The Practice of Local Government Planning*. Washington, DC: ICMA, 2000.

Hofstadter, Richard. *The American Political Tradition and the Men Who Made It*. New York: Vintage Books, 1989.

Hohfeld, Wesley Newcomb. "Some Fundamental Legal Conceptions as Applied in Judicial Reasoning." *Yale Law Journal* 23 (1913): 16–53.

Honoré, A. M. "Ownership." In *Oxford Essays in Jurisprudence*, ed. A. G. Guest, 107–47. Oxford: Oxford University Press, 1961.

Hopping, Jason. "High Court's Eminent Domain Ruling Touches a Nerve." *St. Paul Pioneer Press*, July 24, 2005, B1.

Horwitz, Morton J. *The Transformation of American Law: 1780–1860*. Cambridge: Harvard University Press, 1977.

———. *The Transformation of American Law: 1870–1960*. Cambridge: Harvard University Press, 2006.

Hume, David. *Moral and Political Philosophy*. New York: Hafner Press, 1948.

———. *A Treatise of Human Nature*. New York: Oxford University Press, 1980.

Hunt, G., ed. *The Writings of James Madison*. New York: Putnam, 1906.

Hurst, James Willard. *The Growth of American Law*. Boston: Little, Brown, 1950.

Karlin, Adam. "Property Seizure Backlash." *Christian Science Monitor*, July 6, 2006, 1.

King, Martin J. "Rex Non Potest Peccare??? The Decline and Fall of the Public Use Limitation on Eminent Domain." *Dickinson Law Review* 76 (1972): 266–81.

Kirkpatrick, David. "Ruling on Property Seizure Rallies Christian Groups." *New York Times*, July 11, 2005, A16.

Koppel, Nathan. "There Goes the Neighborhood: A Fight over Defining Blight." *Wall Street Journal*, April 30, 2009, A11.

LaBerge, Suzanne. "The Public Use Requirement in Eminent Domain: A Constantly Evolving Doctrine." *Stetson Law Review* 14 (1985): 649–64.

Landry, Mark C. "The Public Use Requirement in Eminent Domain—A Requiem." *Tulane Law Review* 60 (1985): 419–35.

Large, Donald. "The Supreme Court and the Takings Clause: The Search for a Better Rule." *Environmental Law* 18 (1987): 3–54.

Larkin, Paschal. *Property in the Eighteenth Century with Special Reference to England and Locke*. London: Cork University Press, 1930.

Lenhoff, Arthur. "Development of the Concept of Eminent Domain." *Columbia Law Review* 42 (1942): 596–620.

Lenin, Vladimir. "The State and Revolution." In *The Lenin Anthology*, ed. Robert C. Tucker, 311–98. New York: W. W. Norton, 1975.

Lewis, Emily. "Corporate Prerogative, 'Public Use' and Neighborhood Plight: *Poletown Neighborhood City Council v. City of Detroit*." *Detroit College of Law Review* 4 (1982): 907–29.

Lewis, John A. *Treatise on the Law of Eminent Domain in the United States.* Chicago: Callaghan, 1909.

Lewis, John D., ed. *Anti-Federalists versus Federalists: Selected Documents.* Scranton, PA: Chandler Publishing, 1967.

Liensch, Michael. *New Order of the Ages: Time, the Constitution, and the Making of Modern Political Thought.* Princeton, NJ: Princeton University Press, 1988.

Lindblom, Charles E. "The Market as a Prison." *Journal of Politics* 44 (May 1982): 324–36.

Locke, John. *Two Treatises of Government.* New York: New American Library, 1963.

Long, Dennis H. "The Expanding Importance of Temporary Physical Takings: Some Unresolved Issues and an Opportunity for New Directions in Takings Law." *Indiana Law Journal* 72 (1997): 1185–1209.

Madison, James, Alexander Hamilton, and John Jay. *The Federalist Papers.* New York: Modern Library, 1937.

Main, Carla, T. *Bulldozed: "Kelo," Eminent Domain, and the Lust for Land.* New York: Encounter Books, 2007.

Malloy, Robin Paul. *Private Property, Community Development, and Eminent Domain.* Burlington, VT: Ashgate Publishing, 2008.

Marx, Karl. "Manifesto of the Communist Party." In *The Marx-Engels Reader*, ed. Robert C. Tucker, 469–500. New York: W. W. Norton, 1978.

McKeon, Richard. "The Development of the Concept of Property in Political Philosophy: A Study in the Background of the Constitution." *Ethics* 4 (1938): 297–366.

Macpherson, C. B. *The Political Theory of Possessive Individualism.* New York: Oxford University Press, 1975.

McWilliams, Wilson Cary. *The Idea of Fraternity in America.* Berkeley: University of California Press, 1974.

Meidinger, Errol E. "The 'Public Uses' of Eminent Domain: History and Policy." *Environmental Law* 11 (1980): 1–66.

Mensch, Elizabeth V. "The Colonial Origins of Liberal Property Rights." *Buffalo Law Review* 31 (1982): 635–735.

Merriam, Dwight H., and Mary Massaron. *Eminent Domain Use and Abuse: Kelo in Context.* Chicago: American Bar Association, 2006.

Michelman, Frank I. "Property as a Constitutional Right." *Washington and Lee Law Review* 38 (1981): 1097–114.

Munzer, Stephen R. *A Theory of Property.* New York: Cambridge University Press, 1990.

National Conference of Commissioners of Uniform State Laws. *Uniform Eminent Domain Code: With Prefatory Notes and Comments.* Chicago, 1975.

Nedelsky, Jennifer. *Private Property and the Limits of American Constitutionalism.* Chicago: University of Chicago Press, 1990.

Nelson, William. *Americanization of the Common Law.* Cambridge: Harvard University Press, 1979.

Nichols, Philip, Jr. "The Meaning of Public Use in the Law of Eminent Domain." *Boston University Law Review* 20 (1940): 615–41.

Nozick, Robert. *Anarchy, State, and Utopia.* New York: Basic Books, 1974.

Olson, Mancur. *The Logic of Collective Action.* Cambridge: Harvard University Press, 1965.

Paul, Ellen Frankel. *Property Rights and Eminent Domain.* New Brunswick, NJ: Transaction Publishers, 1988.

Peterson, Merrill D., ed. *Thomas Jefferson: Writings.* New York: Library of America, 1984.

Philbrick, Francis S. "Changing Conceptions of Property in Law." *University of Pennsylvania Law Review* 86 (1938): 691–732.

Plato. *The Republic of Plato.* Translated by Francis MacDonald Cornford. New York: Oxford University Press, 1968.

Pocock, J. G. A. *The Machiavellian Moment: Florentine Political Thought and the Atlantic Republic Tradition.* Princeton, NJ: Princeton University Press, 1975.

Preciphs, Joi. "Eminent-Domain Ruling Knits Rivals." *Wall Street Journal*, July 8, 2005, A4.

Proudhon, Pierre-Joseph. *What Is Property?* New York: Cambridge University Press, 1994.

Radin, Margaret Jane. *Reinterpreting Property.* Chicago: University of Chicago Press, 2006.

Reeve, Andrew. *Property.* Atlantic Heights, NJ: Humanities Press, 1986.

Roberts, Thomas E. "Regulatory Takings in the Wake of Tahoe-Sierra and the Iolta Decision." *Urban Law* 35 (2003): 759–82.

———. *Taking Sides on Takings Issues: Public and Private Perspectives.* Chicago: American Bar Association, 2002.

Rousseau, Jean-Jacques. "Discourse on the Origin and Foundations of Inequality." In *The First and Second Discourses*, trans. Roger D. Masters, 77–181. New York: St. Martin's Press, 1964.

———. "Discourse on the Origin and Foundations of Inequality." In *The Social Contract and Discourses*, trans. G. D. H. Cole, 27–114. New York: J. M. Dent and Sons, 1978.

———. "The Social Contract." In *The Social Contract and Discourses*, trans. G. D. H. Cole, 165–278. New York: J. M. Dent and Sons, 1978.

Ryan, Alan. *Property*. Minneapolis: University of Minnesota Press, 1987.

———. *Property and Political Theory*. New York: Basil Blackwell, 1984.

Sax, Joseph L. "Takings and the Police Power." *Yale Law Journal* 74 (1964): 36–76.

Schattschneider, E. E. *The Semisovereign People*. New York: Holt, Rinehart and Winston, 1960.

Scheiber, Harry. "The Road to Munn: Eminent Domain and the Concept of Public Purpose in the State Courts." In *Law and American History*, ed. Donald Fleming and Bernard Bailyn, 615–41. Boston: Little, Brown, 1971.

Schlesinger, Arthur M., Jr. *The Cycles of American History*. New York: Mariner Books, 1999.

Schultz, David. "Comprehensive Plans, Corporate Thuggery, and the Problem of Private Takings." *Government, Law, and Policy Journal* 9 (Spring 2007): 6–12.

———. "Economic Development and Eminent Domain After *Kelo*: Property Rights and 'Public Use' under State Constitutions." *Albany Environmental Outlook Journal* 24 (2006): 43–88.

———. "The Locke Republican Debate and the Paradox of Property Rights in Early American Jurisprudence." *Western New England College Law Review* 13 (1991): 155–88.

———. "Political Theory and Legal History: Conflicting Depictions of Property in the American Political Founding." *American Journal of Legal History* 37 (1993): 464–95.

———. "The Price Is Right! Property Valuation and Damage Awards for Temporary Takings." *Hamline Law Review* 22 (1998): 281–302.

———. *Property, Power, and American Democracy*. New Brunswick, NJ: Transaction Press, 1992.

———. "The Property Rights Revolution that Failed: Eminent Domain in the 2004 Supreme Court Term." *Touro Law Review* 21 (2006): 929–88.

———. "What's Yours Can Be Mine: Are There Any Private Takings After *City of New London v. Kelo*?" *UCLA Journal of Environmental Law and Policy* 24 (2006): 195–234.

Schultz, David, and David Jann. "The Use of Eminent Domain and Contractually Implied Property Rights to Affect Business and Plant Closings." *William Mitchell Law Review* 16 (1990): 383–427.

Schwartz, Bernard. *The Great Rights of Mankind: A History of the American Bill of Rights*. New York: Oxford University Press, 1977.

Shaw, Charley. "Lawmakers Respond to Eminent Domain Ruling." *St. Paul Legal-Ledger*, July 18, 2005, 1.

Siegan, Bernard H. *Economic Liberties and the Constitution*. Chicago: University of Chicago Press, 1980.

———. *The Supreme Court's Constitution*. New Brunswick, NJ: Transaction Publishers, 1987.

Simon, James F. *The Center Holds: The Power Struggle Inside the Rehnquist Court*. New York: Touchstone, 1999.

Smith, Adam. *An Inquiry Into the Nature and Causes of the Wealth of Nations*. New York: P. F. Collier and Son, 1937.

Stemple, Justin W. "Take It or Leave It: the Supreme Court's Regulatory Takings Jurisprudence after Tahoe-Sierra." *William and Mary Environmental Law and Policy Review* 28 (2003): 163–203.

Stoebuck, William B. "A General Theory of Eminent Domain." *Washington Law Review* 47 (1972): 553–608.

Strong, Frank R. "On Placing Property Due Process Center Stage in Takings Jurisprudence." *Ohio State Law Journal* 49 (1988): 591–622.

———. *Substantive Due Process: A Dichotomy of Sense and Nonsense*. Durham, NC: Carolina Academic Press, 1986.

Tannenbaum, Donald G., and David Schultz. *Inventors of Ideas: An Introduction to Western Political Thought*. New York: Wadsworth Publishers, 2003.

Thayer, J. B. "The Right of Eminent Domain." *The Monthly Law Reporter* (September 1856): 241–63.

"They Paved Paradise." *Wall Street Journal*, June 30, 2005, A12.

Timiraos, Nick. "States May Raze Court's Eminent Domain Ruling." *St. Paul Legal-Ledger*, July 18, 2005, 3.

Treanor, William Michael. "The Origins and Original Significance of the Just Compensation Clause of the Fifth Amendment." *Yale Law Journal* 94 (1985): 694–716.

Tully, John. *A Discourse on Property: John Locke and His Adversaries*. Cambridge: Cambridge University Press, 1980.

Waldron, Jeremy. *The Right to Private Property*. Oxford: Clarendon Press, 1988.

Weimer, David L., and Aidan R. Vining. *Policy Analysis: Concepts and Practice*. Upper Saddle River, NJ: Prentice-Hall, 2005.

Wood, Gordon. *The Creation of the American Republic: 1776–1787*. New York: Norton, 1972.

Wright, Benjamin F. *The Contract Clause of the Constitution*. Westport, CT: Greenwood Press, 1938.

———. *The Growth of American Constitutional Law*. New York: Reynal and Hitchcock, 1942.

Wylie, Jeanie. *Poletown: Community Betrayed*. Urbana: University of Illinois Press, 1990.

Index

About the Author

DAVID SCHULTZ is a Hamline University professor in the School of Business in St. Paul, Minnesota, and a senior fellow at the University of Minnesota Law School's Institute for Law and Politics. Professor Schultz is the author of more than 25 books and 70 articles on topics including property law, land use, and eminent domain law. Professor Schultz is a former city director of planning, zoning, and code enforcement who was responsible for an agency that enforced city and state housing laws, and he has served as a housing and economic planner for an Office of Economic Opportunity (OEO) community action agency.